THE HAMMARSKJÖLD FORUMS

Case Studies

on

The Role of Law

in the

Settlement of International Disputes

Race, Peace, Law, and Southern Africa

BACKGROUND PAPER AND PROCEEDINGS
of
THE TENTH HAMMARSKJÖLD FORUM

RITA F. TAUBENFELD

and

HOWARD J. TAUBENFELD
Authors of the Working Paper

JOHN CAREY
Editor

Published for

THE ASSOCIATION OF THE BAR OF THE CITY OF NEW YORK

by

OCEANA PUBLICATIONS, INC

DOBBS FERRY, N.Y.

1968

Library of Congress Catalog Card Number: 67-25906
Oceana Book No. 20-10

PRINTED IN THE UNITED STATES OF AMERICA

Table of Contents

PART ONE

THE WORKING PAPER
by RITA F. TAUBENFELD and HOWARD J. TAUBENFELD

172458

PART TWO

THE FORUM

THE TENTH HAMMARSKJÖLD FORUM

December 5, 1967

Participants

HOWARD J. TAUBENFELD
Professor of Law, Southern Methodist University.

GERSHON B. O. COLLIER
Ambassador Extraordinary and Plenipotentiary, Permanent Representative of Sierra Leone to the United Nations; Chairman, U.N. General Assembly Special Committee on the Situation with Regard to the Implementation of the Declaration on the Granting of Independence to Colonial Countries and Peoples; Member of the English Bar.

DAVID P. DE VILLIERS
Member of the South African Bar; Leader of the South African Legal Team in the 1966 South West Africa Cases before the International Court of Justice; Member of the South African Delegation to the 21st Session of the United Nations General Assembly.

EDITOR'S FOREWORD

Of the crises that have afflicted the United Nations in 1967, not the least trying has been that of South West Africa. There, despite the 1966 decision of the International Court of Justice, the Organization's legal interest was the most clear-cut in all of racially tense southern Africa, because of the U.N.'s role as successor to the League of Nations. There the U.N. took perhaps its most far-reaching action—on paper at least—by undertaking to administer a territory whose *de facto* rulers have, so far as appears, the will and means to repel any U.N.-mounted invasion now in sight. There, consequently, the most successful attempt at world order to date may be running its greatest risk of frustration.

Since the Tenth Hammarskjold Forum in December 1966, events respecting the South West Africa part of southern Africa moved rapidly at the U.N. until overshadowed by the Middle East explosion. At the end of March the *Ad Hoc* Committee set up "to recommend practical means by which South West Africa should be administered" gave up trying to agree on one plan. In late April began a Special Session of the General Assembly, which the following month voted to establish a U.N. Council and Commissioner to administer the territory prior to independence in 1968. In June the Special Session elected to the Council: Chile, Colombia, Guyana, India, Indonesia, Nigeria, Pakistan, Turkey, United Arab Republic, Yugoslavia, and Zambia. U.N. Legal Counsel Constantin A. Stavropoulos was appointed Acting U.N. Commissioner for South West Africa.

The legal unfoldment of southern Africa's racial problems is thus a continuing process. The Tenth Hammarskjold Forum could do no more than examine the situation at a given moment. The examination had the benefit of sharply conflicting viewpoints: the White South African plan to protect white hegemony by a species of partition, the Black African insistence on unified states with majority rule, and the outside observer's proposal for compromise through a "fair" partition. Through these contrasting presentations, the Forum employed the adversary method for developing the legal issues. In similar fashion, the issues of "Law and Policy-Making for Trade Among 'Have' and 'Have-Not' Nations" were developed at the eleventh Hammarskjold Forum in April 1967 and the issues in the Middle East crisis are to be developed at the twelfth Forum in December.

The Committee which arranges the Forums is pleased that Mr. James N. Rosenberg, a founder of the Series, has accepted appointment as Honorary Chairman. The Committee's gratitude goes as always to the Staff of The Association of the Bar of the City of New York for its cooperative assistance and especially to Mr. Anthony P. Grech, Reference Librarian, who compiled the bibliography appended to outstanding working paper by Professor and Mrs. Howard J. Taubenfeld.

New York, August 1967

John Carey, Chairman
Special Committee on the Lawyer's Role in the Search for Peace, The Association of the Bar of the City of New York

PART ONE

THE WORKING PAPER

Race, Peace, Law and Southern Africa

RITA F. TAUBENFELD and HOWARD J. TAUBENFELD

> The prevention of war, like the prevention of revolution
> within the state, does not depend on legal procedures,
> but on the art of adjustment. Gerhart Niemeyer, *World
> Order and the Great Powers,* p. 48.

As the title of this paper suggests, we have undertaken the intellectually hazardous and academically unfashionable assignment of discussing a highly emotive and sweeping set of issues, race and southern Africa,[1] in the context of a highly generalized, abstract conceptual framework, the evolving international legal and peace-keeping system. In this fall of 1966, the problems of southern Africa have matured into a dominating political issue at the United Nations and events can be expected to outrun any attempt merely to survey the historical facts and current events. There are nevertheless even better reasons for analysis of these issues in a broader perspective.

The detailed facts of life in southern Africa have been carefully surveyed elsewhere. Apartheid has been discussed in principle and examined in practice. It has been found "odious," "intolerable" and labeled a "pathological" aberration by heads of governments, including President Johnson, and by scholars outside South Africa.[2] It has been labeled by most of the UN's members as an offense to humanity, a disease which, in principle, they have agreed must not be permitted to spread to South West Africa and Rhodesia.[3] It has been described as a direct threat to world peace.[4] This case does not have to be made now. In surveying and summarizing the available material, the hazards are few; it is easy to side with the angels. The hazards commence when the policy questions are submitted to analysis; what can be done about these issues within the present international system and with what prognosis? As the decision-makers put it: "What are the real options?" and "Which appear optimal, given the overall aims and preferences of the decision-makers?" At this juncture in history, it seems irresponsible to discuss southern Africa and not to face at least the first of these hazardous sets of questions.

5

One caveat must be offered. It is sometimes said that area specialists fail to "find the forest" because they "lack ignorance." Here, with all modesty, we can claim some advantages. We are not specialists in African problems and we rely heavily on information provided by such specialists. Our long-run interests are in the development of international organization and law, and, of course, in a civilized and peaceful world.

For these reasons, our major focus here is on the interrelations between the bitter, intransigent problems of southern Africa and the orderly development of an international system capable of providing at least the necessary minimum of world order and security with justice required to permit us to retain a hope for human survival. In attempting this, we cannot hope to uncover in this paper the optimum overall policy response for next week's international crisis. We seek rather to identify and address ourselves, however briefly, to the underlying issues which the problems of southern Africa raise, and promise to raise, for the international system and the United States as well as the general, long-run, overall policy alternatives these imply.

At this level of abstraction, the important conflicts, dangers and possibilities will not, we believe, change by next week or next year.

First, then, we briefly describe the regions in question, the reported "intolerable" conditions under which their majorities live, and the UN's long-standing concern with each. Then we will attempt to identify the most important legal, conceptual, political, moral and systemic conflict issues which have emerged. Last, we will explore some possible approaches to a solution or solutions for the area and their implications for the international system.

Before turning to the countries separately, it may be well to point out their links. South Africa, Southern Rhodesia and Portugal have demonstrated that they are aware of their common cause as white-dominated societies on the periphery of a raging black Africa. They have provided each other with mutual assistance; both South Africa and the Portuguese colonies have helped sustain Rhodesia against world economic sanctions. South Africa and Portugal vote together, sometimes against the world, at the UN. The loss of any one of them is likely to be a psychological and a strategic blow to the others. Indeed, some Western governments have urged a "one-at-a-time" policy for southern Africa on the analogy to a self-supporting line of dominoes or a house of cards.[5]

It is nevertheless also essential to distinguish between these natural allies. The most important conceptual distinction separates the problems of the Republic of South Africa from the others. The central issues in the Portuguese territories and even in South West Africa and Rhodesia can be construed as colonial, with, of course, important racial overtones. The international interest in them can readily be subsumed under the rubric of colonial self-determination. As such, they are the "hard core" cases, the tag end of a process of decolonization which, as one diplomat has noted,[6] has culminated since World War II in the political independence of states with "two-thirds" the population of the world, under the prodding and the approving eye of the present UN.[7] South Africa presents a different, far more troublesome and important set of issues; the Republic is a sovereign member of an international society of sovereigns.

For the existing international system, then, southern Africa is the present point of confrontation between two basic and fundamentally inconsistent international positions. One is the accumulating insistence on international action to assure certain group and individual human rights, even against the will of a legitimate sovereign. These rights include *inter alia* both the "self-determination of peoples" and internal non-discrimination on racial and ethnic lines. The other conflicting tenet is the traditional sanctity of the sovereign national state to pursue its own domestic policy and to design its own way of life and domestic political system free not only of interference from other states but from the international community as well. Both the concepts of sovereign independence and immunity from interference, on the one hand, and of human rights, on the other, are enshrined in the Charter, and South Africa, in pursuing its domestic policy in contravention of some of the most fundamental standards of currently

7

agreed international morality rests its case at base on the "illegality" of other states either individually or through the United Nations in concerning themselves in her affairs.

Such conflicts among basic norms and cherished values, which usually embody and reflect other conflicts of interest of groups or individuals, are common in all constitutions, including those of relatively stable, well-organized societies with well articulated government institutions where they are normally resolved peacefully by binding legal or political decision machinery.[8] Conflicts of important and valued norms are common in the Charter system.[9] Such conflict implies the necessity of choosing between or preferably, if possible, reaching a compromise between the incompatible norms and aims. However, the conflict between the traditional concept of inviolable sovereignty and international intervention in the name of human rights strikes at the heart of the present international system of sovereigns.

In a sense, it is the contest for ultimate governmental control. Historically, sovereignty has been the chosen champion. A general international organization which could effectively and consistently impose a world consensus on human rights on a state would be far more like a federal government than any sovereign has thus far been willing to contemplate. In short, forceful UN intervention against apartheid in South Africa could represent a momentous and portentous, if small, break with international legal and organizational traditions.

Even if we agree that this path should be trod, and that South Africa is the ideal case with which to begin the long climb to, hopefully, a more "just" world, one safer for the individual, safer from genocide, it seems obvious that so crucial a departure from the past should be designed as carefully as possible to assure that the achievement of these important purported ends will, indeed, be likely. Anything else promises at a minimum to compromise the future possibilities for growth of the organized international community's capacity in the area of human rights and might in fact threaten the survival of the present Organization in general. So far, no solution for South Africa offered at the UN promises to fulfill what we consider to be these minimum requirements. On the other hand, at this point in history, the UN cannot, and would not, ignore apartheid as a "domestic" issue in traditional fashion. Quite aside from the moral issues, in a world hyper-sensitive to race, in which the present Great Powers have been forced to become rivals in their affirmation of racial equality by the proximate debut of a non-white superpower, the existence of a "pigmentocracy"[10] is an ultimate threat to the peace, with, if possible, even more terrifying long-run potentials than all the others.[11] A world of mutual nuclear deterrence, which relies ultimately on the rational mutual cowardice of the giant states for stability must somehow contain the mass hysteria and the fundamental threat to rationality which racial conflict represents.

We turn first to contemporary conditions in southern Africa and to the record of the UN's interest there.

I. SOUTHERN AFRICA IN BRIEF

To speak of southern Africa as one unit for legal and political analysis is of course misleading, despite the basic interdependence of the areas and issues involved and the common cause their governments have made.[12] We here sketch briefly the components; first, the Portuguese colonies, Rhodesia, and South West Africa, in all of which the issue of the right of self-determination is at the fore with race a dominant overtone; last, South Africa, in which an asserted international interest in internal discrimination on a racial basis confronts most directly the claim of all sovereigns to be left alone to deal with internal matters.

The Portuguese Areas

Angola and Mozambique are, in Portugal's view, integral parts of Portugal, just as Algeria was considered by France to be an integral part of France.[13] This view has been expressly rejected by the General Assembly.[14] The territories have a combined area of some 679 thousand square miles and a population of some 12 million, making tiny Portugal today's largest colonial power. Of the 12 million, in the 1950 census, only some 130,000 were European, 55,000 were "mixed," 100,000 were "civilized" or "assimilated" Africans and the other 11½ million, were "indigenous."[15]

While official Portuguese policy is largely free of explicit rac-

9

ism, little progress in economic or political development has occurred for the bulk of the population in these areas. Explicit United Nations political interest in the territories is quite recent; in 1961, uprisings in the various Portuguese areas in Africa led to vigorous Portuguese military action in each of them. In March and June, 1961, the Security Council "deplored" the severely repressive measures employed and called the situation an actual and potential cause of international friction and one likely to endanger the maintenance of international peace and security. Portugal was asked to cease repressive activities and to find a peaceful solution to the discontent of the native majorities.[16] The General Assembly also called on Portugal to introduce measures for the respect of human rights there.[17]

As a result in part of these pressures, Portugal has instituted economic and social reforms to a limited degree. The "Native Statute" and forced labor laws were repealed; Africans were given Portuguese citizenship; compulsory primary education is offered by all schools (since 1964); and an attempt at economic integration within the "escudo zone" is in progress.[18] Guerrilla warfare has nevertheless remained endemic in the Portuguese territories with an estimated hundred thousand Portuguese troops now in Portuguese Africa. Despite the alleged receipt by the rebels of Chinese and Russian weapons, of alleged training in Communist guerrilla schools, and of alleged sanctuary in other African states, especially the Congo,[19] the Portuguese have been perhaps surprisingly successful thus far in controlling the rebellions, though at substantial economic cost.[20] At the moment, only in Portuguese Guinea are the rebel forces reported to be of any immediate consequence.

Pressures from other states directed toward independence for these areas continue unremitting. In 1963, Portugal was expelled from the UN's Economic Commission for Africa by ECOSOC; in November, 1965, she was expelled from the Inter-African Coffee Organization "because it is not an African country;" in May, 1966, she was suspended from all WHO regional activities.[21] The UN also provides assistance to refugees from Portuguese territory and awards scholarships for refuge education.[22]

Of greater political significance, in November, 1965, the Security Council again demanded that Portugal recognize the right of the peoples to self-determination and independence. The Council stated that Portuguese policy "seriously disturbs international peace and security" but refused to take action under Chapter VII.[23] In December, the General Assembly for the first time urged members to take sanctions against Portugal including the termination of diplomatic relations and an embargo of all trade and commerce but over a third of the nations voted no or abstained.[24] NATO members were expressly asked to stop the sale of arms and to refrain from providing any assistance that could be used to continue repression in Africa.[25]

Although the sale of arms to Portugal *for use in the colonies* has reportedly been ended (and one may wonder how such a partial arms embargo can be effectively designed while Portugal retains access to military procurement for other purposes), few non-African states have complied with the call for a trade embargo.[26] Portugal remains adamant against the engulfing anti-colonial tide, refusing to accept as inevitable an ultimate withdrawal from its now almost unique position of colonial suzerain, and insisting that UN action violates the Charter's ban in Article 2(7) on interfering with matters exclusively within Portugal's domestic jurisdiction.[27] It remains difficult in the long run to believe that Portugal alone will be able to withstand the post-War political cauldron in which all other old-style colonial empires have been dissolved.

Southern Rhodesia

Southern Rhodesia also is, in the view of most of the world's nations, technically still a colony under British legal control, though in revolt against the motherland. Here though, the issue is not independence, all parties have agreed to that, but rather the post-independence constitutional bargain and consequently the political control of the country after independence. At present, some 217,000 whites rule Rhodesia's 150,000 square miles and four million natives with near absolute control.[28]

Historically, Rhodesia was never subjected to very firm British control. Conquered by Rhodes on his own behalf, it was long run as a private preserve with order maintained by a private army.[29]

After the First World War, the white population rejected union with South Africa and, instead, in 1923 adopted a constitution according the colony almost complete self-government. Under British pressure, a federation with Nyasaland and Northern Rhodesia was formalized in 1953 with complete independence as a functioning "multi-racial society" and "full membership in the Commonwealth" for the combined entity as the asserted goal. The Federation had a brief life; the vast native majorities, with voting rights, in the other areas were suspicious of Southern Rhodesia's white controlled government, which denied similar voting rights to its non-white majority, from the outset. When that Federation began to break up, Southern Rhodesia adopted a new constitution (1961) removing the UK's reserved powers but retaining British sovereignty. Thus, by 1961, the "colonial" relationship was already largely formal. Nevertheless, legal independence was withheld. The key issue was the lack of adequate constitutional provision for African voting rights and Parliamentary representation.

In 1962, the U.N. first acted affirmatively with respect to Southern Rhodesia, despite Britain's assertion that this was her private affair, when, in June, the General Assembly asserted that the area was a Non-Self-Governing territory and it called on the U.K. to suspend the 1961 Constitutuion and protect the native population.[30] In 1963, agreement with the U.K. was reached to dissolve the Federation as of January 1, 1964 and the U.K., at the U.N., vetoed a Security Council proposal that the U.K. not transfer sovereignty or Federation military forces to the then government of Southern Rhodesia. The Assembly then adopted resolutions with the same terms, asking also that there be no independence without majority rule based on universal suffrage.[31]

In Rhodesia, demands for independence, which was granted by the U.K. to the other two parties to the Federation, grew, but the British, under Commonwealth and African pressure, refused approval since there was still no firm commitment to eventual majority rule. In 1964, the U.K. asserted that it would not accept a unilateral declaration of independence (UDI) and in late spring the Security Council urged all states to ignore any UDI. In October, 1965, as the conflict neared a crisis, the General Assembly condemned any attempt to seize independence and called on the U.K. to suppress any rebellion if one broke out. On November 11, 1965, Southern Rhodesia, under Ian Smith's government, despite urgent British warnings and threats, declared, unilaterally, its independence.

Immediately after the unilateral declaration of independence of November 11, 1965, the General Assembly called on the U.K. to effectively end the rebellion and asked the Security Council to consider the matter. On November 12, meeting at the U.K.'s request, the Council condemned the UDI and called on all states to deny recognition to the Smith regime and to refrain from aiding the rebels.[32] Although the U.K. had theretofore insisted that the U.N. had no competence to deal with the internal affairs of the territory, it now believed the matter of "minority rule" to be of world concern, though still Britain's responsibility.[33] On November 20, in response to the African states' demands, the Council condemned the "usurpation of power," called on the U.K. to bring the regime to an immediate end and to take measures that would allow the people of Southern Rhodesia "to determine their own future." It called on all states not to recognize or establish diplomatic relations with the illegal authority; to refrain from providing the regime with any assistance or encouragement, particularly arms, equipment, and military material; and to sever economic relations and institute an embargo on oil and petroleum products. It also asked the OAU to assist in implementing this resolution.[34] This then was a call for complete economic sanctions against the rebel government, including a petroleum embargo. In early 1966, Prime Minister Wilson predicted that sanctions would end the rebellion "in a matter of weeks;"[35] he was wrong.

Since UDI, the U.K., under great international pressure from the new states, has reaffirmed its sovereignty over the area, has adopted a full range of economic sanctions and, as we have seen, has obtained overwhelming UN support for all nations to do the same, and, pressured by the African members of the Commonwealth, it has now threatened to ask the UN for mandatory (compulsory) economic sanctions to replace the measures now in effect, which remain only voluntary even for UN members, if the "re-

13

volt" is not ended by late 1966. Britain has also made it clear however that no military force will be used to retake the colony, despite demands by the African states.[36] Britain has also made it clear that it would prevent a UN use of force, what Prime Minister Wilson has called a "Red Army in Blue Berets."[37] The U.K. has nevertheless reaffirmed that independence will not be granted unless six principles are met, including:[38]

1. Unimpeded progress to majority rule, already enshrined in the 1961 constitution, to be maintained and guaranteed;
2. Guarantees against retrogressive amendment of the constitution;
3. Immediate improvement in the political status of the African population:
4. Progress towards ending racial discrimination;
5. The British Government would need to be satisfied that any basis proposed for independence was acceptable to the people of Rhodesia as a whole;
6. The "need to ensure that, regardless of race, there is no oppression of majority by minority or of minority by majority."

In April, 1966, two tankers appeared near the port of Beira, Mozambique, apparently loaded with petroleum for Rhodesia. The Security Council, meeting at the U.K.'s urgent request, declared that the "resulting situation constitutes a threat to the peace." It called on Portugal "not to receive at Beira oil destined for Rhodesia" and "not to permit oil to be pumped" through the Beira-Umtali pipeline, and requested all states to divert any of their vessels "reasonably believed" to be carrying oil for Southern Rhodesia. In addition the Council called on the United Kingdom to prevent "by the use of force if necessary" the arrival at Beira of vessels "reasonably believed" to be transporting oil to Southern Rhodesia.[39] The Council thus, for the first time, authorized a state to carry out a Council decision taken, it seems reasonably clear, under Chapter VII (Action with Respect to Threats to the Peace, Breaches of the Peace and Acts of Aggression) of the Charter.

The U.K. succeeded in preventing the unloading of these tankers but the Smith regime, bolstered by receipt of supplies, especially petroleum, from and through South Africa and Mozambique, has been repeatedly reported to have the internal economic situation well under control.[40] And sanctions have re-

14

portedly rallied the country behind the regime.[41] A few early internal strikes and disorders connected with UDI were quickly and easily crushed; potential native resistance is hampered by internal divisions in native leadership; and a few "invaders" to date, allegedly armed with Chinese and Soviet weapons, have apparently been summarily dealt with by security forces (which include native troops).[42] Internally, the regime has resorted to wartime repressive policies including strict censorship, import and export controls, a ban on strikes and demonstrations protesting independence now, and an increase in restrictive arrests.[43] In response to the economic sanctions, it has elevated economic information on its current markets and sources of supply to the status of state secrets. Thus far, the special restrictions on the native population do not resemble in quality or scope those of South Africa's apartheid and an ultimate goal of majority rule, in some form, is admitted. Nevertheless, a white minority controlled state for the foreseeable future and the preservation of special economic benefits that implies for the controllers is the stated objective of the rebellious government, reportedly spurred on by current African crises in such states as Nigeria and Ghana.[44] Land reserves, for example, are divided roughly equally between whites and blacks, though the latter outnumber the whites by eighteen to one.

Whether we class Rhodesia, like Angola, as basically a colonial issue, or with South Africa as a racial tyranny is perhaps factually unimportant. But legally, and, therefore, in political strategy, the distinction is clear and valuable to the African cause. The pressure from the African states to take aggressive action, to punish South Africa and Portugal for aiding the revolt, and even to punish the U.K. if the revolt is not soon ended has been constant and unremitting.[45] The U.K.'s indication at a Commonwealth meeting in September that it would seek mandatory sanctions, but not military action, if an accord was not reached by late 1966[46] clearly left many Commonwealth members unhappy. Indeed, it is difficult to believe that such a move could be effective unless South Africa and Portugal can be expected to risk Rhodesia's failure, which seems unlikely, or can be forced to deny Rhodesia all aid, which implies at least a comprehensive blockade of all southern

15

Africa and probably several years of patience and economic and political self-restraint by all.[47] For many reasons then, the prospects are dubious without military action.[48]

The absolute determination of the African states was again demonstrated in October, 1966, when the General Assembly condemned out of hand continuing talks between Smith and U.K. representatives. This suggests that they are unlikely to accept any negotiated settlement allowing sovereign independence to Rhodesia precisely to avoid converting the Rhodesian issue from a decolonization case into a legally more difficult "South Africa type" case. Can the U.K. be barred from coming to a settlement and granting independence with ostensibly enforcible guarantees? If not, need other states accept it? Non-recognition seems possible, indeed likely. In their present mood, and with the South West Africa victory in the General Assembly to whet their appetites, the Afro-Asian bloc might well vote Rhodesia a UN territory too.

All in all, Rhodesia, like the Portuguese territories, appears inevitably destined, perhaps after trouble and bloodshed, to have to submit eventually to decolonization with majority rule; the population figures against the "Europeans" are too irreversibly disproportionate though at the moment the white regime is in apparently firm control,[49] the African states lack the military force to act on their own,[50] and the U.K. is still very much interested in negotiating a settlement which may yet emerge. Yet as even the name, Rhodesia, itself reminds us, the white rulers are quixotic outcasts, determinedly pioneering in the wrong continent, in the wrong century, at the wrong end of an essentially ignoble and now politically unviable imperial experience, Once seized of the issue, no international organization purportedly representing the world's peoples could tolerate their ultimate victory over the massive native majority. To paraphrase a familiar slogan, the UN has little choice but to repeat, over and over, in effect, "Europeans go home" until they do.

South West Africa

South West Africa, a German colony before the First World War, was captured by South African forces in 1915. In 1917, the

16

British Cabinet decided that South Africa should be allowed to annex the area but in the peace settlement President Wilson's concept of no territorial aggrandizement prevailed and the territory was formally transferred for *administration* to the Union of South Africa by the Principal Allied and Associated Powers, acting on behalf of the League.[51] The League Council confirmed and defined the transfer as a Class C Mandate, to be administered as an integral portion of the Mandatory, with relatively few specific obligations on the Mandatory which was, however, to promote the well-being of the inhabitants and to make reports and submit certain disputes to the P.C.I.J. and was barred from modifying the status of the Territory without the Council's consent.[52] The international concern with South West Africa was thus formalized and has continued for almost fifty years.

Of the former Mandates, South West Africa was the only one which neither achieved independence directly nor was placed under the Trusteeship System of the United Nations. Indeed, in 1946, South Africa argued at the UN for full incorporation of the territory into the Union. The General Assembly refused to accede to the request and the Union Government decided then not to proceed with incorporation but to maintain the *status quo*.[53]

It is today an area of over 317 thousand square miles of difficult country inhabited by some half million people, 73,000 of whom are white, making the racial ratio about one white in seven.[54] The non-whites are associated with some eight or nine tribal or ethnic groups, several of which are from time to time in conflict with the others. Most of the Territory is desert or semi-desert; much was vacant land in 1920, the population having doubled since then.

South Africa has concentrated development in a so-called Police Zone and land was sold to white farmers in that area. As part of its admitted program of "separate development" along racial and ethnic lines in the Mandate, South Africa admittedly applied laws to the Mandate which classify persons as White, Native, Coloured and Asiatic and which make rights and duties dependent on the classification. Laws prevent Natives from being permanent residents or owners in the *urban* areas of the Police Zone, limit mineral prospecting in the Police Zone, except for native reserves, to Europeans, limit the jobs a Native can hold in min-

17

ing, the Civil Service, fishing, railroads and harbors, limit residential leaseholds by Natives, limit union and labor dispute rights of Natives, make it a crime for a Native to fail to perform labor contracts, exclude non-Whites from all important elections and offices, permit arrests of Natives freely as "idle persons," no doubt as a means of "encouraging" their employment and their circumspect behaviour in general, limit the travel and movement of all Natives and provide completely segregated and limited education for Natives.[55] While South Africa has delayed in implementing the so-called Odendaal study report, which called for even more formal "apartheid" policies, the facts of separate treatment, rights based on race and, indeed, implicitly forced labor are evident.[56]

Ever since the UN refused, in 1946, to accept South African annexation of the Mandate, questions concerning the status of the Territory have been before the UN in one way or another. In the history of this organized, determined international interest, of greatest importance are the several decisions of the International Court of Justice (ICJ) concerning the Mandate.

When the League was dissolved by its Members after the Second World War, it did not make specific provision for the future of the Mandates, perhaps on the assumption that they would all become Trust Territories through the voluntary action of the Mandatories. South Africa, as noted, made no such transfer and over the years denied at first a continuing substantial international interest in South West Africa while more recently it has been urging that the Mandate is extinguished.

To test and contest the South African position, the General Assembly asked for an Advisory Opinion from the ICJ on the status of South West Africa. On July 11, 1950, the Court held unanimously that the Territory remained an "international Mandate" and that the Union, "acting alone, has not the competence to modify the international status of the Territory" for to do so required UN consent.[57] By 12 votes to 2, the Court decided that South Africa "continues to have the international obligations stated in Article 22 of the Covenant . . . and in the Mandate . . . as well as the obligation" to transmit petitions and make reports under UN supervision. By a much narrower vote of eight to six, however, it was also held that South Africa was not obliged to place the Territory under the Trusteeship System, though all the Judges agreed she could do so. The Court was quite clear overall that the Mandate had not lapsed.

In additional Advisory Opinions in 1955 and 1956, the Court dealt with questions of voting in the UN concerning South West Africa and of the hearing of petitions from the Territory[58] but South Africa, while taking pains to preserve a separate status of sorts for the Mandate, gave no evidence of acceptance of the import of the 1950 Opinion, never reporting, for example, on conditions in the area as other states did for Trust and Non-Self-Governing Territories. To counter the lack of response to these Advisory Opinions, most of the UN members urged the African states which had been Members of the League to bring a contentious case against South Africa over the Territory presumably with the idea that, if they won and South Africa refused to comply with the Court's decision, the matter could be brought directly to the Security Council for action under Article 94(2) which provides:

> If any party to a case fails to perform the obligations incumbent upon it under a judgment rendered by the Court, the other party may have recourse to the Security Council, which may, if it deems necessary, make recommendations or decide upon measures to be taken to give effect to the judgment.

This Article has never been invoked and its meaning is not clear. Nevertheless a victory would have cleared up the issue of enforcement, of who could do what with respect to the already Court-recognized international rights of the peoples of the Territory. This, it was felt, would make further, more vigorous action easier to support and to explain at home for states traditionally imbued with a respect for courts and law and legal remedies, most particularly the United States and also, perhaps, the United Kingdom, states which might otherwise be reluctant to see the organized international community interpose itself forcefully between a sovereign and its "wards" in enforcement actions in which they might well be called upon to bear much of the contributions and sacrifices.

Thus, on November 4, 1960, the Governments of Liberia and Ethiopia filed identical Applications against South Africa asking the Court to adjudge that South West Africa is a territory under the Mandate; that the Respondent continues to have the international obligations stated in Article 22 of the Covenant of the League of Nations and in the Mandate for South West Africa as well as the obligation to transmit petitions from the inhabitants of the territory; and that the supervisory functions are to be exercised by the United Nations to which the annual reports and petitions are to be submitted. All these were essentially matters already covered by the earlier Advisory Opinions. In addition, perhaps the most important claim was that South Africa had failed to perform her prescribed duties in that she practiced apartheid in South West Africa (discriminated on a racial basis), adopted arbitrary and unjust laws for the area, placed military bases there, and in other ways failed to fulfill her obligations adequately.[59] Under Article 7 of the Mandate Agreement, it was asserted that South Africa was obliged to litigate these questions with interested League Members. Significantly, South Africa made its appearance to contest the case.

At first, South Africa resisted on jurisdictional grounds urging, *inter alia,* that these states lacked standing to sue, at least with respect to the general question of treatment of persons within the Territory. In 1962, by vote of 8 to 7, the Court asserted that it did in fact have jurisdiction to hear the matter, that these states could bring this suit.[60] South Africa, perhaps surprisingly, continued to contest the case, now on the merits and, over the next four years, the merits of the questions were debated and investigated at length before the Court.

Then, on July 18, 1966, the Court, after six years of proceedings, 336 hours of oral testimony, 3,756 pages of evidence, and 112 court sessions, dismissed the case on the ground that the applicants had no legal right or interest in the subject matter of the claim.[61] That interest, by implication, lies only in the now defunct Council of the League or, *perhaps,* in the United Nations as an entity, an entity which cannot, however, under the Charter of the Court, bring a litigous action. By vote of 8 to 7, with the President, Spender, having cast a double vote to break a tie, the minority of 1962 on the issue of jurisdiction became the majority[62] and the Court's Opinion did not reach the merits at all. The

Court's Opinion, the concurring opinion of Judge Van Wyk and the several vigorous dissents all devote most of their efforts to the meaning of Article 7, paragraph 2 of the Mandate Agreement, to the meaning of the Mandate System, the initial obligations thereunder and related questions, and to who may enforce the present content of the Mandate obligations, if any persist. Technically, the results of the 1962 and 1966 Opinions seem to say that, while Ethiopia and Liberia had standing to bring the suit, they lack standing to obtain a judgment, an example of "the legal mind at work" in a manner to baffle even the initiated and leading Judge Jessup to describe the 1966 Judgment as absurd. While doubtless of considerable interest in law, the decision cannot be discussed in depth here; we focus at this point rather, on the most important implications and aftereffects for purposes of our discussion, returning to the decision again later within the context of our discussion of human rights.

Clearly the most significant political result of the decision was the immediate return of the question of South West Africa to the organized international political arena. The African states, which had been urged over the years by the West to wait patiently for the expected orderly, legal defeat of South Africa were outraged. The Court's action was called one "to confound its advocates and give joy to its opponents,"[63] an "abdication of responsibility," a "slap in the face."[64] Retribution has been threatened against the majority judges.[65] There have been expressions of disillusion with the UN system and demands that all organs of the UN be reorganized to meet the needs of modern times.[66]

For some fifteen years, the UN had tried to gain supervision over the Territory with no success.[67] In 1965, at the UN's twentieth session, the General Assembly had again condemned South Africa over its actions in the Territory, condemned apartheid, warned that partition of South West Africa would violate the Mandate and that annexation would be aggression, and asked the Security Council to watch over this "serious threat to international peace and security."[68] During the first weeks of the 21st session, almost every nation demanded that the UN should assert control over South West Africa with the African and some other states insisting on the immediate creation of a UN authority there. Even those states which usually counsel caution, such as the United States, were equally clear that the Mandate persisted; that apartheid was reprehensible and intolerable; and that South Africa, having failed in her duties, should be ousted as Mandatory.[69] As a result, on October 27, 1966, the General Assembly by 114 to 2 (Portugal, South Africa) with France and the U.K. abstaining, resolved that the Mandate was terminated; that South Africa had, "in fact, disavowed the Mandate," and that the Territory is henceforth "a direct responsibility of the United Nations."[70] The fact that Ethiopia and Liberia, in losing the case on "legalistic" procedural grounds had exhausted all presently available legal remedies has, if anything, expedited and increased the decisiveness and definitive nature of the will of the General Assembly majority concerning South West Africa and has served to escalate the UN pressures on all southern Africa.

Since it was apparent that the Security Council was unlikely to authorize the use of force at this stage,[71] the Afro-Asian states modified their demands for the immediate appointment of a UN administering authority and accepted the creation of a 14-nation special committee to study practical means for UN administration which is to report by April, 1967. The United States has expressed willingness to serve on such a commission which will have the formidable task of trying to secure South Africa's acceptance of the UN action. South Africa has already stated that it regards the resolution as illegal; that it will not discuss any change in the Territory's status; that the commission will not be permitted into the area; and that it is reexamining its position as a UN member. Moreover, the South African Foreign Minister has stated that South Africa: "will resist with all the power at its disposal any attempts which endanger the safety of our country or of the peoples committed to our care."[72]

Despite South Africa's anticipated immovability, the issue remains more akin to the eviction of an old-style colonial overlord rather than to direct intervention into the domestic territory of a state on grounds of a supervening international standard. There are relatively few white settlers and they might readily be absorbed into the Republic proper; they are in general fairly recent arrivals in the territory; they are largely South African. They do have a place to retreat to in extremis just as the "colons" returned from Algeria to France. Although South Africa's bellicosity and expressions of self-righteousness have increased as a result of the "victory" at the Court, the facts that South Africa has historically acted more cautiously vis-à-vis South West Africa than at home in extending formal apartheid, in refraining from building military bases, and indeed in arguing before the ICJ, and that she has good reason to avoid direct, forceful international intervention in the Territory which might readily spill over into South Africa proper, suggest that she might, in time, be induced to yield on the Mandate in ways that would be unthinkable, in white South African eyes, for the foreseeable future with respect to the homeland. We return to these prospects in the last part of this paper.

The Republic of South Africa

South Africa itself, the most prosperous and technologically advanced nation on the African continent, presents a quite different legal setting from these other three colonial areas. South Africa is an unquestionably independent state whose internal policies and the ethos they employ differ so markedly from those professed by other nations that most of the UN members have voted to call for a change in her domestic constitutional arrangements and her prevailing domestic ideology and ethical system with some states, at least, advocating the use of international force if needed to impose the demanded internal political changes.[73] It is here that the clash between national sovereignty as the foundation stone of the present world system and a demand for an overriding internationally enforcible standard of minimum human rights comes most sharply into focus.[74]

South Africa has been described as beautiful. It is a country of mild climate and rich treasures whose major products include diamonds and, in company with the Soviet Union, most of the world's new monetary gold. The few dozen Dutch traders who established a village at the Cape of Good Hope in 1652 were the first white men to settle in the reportedly then empty area in the southern extreme of the continent. There are now some 3.4 million whites who rule some 12 million "Bantu" (Blacks), 1.5 million Coloureds (mulattoes) and a half million Asians.

23

During the Napoleonic Wars, England seized Capetown from the Dutch who had already begun to move inland. Gold and diamonds were discovered in the 1870's and 1880's and, as the British moved in in the South, the Boer (meaning farmer) descendants of the Dutch moved farther inland, for they came to the land as settlers, not as colonial overseers, fighting and pressing back the Bantu who made their appearance along the frontier. The Boers established the Republic of Transvaal and the Orange Free State in the north while the British formed Natal and the Cape Colony in the south. In a war from 1899–1902, the British defeated the Boers and unified the country.

In conformity with the Commonwealth concept, then primarily for European-stock self-governing members, South Africa became largely autonomous by the end of the First World War. After the Second World War, the Afrikaner-dominated Nationalist Party obtained parliamentary control and the policy of apartheid (official separate development) became the rule of the land, formalizing and further elaborating in law the already existing white discriminations and control and intensifying and sanctioning in law all types of racial segregation. In 1961 the Republic of South Africa was born as the country left the Commonwealth after being denounced on the apartheid issue.

In the concept of apartheid, the South Africans stress the notion of *separate* development. In the current South African view, it includes "self-determination" and "self-government" of each major racial group within its own separate enclaves. The division of the lands is of course made by the central government and, as is traditional in such political circumstances, it has been changed at times to accord with newly discovered needs of the white minority when they emerge. Native enclaves called Bantustans are scattered throughout South Africa. They amount to 13 per cent of the land for 80 per cent of the people and include little of South Africa's special resource riches. Ordinarily "white" private capital is not permitted to invest in them, to preserve the inviolability of the separation; this also of course perpetuates their underdevelopment. Since the Bantustans could not support more than a fraction of the people now allotted to them, it has been argued that even if a true internal partition of the country were accomplished in this manner the inhabitants of the Bantustans would remain largely dependent on employment in the white areas for survival.[75]

In South Africa, at times even the classification of races accords with the needs of the controlling minority: Chinese, for example, are non-whites; Japanese (whose interest in trade is high) are according to the press, "honorary Aryans." [76] Control over all activities of non-whites is complete; their presence in white areas is "migratory."[77] The Bantu Laws Amendment Act and Bantu Labour Act of 1964 provide the controlling mechanisms which regulate all details of the non-white's life: where he can live, at what he can work, how he can find a job if out of work, how (if at all) he can vote, what land he can own, restrictions on his marriage, political associations, how he is educated, and the like. Any privilege can be canceled at any time. And every facility is separate and segregated: housing, transport, public amenities of all sorts, and education.[78] Nor may the African strike to improve his lot at work.[79]

For *all* South Africans, there are over twenty-five kinds of banning orders available under the Suppression of Communism Act and the Minister of Justice's interpretation of that act cannot be challenged. The "180 day law" permits imprisonment, incommunicado and without charges, of any person as a possible witness in a security case. The Government also possesses almost unlimited power to ban organizations, to ban persons from political activity, to make it a crime to publish anything any such person says or writes, to keep them under constant house arrest, to remove the right of habeas corpus, to use renewable periods of 90 days solitary confinement to obtain information, and has other similar rights as well. The availability of funds and counsel for defendants in cases involving state security has been drastically curtailed.[80] The movement of large numbers of people from their established homes to accord with concepts of separation of each of the racial groups has occurred. Yet the Bantu of necessity form a large part of the work force and, even after the Bantustans are complete most will form part of the work force of the general economy. As the Legums have written: "There is no real Separate Development, only racial discrimination in an integrated economy."[81] Thus, in sum, South Africa is what Lancelot Hogben once called a "pigmentocracy"[82] in which the "discrimination is racial and unashamed"[83] and the status, rights, duties, opportunities and burdens of the population are determined and allotted arbitrarily on the basis of race, color, and tribe, in a pattern which ignores the needs and capacities of the groups and individuals affected, and subordinates the interests and rights of the great majority of the people to the preferences of a minority. Yet South Africans assert that they are much concerned with human rights and that "In South Africa oppression is as much contrary to law and morals as in any country on earth."[84]

Signs of unrest have been rapidly and ruthlessly suppressed as at Sharpeville in 1960 and internal opposition by the native population, divided within itself in any event, has been curbed by arrests, banning orders and constant harassment almost to the point of invisibility.[85] Indeed the ineffectiveness of local black opposition no doubt contributes to the demands by African states that the UN and the major powers act. Despite the UN's concern, foreign investment is heavy, and continuing, with the UK's total commitments in the area alone estimated at perhaps $3 billion, and white immigration continues, presumably attracted by the economic opportunity in Afrikaanerland where a renewed boom has been in progress since 1961 and where foreign investment earns high returns and a white man has a good life and cheap native help.[86] Moreover, in response to Black African and international pressure to achieve a "non-racial" society, South Africa has unified under the Afrikaner banner.[87] The late Dr. Verwoerd's Nationalist Party won a three to one majority in the general election held in early 1966 with white opposition parties all but disappearing.[88] A bill to ban political parties permitting Bantu participation and to forbid the *discussion* of politics in any racially mixed group has been at least temporarily shelved[89] but, the present solidarity of all major white groups, Afrikaner and English, behind the Government is clear. Indeed, as with Ghandi on another continent, the assassin of Prime Minister Verwoerd in September, 1966, was apparently an extremist right-winger, a member of the new right wing extremist Republican Party which claims that too much has already been done for the Bantu.[90] And

Dr. Verwoerd's successor, Mr. Vorster, has reaffirmed the sanctity of apartheid.[91]

The UN's interest in this rich, extraordinarily dynamic, frankly racist, society has been evident from its first sessions.[92] In 1946, India brought to the General Assembly a complaint about the treatment of people of Indian origin in South Africa. Discriminatory measures against the Indians, leading to passive resistance movements led by Ghandi in 1907 and 1913 were followed by agreements between India and South Africa in 1927 and 1932 but additional discriminatory legislation in 1943 and 1946, in particular, led to Indian protests, the withdrawal of the Indian High Commissioner to South Africa and a trade embargo by India. At the UN, India urged that this was both an international dispute and a violation of the U.N. Charter provisions barring racial discrimination. South Africa argued that Article 2(7) prevented even discussion of the matter and that, in any event, the Charter did not define human rights so that the issue should die for lack of legal certainty as to the rights to be protected or that the question of the General Assembly's competence should go to the International Court of Justice.[93] India urged that "fundamental violations of the principles of the Charter" could not be matters of domestic jurisdiction[94] and several other representatives asserted that Article 2(7) was no barrier and that human rights were not "essentially within the domestic jurisdiction of the state."[95] The Assembly adopted resolutions on these issues at almost every session through the Sixteenth, at which time the question was merged into that of apartheid. Positions have not subsequently changed.[96] South Africa was urged to negotiate with India and to ameliorate the economic, legal and social condition of those of Indian descent in her population but South Africa has not yielded at all on this issue.

The apartheid question as such has been before the U.N. since 1952 when thirteen Afro-Asian states requested that the question of race conflict in South Africa be put on the General Assembly's agenda as a threat to international peace and a violation of basic principles of human rights and fundamental freedoms.[97] South Africa insisted that Article 2(7) used the term "nothing" and meant it and argued that even discussion was improper intervention in this purely domestic issue.[98] It was denied that any threat to international peace existed, the only situation admittedly overriding Article 2(7). Initially, Australia, Belgium, France, New Zealand and Britain supported the South African view while the United States, Canada and the Scandinavian countries felt that the matter could be discussed but that only general appeals for the observance of human rights could issue. Other countries rejected South Africa's position completely.[99] The outcome of the discussion was that a three member Commission was appointed to study the racial situation in South Africa.[100] That Commission, in its Report of October 3, 1953, concluded that action of the Assembly with respect to human rights was not "intervention" within the meaning of Article 2(7) and that South Africa's racial policies violated the Charter and the Universal Declaration of Human Rights which were said to ban discrimination on racial lines, and also impaired friendly relations among states.[101]

The General Assembly discussed and adopted resolutions on South Africa's racial policies at every session thereafter and the Security Council has, less frequently, acted as well.[102] On April 1, 1960, after the Sharpeville massacre, the Council recognized that the situation in South Africa had led to international friction and, if continued, might endanger international peace and security and it called for measures to bring about equality and racial harmony.[103] In 1961, the Assembly also resolved that South Africa's policies had led to international friction and that they endangered international peace.[104] A proposal at this time to recommend economic sanctions failed to obtain the needed two-thirds vote. In November, 1962 however, the Assembly verbally chastized South Africa for its "determined aggravation" of racial issues and requested Members to end diplomatic relations with South Africa, to close their ports and airspace to her ships and aircraft and to impose an embargo on imports from and exports to her, especially arms.[105] A Special Committee on Policies of Apartheid was established to keep South Africa's racial policies under review and report regularly to the U.N. The Security Council was asked to take appropriate measures, including sanctions, to secure South Africa's compliance with U.N. resolutions. Among the sixteen states voting against the resolution however, were South Africa's chief trading partners, Britain, the United States, France, Canada, Australia, Japan and Belgium and all the recommended economic and diplomatic sanctions to date have had little perceptible effect on South Africa's economy,[106] or on her political policies.

In August, 1963, the Security Council called on States to cease the sale of arms, munitions and military vehicles to South Africa;[107] in October, the Assembly called for the release of South African political prisoners; and in December the Council asked for the establishment of a Group of Experts to examine the whole problem.[108] In April, 1964, that Group called for the convening of a truly representative national assembly, on the basis of one man, one vote, to alter South Africa's constitutional structure to provide an integrated non-racial society. The Commission recommended the use of mandatory economic sanctions if South Africa failed to agree. The General Assembly accepted this Report and its suggestions for the internal political reorganization of South Africa.[109] Needless to say, the South African government has not complied and no mandatory sanctions have been ordered by the Council.

In March, 1965, a study of economic sanctions, prepared by a Committee of Experts at the request of the Security Council was presented to the U.N.[110] Here, the nature of the South African economy was explored at length and its peculiar strength as a well industrialized, if small, country and as an exporter of gold and diamonds, both light in weight and greatly sought after, were noted. It was also suggested that, for an economic break to have any substantial effect, it would have to be sharp and total both as to goods and countries involved, that it probably needed at least a naval blockade to make it effective and that, in addition to the costs of such a naval campaign, which are high, it would doubtless be costly to many of the participating states due to losses of trade and prospective South African countermeasures with respect to foreign investments and property. That properly conducted economic warfare could have some effect on the economy was never doubted however[111] and South Africa has heeded all the warnings in these studies and UN actions, in a sense, by stockpiling, intensifying the search for reliable access to resources, especially oil, at home, in Angola, and elsewhere, and in other ways making ready, with apparent effectiveness, for all eventualities.[112]

In 1965, the General Assembly again deplored the military build-up in South Africa and the continued growth of foreign investment there, requested an arms embargo, called the continued existence of apartheid a threat to international peace and security and called anew for at least economic action by the Security Council under Chapter VII. [113] An attempt to enlarge the Committee on Apartheid during 1966, no doubt in an attempt to involve those states which had not approved earlier calls for sanctions against South Africa, was frustrated by the refusal to serve of the U.S., the U.K., France and 12 others. This precipitated further attacks on their "participation" in apartheid. Some, like France, which has not even agreed to the arms embargo with which the other major powers are officially cooperating, opposed generally the interventionary aims of the U.N. in this case; others, while supporting the ends, apparently objected to the somewhat precipitous ways in which the Committee conducted its investigations and made its condemnations.[114]

While 61 states have apparently applied an economic embargo, the major Western powers have not limited trade, except in arms. Any obligatory enforcement action under Chapter VII has been resisted for economic reasons, the fear of disastrous loss of trade and investment, especially in view of the probable ineffectiveness of economic measures if used alone, and their unwillingness to go beyond economic measures to the use of force and the supplying of men, ships and arms for a potentially bloody fight,[115] and on the ground that "in terms of Article 2(7) of the Charter, the United Nations is precluded from considering the issue [of apartheid]," [116] or because no immediate threat of hostilities exists.[117] The Council's resolutions have been worded in terms of Chapter VI which deals with the "peaceful settlement" of disputes and does not provide for mandatory action.[118]

Current U.N. action continues to include attacks by the Special Committee on Apartheid,[119] a Programme for the Education and Training Abroad of South Africans, a U.N. Trust Fund to provide legal assistance to victims of racial discrimination in South Africa,[120] attacks on South Africa's policies by the UN's Committee on Decolonization, and special informational activities such as the Seminar on Apartheid, held in the summer of 1966 in Brazil, which blistered South Africa (and the West in general).[121] Yet the South African government has not yielded nor, since many Afrikaners at least believe South Africa's racial policies to be both moral and correct in divine eyes,[122] and since spokesmen and writers have made it clear that the white population, Afrikaner and English-speaking alike, considers that its stand is necessary for the survival, not to mention the survival in comfort, of those whose interests it represents, is it likely to yield in its confrontation with the UN. The experts are also pessimistic. They express grave doubts as to the capacity of the legally repressed native majority to arise, nor do the new African states possess sufficient power, even if they were free from internal strife, to mount, at present, a successful attack on their own against the major African armed force south of the Sahara, and perhaps in all Africa. Yet time moves rapidly, even in Africa.

Having looked at southern Africa and the UN's role to date, we must still come to grips with the more general legal and political issues involved. For our purposes, perhaps we can state the legal problems sequentially this way: are there, today, norms of binding law protecting the right of "peoples" to become nations and protecting the "human rights" of individual humans, as such, even against their own states? If not, are such norms emerging? If so, what is their present and future standing in the hierarchy of international legal norms, especially vis-à-vis that cornerstone of the present system, national sovereignty? If they exist, who may enforce them, and by what methods?

II. SOVEREIGNTY AND NON-INTERVENTION

While, as we will see in the next section, an increasing number of states has been willing to accept as law an emerging, highly circumscribed, international interest in the protection of human rights, *all* states accept as the cornerstone of the present international system for all usual purposes the concept of the sovereign authority of the national state. Indeed, many nations most actively supporting intervention in southern Africa by the UN and by

African states, if appropriate,[123] are the strongest supporters of non-intervention in domestic affairs when all other questions are discussed.[124] And by near unanimous vote on December 21, 1965, the General Assembly adopted a resolution[125] on intervention declaring that no state had a right to intervene in the "internal or external affairs" of another state by *any* form of interference or coercive measure. This resolution barred aid to subversive activities designed to overthrow a government as well.

Admittedly, then, the cornerstone of the present international system remains the sovereign authority of the national state. Statehood implies the right to near-absolute control over persons, things and acts on the national territory[126] and the right to be free from "dictatorial intervention" or interference from other states and even from groups of states organized into international organizations.[127] In the words of Vattel:[128]

> No sovereign state may inquire into the manner in which a sovereign rules nor set itself up as a judge of his conduct nor force him to make any changes in his administration. If he burdens his subject with taxes or treats them with severity it is for the nation to take action; no foreign state is called on to mend his conduct and to force him to follow a wiser and juster course.

And Brierly, three centuries later, could write that:[129]

> [Sovereignty] stands for the power of modern States, the power of their governments to decide and to act without consulting others and without concern for anything but their own interests as they themselves conceive those interests . . . .

Or in the words of Chief Justice Marshall in Schooner Exchange v. McFaddon:[130]

> The jurisdiction of the nation within its own territory is necessarily exclusive and absolute. It is susceptible of no limitation not imposed by itself.

These strong statements demonstrate that the consistency of sovereignty with any binding international obligations requires explanation. Indeed, it is difficult to dispute the logic of Morganthau's conclusion that this conception of sovereignty (which he shares) both requires and is consistent only with "a decentralized, and hence weak and ineffective international legal order. For national sovereignty is the very source of that decentralization, weakness and ineffectiveness." Consequently, in such a system:

> Only a relatively small number of rules of international law do not owe their existence to the consent of the members of the international community. They are either the logical precondition for the existence of any legal system, such as rules of interpretation and rules providing sanctions, or they are the logical precondition for the existence of a multiple-state system, such as the rules delimiting the jurisdiction of individual states.[131]

He goes on:

> Rules of this kind are binding upon all states, regardless of their consent, and might be called the common or necessary law, the *jus necessarium* of the modern state system. Their binding force does not affect the sovereignty of the individual nations. Indeed it makes sovereignty as a legal concept possible. For without the mutual respect for the territorial jurisdiction of the individual nation, and without the legal enforcement of that respect, international law and a state system based on it could obviously not exist.

Many scholars, particularly those who espouse the growth of the international legal regulation of human rights, of course take a less narrowly positivist position.[132] Furthermore, the consistency of the existence of international organizations capable of taking decisions by any binding majority rule with the continued existence of sovereignty also requires explanation. To this, Morganthau states simply (if non-operationally) that: "unequal representation and majority rule [in international organizations] may or may not be compatible with sovereignty. The answer would depend on whether or not this deviation from the rule of unanimity transfers supreme authority from the national government to an international agency." He concludes that none of the present international organizations with their "elaborate safeguards" affect the sovereignty of the individual states. This seems certainly true for those states with vetoes in the Security Council. The nature of the circumstances in which he feels sovereignty would be "lost" to an international authority are once again interesting and typical of scholarly opinion:[133] "The nation would have renounced its sovereignty if it had consented to submit to the majority vote of an operating international agency such matters as amendments to the constitution, declaration of war, composition of the government and financial policies. Then by virtue of the international agreement establishing majority rule, the decisive political power would have shifted from the natural government to the international" agency, which would then exercise the supreme law giving and law-enforcing authority, *i.e.*, sovereignty within the national territory.

The League of Nations was based firmly on the concept of the sovereign equality of its Members; in principle, no action could be taken by its Council or Assembly without the unanimous concurrence of all Members, thus presumably preserving each from inroads by the others. The UN was likewise designed of course as an organization of sovereigns. Article 2(1) proclaims "the principe of the sovereign equality of all its Members" and Article 2(7) provides that:

> Nothing contained in the present Charter shall authorize the United Nations to intervene in matters which are essentially within the domestic jurisdiction of any state or shall require the Members to submit such matters to settlement under the present Charter; but this principle shall not prejudice the application of enforcement measures under Chapter VII.

Some scholars have suggested that this clearly eliminates UN intervention on human rights grounds.[134] In a hierarchy of norms confirmed in the Charter, "domestic jurisdiction" for them outranks human rights though we must bear in mind one important point—a human rights issue which developed into a "threat to the peace, breach of the peace or act of aggression," the language of Chapter VII, would permit intervention by the Charter's own terms.

Over the years, various states have argued that even UN discussion of what they regard as their "domestic" concerns constitutes unlawful intervention in their internal affairs.[135] Such arguments have been made in decolonization situations, for example, in the cases of the Netherlands and Indonesia, France and Algeria and Portugal and her African colonies. They have been urged by South Africa in questions of human rights. They were made by the Soviet Union concerning the rights of Soviet women, the Czechoslovakian case and the Hungarian intervention of 1956. They have been pressed by France and other countries on various occasions as well.[136] The near-uniform practice in the UN has been to ignore this claim when raised as an objection and to discuss the matter and adopt resolutions relatively freely, though, except in the long-run effects on decolonization, such activities have not always had any great impact on the offending state.

It must also be remembered that the UN, like the League, was initially designed primarily to maintain peace, the status quo, and that the constitutional structure of a "peaceful" Member is normally considered in the Charter to be outside the scope of the Organization's action potential. For example, the Charter does not itself specify the type of state eligible to membership. There was no such qualification for the fifty-odd original Members, including South Africa, and the qualification raised in Article 4, that applicants be "peace-loving" has proved both undefinable and unimportant since the Organization has for a decade admitted all nations seeking entry with the few well-known political problems including Germany and Korea and the appropriate representation for China still unresolved.

The one effort to bring pressure to bear against a State (a non-Member) to force a change in constitutional structure occurred with Spain in 1946 and following years and was a total failure. While technically based on the "finding" that Fascist Spain constituted a threat to world peace, it was clear that Spain was not in fact then engaged in aggression nor breaching the peace nor did it, considering its power base, actually present a direct threat to any other State, not even to Gibraltar. What was frankly desired by the leaders of several nations was to force a change in Spain's government, to oust the Fascist government in office and thus change the constitutional structure of the country.

The definition of an "acceptable" government was indeed a model, one that at least four-fifths of the present U.N. membership could not match, in its call for a government:

> which derives its authority from the consent of the governed, committed to respect freedom of speech, religion and assembly, and to the prompt holding of an election in which the ... people, free from force and intimidation and regardless of party, may express their will ...

This definition would seem to rule out the majority of U.N. Members if they were to be put to the test.

The recommended measure, an embargo on diplomatic relations with Spain, seems to have had the effect of strengthening

Franco against the "common enemy" and clearly did not weaken his grip. Furthermore, it is useful to note that, though the General Assembly, in Res. 39(1) of 1946 and Res. 114 (II) of 1947, recommended that the Security Council consider "adequate measures to be taken" should certain conditions not obtain in Spain, the Council refused to discuss either resolution and thus to consider further action. While they were not anxious to insist on defiance of the Assembly's recommendations, the Western Great Powers were also obviously unwilling to move to change a domestic order and to convert Franco from a minor annoyance into a major issue.[137]

In general then, while the norm of "domestic jurisdiction" does not bar the UN's exhorting members to do right or putting pressure on them to conform to some other *agreed* norm, there nevertheless remains a bar to *this* Organization's acting as the scourge of the Lord to punish some special group even in the case of a generally agreed *domestic* wrong, unless, of course, it is so flagrant as to offend "basic principles of justice." It is the implications of this exception to which we turn next. Furthermore, since the Charter is a constitution, whether some states would have it so or not, we will expect to find that the division between two of its norms, domestic jurisdiction and the international interest in human rights, is and will continue to be a shifting one. Yet the example of Spain warns us of the perils that international intervention against a government regime can be both purely political and, unless backed by a will to succeed and genuine force, ineffectual or worse.

The fact is that sovereignty is a political reality. It exists in the power of the individual states to defend effectively their final control over their territory and populations; it is this practical fact which gives rise to the legal conception and the limits it implies for collective actions by an international organization. As Toynbee has said: "The only point in having law is to make life work. Otherwise there will be explosions." The present sanctity of the sovereign, expressed in the concept of domestic jurisdiction, against most intervention by a general international organization is merely a reflection of the current state of the international community and serves to make international collective life workable.

III. *LAW: THE INTERNATIONAL PROTECTION OF HUMAN RIGHTS*

While the quest for international protection of human rights has received dramatic impetus in the last two decades, the concept as already indicated is much older. In 1650 for example Grotius, drawing on examples from history including threatened interventions to prevent persecution of Christians, concluded that humanitarian intervention to preserve human rights was permissible. He wrote that a state could intervene forcibly in another "for the justifiable purpose of protecting the inhabitants of another state from treatment which is so arbitrary and persistently abusive as to exceed the limits of that authority within which the sovereign is presumed to act with reason and justice." [138] He was at once attacked by Vatell [139] on this issue and admitted that the sovereign was normally the "supreme judge in his own kingdom" but held to his basic view. While the issue of "just" wars has been debated ever since, this view has certainly not been the accepted norm in past centuries nor is it the favored norm of those positivists who stress the sovereign as the source of law and of enforcement except, perhaps, in exceptional cases. There are nevertheless numerous examples of international arrangements designed to protect the life and decent survival of humans, at least against the actions of states of which they were *not* nationals. We can cite such examples as the early treaties dealing with the conduct of hostilities, the humanitarian conventions of the 19th and early 20th centuries, the Capitulations and other treaties designed to protect co-religionists in other countries, the arrangements concerning the slave trade and many others. [140]

While the Covenant of the League of Nations made no mention of the rights of individuals, it did formalize, in the Mandates System, the concept of an international interest in dependent peoples, which we will examine again shortly. [141] In addition to the Mandates arrangements, many of the roughly 25 million people in Central and Eastern Europe who were ethnic minorities in the post-World War I national states came under special international arrangements in the Minorities Treaties. The fact that President Wilson's view of self-determination, the release of "peoples" from the control of the Hapsburg and Turkish empires,[142] was largely achieved did not, of course, eliminate the problems of the "self-determination" of still smaller groups of "peoples" who were left as minorities in the balkanized Balkans and Eastern Europe. This type of conceptual problem is indeed inherent in the concept of self-determination and has reappeared regularly when that concept has been used operationally. It presents itself repeatedly in contemporary southern Africa as well.[143]

Nevertheless, over a dozen arrangements concluded as part of the overall peace settlement provided for varying guarantees that differences of race, language and religion would not work to the prejudice of any minority group.[144] The League Council was the "guarantor" of these provisions. Moreover, on September 21, 1922, the League's Assembly asked League Members not otherwise subject to the arrangements to treat their minorities in accordance with these standards.[145] Yet in only a limited number of cases could petitions be brought to the League. Despite the complete protection of the lives and rights of minorities ostensibly provided by these arrangements and the League's guarantee to "persons belonging to racial, religious or linguistic minorities," the regimes provided have on the whole been considered to have failed to provide effective protection,[146] despite some modest successes in permitting individuals to bring claims even against their own states in Upper Silesia.[147] Indeed, there is evidence that the treaties were considered an intolerably offensive derogation from the sovereignty of the affected states. Enforcement through collective intervention was certainly no part of the League's system nor could it have been expected at the time.[148] And the Great Powers had been specifically unwilling to include principles of religious toleration and racial equality in the Covenant.

Intervention for ethnic or similar reasons in the League period was in fact confined to protecting one's own nationals or descendants of the intervenor's ethnic background. And some of the minorities created by the World War I settlement provided the political handle for intervention south and east by Hitler, the

Sudeten Germans, the Danzig German "majority." Such "effective" protection of ethnic minorities has been of this type in the post-World War II period as well and the rapid formation of new states in the past two decades promises many more such conflicts. We note below, for example, the problem of Cyprus.

But the UN period is marked by a different approach in general to these issues. First of all, it was recognized that even the extent of balkanization achieved at Versailles had been politically disruptive, producing highly competitive and not always politically and economically viable small states which became pawns or mischief makers of international politics depending on the point of view.[149] Hence initially there seemed to be a new approach to self-determination which itself was qualified by some implicit bias towards viability of the resultant sovereigns: larger, even potentially great states such as India, Pakistan and Indonesia were preferred. Since they were inevitably composites, self determination was denied the sub groups and the implied minorities issues were obvious.

Second, the limited utility of minorities treaties and "entrenched constitutional guarantees," imposed as derogations to be enforced against unwilling sovereigns, was apparently generally understood. Though included in a few peace treaties and in a few other unsuccessful instances, such as Cyprus, this approach has been largely abandoned. An alternative approach to the minorities problem, partition, was applied where insisted on by the "peoples" concerned, preferably again where, as with the Indian subcontinent, this would leave large, potentially viable states. Elsewhere, for the bulk of the new states the issue of the rights of component peoples was in fact simply ignored. During the decolonization struggles, the ultimate problems for the component "peoples" of the new, non-integrated states were in part masked, but, as with the Congo and with Nigeria today, to note just two examples among many, not for long. To the aftermath of qualified "self-determination" stressing, if possible, viable units, usually on historical colonial lines of administration without provision for effective minority protection we return, of necessity, below.

As seems fitting in the case of so widespread a set of problems, the approach to an international interest in human rights under the UN has been turned from the particular to the general. There were few specified minorities derogations in this peace settlement but the Charter, unlike the Covenant, makes direct reference to human rights and freedoms. It thus has been said to bring individuals more directly into the international legal arena.[150] The Charter affirms in its Preamble,[151]

> faith in fundamental human rights, in the dignity and worth of the human person, in the equal rights of men and women.

A stated purpose of the Organization is:

> the achievement of international cooperation is promoting and encouraging respect for human rights and for fundamental freedoms for all without distinction as to race, sex, language or religion.[152]

To this end, the General Assembly is to initiate studies and make recommendations "for the purpose of assisting in the realization of human rights and fundamental freedoms"[153] and, under Article 55, the Organization is to promote "universal respect for, and observance of, human rights and fundamental freedoms for all without distinction as to race, sex, language or religion." The Economic and Social Council is authorized to make recommendations to the General Assembly and/or the Members and the Specialized Agencies "for the purpose of promoting respect for, and observance of, human rights and fundamental freedoms for all" and it was also to set up Commissions for the promotion of human rights,[154] which it did soon after the U.N. was created.[155] One of the objectives of the Trusteeship System as well is the encouragement of respect for human rights.[156] And in Article 56, "All members pledge themselves to take joint and separate action in cooperation with the Organization for the achievement of the purposes set forth in Article 55." No further specific provisions for implementing these provisions are included.

From the outset, there was no scholarly agreement as to whether or not the Charter provisions placed any affirmative obligations on members with respect to human rights. Some writers argued that these provisions "do not constitute legal norms, but only guiding principles," that there is no way in general to protect these rights unless the "violation of human rights constitutes a danger to peace";[157] and that the "Charter does not impose upon the members a strict obligation to grant to their subjects the rights and freedoms mentioned in the Preamble in the text of the Charter" and that members are not "under legal obligations regarding the rights and freedoms of their subjects." [158] On the other hand, it was also said that

> it is already the law, at least for members of the United Nations, that respect for human dignity and fundamental human rights is obligatory.

even if international enforcement was not provided for, a not unusual circumstance in international law.[160]

Outside the UN, a developing interest in the protection of individual human rights has also grown, in some regions, even more quickly. Indeed, for Western Europe, where the states could achieve a consensus on these issues relatively readily, the first major hurdle, the creation of a court available to citizens directly for certain types of actions even against their own states, has already been passed.[161]

In addition to the general provisions, as after the First World War, some defeated enemy states were obliged in peace treaties "to take all measures necessary to secure to all persons under its jurisdiction without distinction as to race, sex, language or religion, the enjoyment of human rights and fundamental freedoms including freedom of expression, of the press and publication, of religious worship, of political opinion and of public meeting." [162] Attempts by the Western Powers to secure compliance with these guarantees by the Communist states through individual diplomatic pressures, exclusion from the UN in its early years, condemnation in the UN and attempts to bring them before the ICJ have met with no success.[163]

UN Activities Related to Human Rights Issues

Under the League, as we have noted, while the "sacred trust" was duly made a part of the Mandate System, little direct supervision existed. Under the Charter, as stated above, the Trusteeship System contained, as one of its purposes, "to encourage respect for human rights" [164] and the Trusteeship Agreements contained provisions and guarantees to this effect. Indeed the Agreement for Somaliland, placed by the Assembly under Italian tutelage for a fixed ten-year period, contained elaborate guarantees as to freedom of speech, press, assembly, petition, conscience and worship as well as prohibitions on slavery, child marriage and forced labor and had a "Declaration of Constitutional Principles" attached to it as well.[165] It is in part through the Trusteeship System, and through the far more widespread opportunities to exert pressure contained in the Charter provisions for reports on conditions in all Non-Self-Governing Territories[166] that the astonishingly rapid decolonization of the last two decades has been achieved.

In the course of its activities, the United Nations has also dealt extensively with human rights through declarations, the preparation of conventions, and recommendations to states generally.[167] Of the Declarations, perhaps the best known is that adopted on December 10, 1948 by the General Assembly, the Universal Declaration on Human Rights. Only the Soviet bloc, Honduras and South Africa abstained on the vote.[168] White it was greeted warmly by the assembled delegates, they made it quite clear that they were not attempting to create instant legal obligations.[169] As Mrs. Roosevelt, the U.S. representative put it:

> The draft declaration was not a treaty or international agreement and did not impose legal obligations; it was rather a statement of *basic principles of inalienable human rights* setting up a common standard of achievement for all peoples and nations." [170] (Emphasis added)

The Soviet bloc argued persistently nevertheless that many Articles violated the Charter because they were contrary to the principle of non-intervention in domestic matters.[171] Their fears were not unreasonable in the sense that, for many national spokesmen today, the Declaration has come to represent something closer to principles of law than to mere aspirations. Except perhaps for strict positivists, the distinction between "basic principles of inalienable human rights" and "the general principles of law recognized by civilized nations," found in the I.C.J.'s Statute, Article 38, as a source of law to be applied by the Court, is unclear.

The Declaration's first 21 Articles affirm traditional civil and political rights: to life, liberty, security of person, recognition as a person, presumption of innocence, freedom to leave and return to a country, to seek asylum, to nationality, to freedom of thought, conscience, religion, opinion, expression, assembly, and privacy, to freedom from slavery, torture, cruel treatment, arbitrary arrest, detention, exile and others. Articles 22-27 are concerned with economic and social rights: to social security, to join trade unions, to rest and leisure, to education, to an adequate standard of living, etc.[172] The Declaration is obviously sweeping; it was to be made effective by a covenant on human rights.

In 1952, the Assembly authorized two draft covenants, one on civil and political rights, the other on economic, social and cultural rights. Work has been in progress since. Each draft covenant, for example, reaffirms in its first Article the right of "peoples" to self-determination. Drafts were approved by the Commission on Human Rights in 1954 but drafting problems, now centered on the creation of enforcement procedures, have prevented the conclusion of final drafts in the Third Committee to the date of this writing.[173]

Even without the covenants, it has been urged that the Declaration, while not binding as such, is authoritative as an interpretation of the human rights provisions in the Charter.[174] Later U.N. resolutions, in alleging human rights violations in southern Africa and elsewhere, have repeatedly tended to refer back to the Declaration as a standard for action as we have seen.

The U.N. has also been responsible for the drafting of some dozen conventions covering such aspects of human rights as the rights of women,[175] of refugees,[176] of news media.[177] Especially relevant for this discussion, it has also prepared the Convention on Genocide, discussed below and, in 1965, the International Convention on the Elimination of all Forms of Racial Discrimination.[178] This important treaty is the first completed UN convention in the field of human rights to contain measures for implementation, including a Committee of Experts, the right of states to lodge complaints for violations by a state of its own citizen's rights under certain circumstances, a right of petition by individual citizens, and techniques of conciliation.[179] It is not yet in force; the United States, with some fanfare, has signed it.[180] A proposed Convention on the Elimination of All Forms of Religious Intolerance has had slower going as heated issues, especially concerning anti-Semitism, have proved difficult to resolve.[181]

Just how such a convention against intolerance might be made operational is still not clear.

The General Assembly has also, from time to time, issued Declarations[182] on aspects of human rights and addressed Recommendations[183] to the members on such matters. These are, in law, exhortatory and not obligatory but, combined with other UN activity in the field of human rights, they are part of an insistently developing international interest.[184] Moreover in 1956, the Economic and Social Council established a reporting schedule under which all UN members were asked to report on their progress in protecting human rights, initially every three years but now on a staggered annual basis.[185] Thus far, however, it must be noted that "the vast majority of states ignore the appeal for reports."[186]

At the UN, the United States has often been a leader in working for the preparation of human rights conventions, and has usually been a signatory, but it has not yet ratified any.[187] Indeed with the Bricker Amendment controversy in mind, the United States, during the latter part of the 1950's, was publicly committed to non-ratification.[188] Several conventions are now before the Senate but no hearings have been held. At times this has become reportedly highly embarrassing to United States representatives at international meetings,[189] especially since large numbers of states, including the Soviet Union, have become parties to the Genocide Convention and others as well.

Some Human Rights "Cases" Before the United Nations

It should be evident by now that the term "human rights" implies a very large table of contents. Indeed it easily covers all types of individual and group relationships, especially *vis-à-vis* governments, ranging from child labor, to marriage laws, to self-determination of peoples. The emphasis remains on defining agreed minimal standard "inalienable rights," to which all human beings and collectivities can be viewed as entitled and by which the performance of the governments can be measured. That some international law of this type in favor of individuals has long existed is also obvious, for example, the rules of war, including the rights and duties of prisoners of war. For the purpose of a brief review of some of the more relevant human rights cases before the UN we are primarily interested in what might be called for convenience the political human rights issues, or, more simply, political (including civil) rights. We ignore instances in which other economic, social or legal humanitarian (*e.g.*, refugee) human rights issues may have been important or predominant. Even so our coverage must be brief and partial.

1. *Self-Determination and Decolonization*

In our consideration of cases involving the claim of human rights before the UN's organs, it seems appropriate to return to the admittedly uneasy division between claims brought on behalf of "peoples" to be free of "foreign" domination, though they may have traditionally been viewed as subjects of these colonial overlords, and those brought to protect groups and individuals against their "own" governments. In both kinds of cases, the alleged bar of Article 2(7) of the Charter has normally been raised.

During and immediately after the First World War, the concept of a formalized international interest in the welfare of at least certain "peoples" took the form, in President Wilson's words, of a principle of "self-determination." As the concept was used at that time, it was applied to the minority peoples in Eastern Europe, primarily in the former Austro-Hungarian Empire but also including Poland and the areas formerly under Turkish rule.[190] When the League Covenant recognized the dependent status, the need for tutelage and a "sacred trust" to educate the backward peoples of the world, it was only those "peoples" to be detached from German and Turkish rule and placed under the Mandates System to which these concepts applied. Unlike the Charter, the "rights" of dependent peoples in colonies and other dependencies were not within the purview of the League; even with the Mandated territories, it was only the Class A Mandates which were acknowledged as approaching readiness for independence. Moreover, as noted above, the League's supervisory powers over the Mandatories were very limited; petitions to the League's Mandates Commission, for example, were sent in only through the good offices of the Mandatory, and the League's Mandates Experts had no right of visitation as the Trusteeship Council does.

45

Yet the Mandate System, with all its flaws, was revolutionary. In the case of the "A" Mandates, it brought a direct promise of freedom. It pronounced and institutionalized a formal, visible international concern in some dependent areas of the world, a limitation which at the beginning was slight and partial on the colonial "overlord." In fact, by hindsight it appears to have been a definitive breach in the dike. Impartial, expert, international discussion of conditions in one set of territories could not but reveal conditions in and set standards for them all. Other League-related programs, such as that of the International Labour Organization, also served to alert other dependent peoples to the changed world of the inter-War period.[191]

How much the idea had matured is revealed in the UN Charter which pronounces, in Article 1(2) and 55, the concept of the "equal rights and self-determination" of peoples, this time meaning all peoples.[192] This principle has become the ideological rallying cry of the emerging nations, each helped on by those which came before and stayed on to join the chorus. Under the Charter, *all* colonial regions are the subject of UN interest either as Trust Territories, or as Non-Self-Governing Territories, with reports due in each case and, in the case of Trust Territories, with international rights of review, direct petition and visitation. And UN support has helped to legitimatize the struggle in the colonial areas which turned to armed self-help for freedom.

Since 1945, the movement towards independence has reached a flood tide. At the UN, the claim of a "right" to self-determination has been formally raised on behalf of colonial peoples everywhere, and was argued at length in such cases as Indonesia,[193] Algeria,[194] and, of course, southern Africa. In most cases, the right of the UN even to consider the matter, much less to act, has been resisted by the overseas government on the ground of "domestic jurisdiction" but the organs of the UN have nevertheless felt free, as we have indicated to discuss, to advise and in many cases to act in many varied ways.[195] Indeed, it is now "almost exclusively established that a matter involving the issue of self-determination cannot be excluded from the jurisdiction of UN organs on a plea of 'domestic jurisdiction'."[196]

The view of the present U.N. majority is evidenced in the

Declaration on the Granting of Independence to Colonial Countries, adopted on December 14, 1960, by the General Assembly,[197] which provides expressly that

> "1. The subjection of peoples to alien subjugation, domination and exploitation constitutes a denial of fundamental human rights, is contrary to the Charter of the United Nations and is an impediment to the promotion of world peace and co-operation.
>
> "2. *All peoples* have the right to self-determination; by virtue of that right they freely determine their political status and freely pursue their economic, social and cultural development.
>
> "3. *Inadequacy of political, economic, social or educational preparedness should never serve as a pretext for delaying independence.*
>
> "4. All armed action or repressive measures of all kinds directed against dependent peoples shall cease in order to enable them to exercise peacefully and freely their right to complete independence, and the integrity of their national territory shall be respected.
>
> "5. Immediate steps shall be taken, in Trust and Non-Self-Governing Territories or all other territories which have not yet attained independence, to transfer all powers to the peoples of those territories, without any conditions or reservations, in accordance with *their freely expressed will* and desire, without any *distinction as to race, creed or colour,* in order to enable them to enjoy complete independence and freedom.
>
> "6. *Any attempt aimed at the partial or total disruption of the national unity and the territorial integrity of a country* is incompatible with the purposes and principles of the Charter of the United Nations.
>
> "7. All States shall observe faithfully and strictly the provisions of the Charter of the United Nations, the Universal Declaration of Human Rights and the present Declaration on the basis of equality, non-interference in the internal affairs of all States, and respect for the sovereign rights of all peoples and their territorial integrity."

Some potentially conflicting or difficult concepts have been italicized. There were no negative votes but the United States, together with Australia, Belgium, the Dominican Republic, France, Portugal, Spain, South Africa and the U.K. abstained.[198] Note that this Declaration speaks only of "independence," not the "self-government" that is also featured in the UN Charter; some feel that it, and the political pressure it represents, have already had a profound influence in carrying out the process of decolonization.

In any case, in the remarkably short time of two decades, the empires of Britain, France, Belgium and the Netherlands have been largely dissolved and most of the Trust Territories are now independent. This successful drive towards the dissolution of

47

colonialism has left only a hard core of still-colonial areas in southern Africa, together with several small sparsely populated, often remote territories in the Pacific, Atlantic, and Indian Oceans and in the Caribbean. In 1965, for the first time, these remaining territories, ranging in population from Mozambique's 6.9 million to Pitcairn Island's 80 or so persons came under scrutiny as separate entities of the UN's "Committee of 24"[199] to which we have already referred. It is this group which is now overseeing efforts to establish independence and majority rule in the "hard core" cases of Angola, Mozambique, Rhodesia and, at least until this fall, South West Africa. It has held meetings in Africa and heard numerous petitioners from the subject peoples. It issues reports on the areas and seeks to lead opinion in the U.N. In a resolution of June, 1966, for example, it recommended that the Security Council employ obligatory measures under Chapter VII of the Charter against Portugal, South Africa, and Rhodesia. It also condemned the "activities of the financial interests operating in these territories," and called for an end to military bases in the areas. In addition, it recommended cooperation with "liberation movements" there and asked all states and international organizations to end assistance to Portugal and South Africa "until they renounce their policy of colonial domination and racial discrimination."[200]

The Limits of Self-Determination: Present Conceptual Style and Scope

This newer concept of self-determination as a politically achieved "right" ends, in the eyes of many (or perhaps all) of the Afro-Asian countries, and certainly of the Soviet bloc, with decolonization, "old style."[201] The newly emerged countries have placed the traditional iron wall of sovereignty around their own new borders, regardless of the demands of *their* internal minorities, for example, Indonesia and the "peoples" of the South Moluccas.[202] Similarly, India could urge that the question of Goa, after her armed forces "liberated" the area, was now solely within her domestic jurisdiction.[203]

Moreover, it is well documented that intermittently throughout its history the Soviet Union has crushed "independent" republics and peoples and scattered them within the Soviet Union,[204] asserting that "self-determination" is inferior to the right to keep a Communist state intact.[205] Nevertheless, to them intervention is legal when it is in "anti-colonial wars of national liberation" and they urge that intervention is itself legal where its end is the termination of a situation contrary to the right of self-determination. Thus, a new "socialist" form of the "just war" concept has emerged, supported by many of the newer nations in cases where old-style colonialism is at issue, despite the Charter ban on the use of force.[206]

Both experience and the logic of the view of self-determination which has been adopted and implemented by those most committed to the concept, the Afro-Asian states who have often been joined by the Communist bloc to form a voting majority in the UN, suggest that the "new" minorities within the new states will have to look to other sources for protection, to some defense of their rights other than their separation into a new state. Their problems are real; in addition to such widely publicized attacks as those on white groups in some parts of the Congo, there have been several recent international movements of African populations to escape genocidal-type onslaughts at home, including those in the Sudan, Mozambique, the Congo, Ghana, Uganda, the Ivory Coast and Nigeria.[207] Some half the Tutsi tribe, the former overlords in Rwanda, have been killed or have fled the country, according to reports.[208] India has had a succession of language and ethnic riots and many groups there apparently support anti-Muslim parties as well.[209] While the reports do not clearly indicate an ethnic base for the attacks, it appears that a half million Indonesians may have been put to death in the past year as well.[210] The African countries and the UN largely ignore these "domestic" issues in the sense of taking action[211] but, although conditions are reportedly not uniformly bad, it is clear that the white populations in southern Africa are well aware of the risks these manifestations imply for their own future.[212]

Yet perhaps the real yearnings of these new states for human rights protection is demonstrated less by these domestic acts than by their vigor in international negotiations on human rights issues. They demand and seek out a dignity for all peoples which

49

they presently do not afford at home where tribalism, discrimination, truncated "justice" and dictatorial rule are often still endemic.[213] It seems important to try to remember that this is often admittedly pathological; it is not a chosen way of life.

2. Cases Involving Individual Human Rights at the UN

While the issue of race and South Africa is the most persistent case before the UN based on the dignity of man as man rather than as a member of a "people," there have been other matters of a somewhat similar nature. In 1947 and 1948, for example, the Soviet Government prohibited Soviet women, married to foreign subjects, from leaving Russia. The Economic and Social Council deplored this act in a Resolution of 1948.[214] In that same year, the Chilean delegate, who had had a personal experience with the ban, brought the matter to the General Assembly, charging a violation of fundamental human rights.[215] Chile, supported by several other states, urged that the Charter, the Universal Declaration of Human Rights and the ECOSOC Resolution referred to above, made this a matter of international concern and not subject to the domestic jurisdiction limitation.[216] The Soviet Union argued that this matter was exclusively within its domestic affairs and that, in any event, the law was designed "to defend human rights" in keeping Russian women from going abroad where they would be ill-treated and unhappy.[217] While the Soviet bloc supported this position, the Assembly adopted a resolution recalling the Preamble, Articles 1(3) and 55(c) of the Charter, the Universal Declaration and the ECOSOC Resolution, declaring that action such as that taken by Russia was not in conformity with the Charter, and recommending that Russia withdraw the law.[218] While Russian policy has been ameliorated, it is not clear whether this airing of the matter at the UN had any direct effect.

In another case as well, the question of "the observance of human rights and fundamental freedoms in Bulgaria, Hungary and Roumania," the issue of domestic jurisdiction was also raised. In the debates, it was clearly suggested by most states that, even absent the Peace Treaties, and even if the states were not members of the UN, issues involving human rights were not solely domestic, and condemnatory resolutions were adopted.[219] Despite the treaties and this UN action, the states involved did not modify their policies in response to these international demands (though recent years have seen some ameliorative changes for other reasons). Similarly, UN condemnation of the violation of human rights in Tibet was resisted by the Soviet bloc on grounds of "domestic jurisdiction" and the UN action has had no observable effect.[220] Thus, while these few cases need not be taken as definitive, they do indicate the generality of the UN assertion of its competence and the probable general incompetence of the Organization to affect the internal policies of even determined small states, and certainly of Major Powers in the short run of the case being examined, despite a large consensus in the UN on the need to protect the human rights of *minorities* within those countries. The long run effect of all the persistent interest in and airing of and frequent condemnation of "internal" political conditions is obviously non-measurable. Nevertheless, it is also appropriate to note that the General Assembly has not lost faith in the utility of its nagging persistence. It seems already to have paid off in decolonization. In Professor Henkin's terms, while "governments may continue to claim that how they treat their own inhabitants is of concern to them alone; increasingly it is a losing claim. . . . The political organs of the United Nations hardly refrain from discussing any human rights issue which any Member puts on the agenda . . ."[221]

Taking all of this burgeoning human rights activity together, the cases, the conventions and declarations, the supervision of colonial areas, and all the other UN efforts partially surveyed here, it is clear that a slow process of constitutional growth in the relationship between the individual and the organized international community is under way. Looking back to the minimal roles the League was given and the minimal interest League members exhibited even in grave human rights issues, the pace and effectiveness of the development of this constitutional change over the last twenty years should not look discouraging. In all:

> The human rights program of the United Nations represents a tremendous collective effort, by the formulation of accepted principle

and the establishment of new procedures, to extend protection of basic individual liberties, most broadly conceived, to levels of effective authority higher than the nation state.[222]

3. *Human Rights and International Tribunals*

One major thread of new development in international law in the mid-20th century, the protection of certain crucial human rights of groups, especially the right to be free from a conspiracy to exterminate them, must be noted here. For the violation of these few crucial rights of peoples, there has developed an increased international willingness to set penalties, at least for individuals culpably responsible.

As suggested above, during the interwar period, despite the existence of the League, no more than occasional expressions of shocked sensibilities were levied against atrocities committed, for example, against the Jews in the Soviet Union in 1918.[223] They were not expressly protected by any minorities treaty; no other country claimed the right on general legal grounds or on political grounds, as former kinsmen, to protect them against their own sovereign. No country intervened on behalf of German victims of Nazi oppression; the British Government rejected suggestions of a protest on the grounds that there was a lack of evidence that such atrocities were being committed and that, in any event, it was against the rules of international law to object to another state about treatment meted out by that state to its own nationals.[224] Yet at Nuremburg, these same acts by the Nazi government formed part of the basis for the charge of "Crimes Against Humanity" which was defined as including:[225]

> murder, extermination, enslavement, deportation and other inhumane acts committed against any civilian population before or during the war, or persecutions on political, racial or religious grounds in execution of or in connection with any crime within the jurisdiction of the Tribunal, whether or not in violation of the domestic law of the country where perpetrated.

International law has long recognized that a few classes of shocking acts could constitute crimes against all mankind for which an individual could be held liable. Thus, the pirate, the coiner of another sovereign's currency and the person guilty of individual war crimes of a traditional nature have all been found subject to international prohibitory rules,[226] though the basis for the subjection remains a matter of scholarly debate.[227] In this way, by punishing an offender, the law upholds the rights of all those protected to be free from unlawful interference in their lives. Yet in none of these classic cases were the rights of individuals protected against their own sovereigns.[228]

Though the concept goes back at least as far as Grotius, the Judgment of the Nuremburg Tribunal, in assessing guilt on the charge of crimes against humanity, clearly reinforces the developing trend towards the effective recognition of an international interest in safeguarding all humans at least from organized abominable behaviour on the part of states. The Nuremburg Tribunal was a court of most of the present Great Powers. As such it is evidence of their views on these matters. It also marks their recognition of the binding nature of some basic non-consensual standards of "justice." Moreover, on December 4, 1946, "the principles of international law recognized by the judgment" of that Tribunal were affirmed unanimously by the UN General Assembly,[229] generalizing and enhancing their status and precedent value.

In a similar vein, the Convention on the Prevention and Punishment of the Crime of Genocide, adopted by the General Assembly on December 9, 1948,[230] and now in force for many nations,[231] also protects groups against their own nations. Genocide is defined as:

> "any of the following acts committed with intent to destroy, in whole or in part, a national, ethnical, racial or religious group, as such: (a) Killing members of the group; (b) Causing serious bodily or mental harm to members of the group; (c) Deliberately inflicting on the group conditions of life calculated to bring about its physical destruction in whole or in part; (d) Imposing measures intended to prevent births within the group; (e) Forcibly transferring children of the group to another group."

While once again no procedures for enforcement have been established,[232] the Convention gives evidence that this need for international protection has been internationally recognized, and that there are no intrinsic legal obstacles to further development of an international concern with human rights. Many African states have sought to apply these precedents by labelling apartheid "a crime against humanity."[233]

In appraising the most important implications of the Nuremburg decision and subsequent developments, we can say that they reaffirm the conclusion that:

> ... there has been and will continue to be nonconsensual external standards which limit a nation's freedom of action. Whether formulated in terms of "Natural Law," or in a philosophy of "Natural Rights," or, as by the abolitionists Channing and Thoreau, in an appeal to the "higher law" in the name of "the sacred and inalienable rights of all men," or on moral convictions that there are "Some Generalities that Still Glitter" [Becker, *New Liberties for Old* 124–150 (1941)] without religious supports, there will remain the standard of "the conscience of mankind" to which to repair so long as man retains his humanity. No theory of international law, no otherwise perceptive useful guide to international politics can be satisfactory to the extent that it fails to accommodate "the growing subjection of governmental action to the moral judgment" [National City Bank v. Republic of China, 348 U.S. 356, 359 (1955)].[234]

In contrast with other non-consensual processes by which customary international rules may develop, however, there are excellent reasons why the scope of such international non-consensual judicial "law-making" or, rather, international non-consensual constitutional review of state conduct respecting the entrenched or inalienable rights of humans should be limited to clearly pathological cases. Metzger argues that:[234a]

> In view of the immense variety of local cultures, customs, human and material resources, and systems of politics and economics of the hundred-odd nations now extant, it is apparent that only the most obviously obnoxious kind of domestic conduct, such as "apartheid," can be the subject of intervention through non-consensual external restraint because it is shocking to mankind's conscience.

If such basic, unspecified, fundamental human rights, binding on all states, do exist, the operational problems of their interpretation and of their enforcement at present remain serious. International tribunals normally require the consent of the states before they can act and it is unwise to assume that the "guilty" state is going to prove a willing defendant.[235] Are pathological domestic actions to be subjected to obligatory constitutional review by the I.C.J., by other regularly constituted tribunals, or by special tribunals as at Nuremburg? Who will be competent to bring the suit? Are they to be subjected only to political review at the UN? In any case, what can the UN do about it legally? The narrow ruling in the South West Africa cases reminds us of the challenging changes in the world legal and enforcement systems which would be necessary to permit effective challenges to sovereigns over their treatment of their own citizens. We turn to that ruling now.

The I.C.J. and the South West Africa Cases: 1966

The problem of South West Africa before the I.C.J. represents a hybrid case. Here it was the right to decent treatment of the humans in the territory which was placed in legal issue by the pleadings of Ethiopia and Liberia, while, in the political background, were the issues both of ultimate freedom for the "peoples" of South West Africa and of human rights for the native majority in the Republic of South Africa itself. Thus, in the developing area of the international protection of human rights, the 1966 decision of the ICJ in the South West Africa Cases of course came as a major disappointment. The Court's Opinion, based on a "strict" reading of the Mandate Agreement and a narrow view of the implications of the Mandate system, did not reach the question of the rights of the Territory's inhabitants. Yet the 1950 Opinion of the Court, which was not formally affected or disturbed by the 1966 Decision,[236] emphasizes the rights of those in the Mandate and of the UN to exercise the League's supervisory functions "to safeguard the sacred trust of civilization" in the Mandate.[237] As the Court said in 1962:[238] "[T]o exclude the obligations connected with the Mandate would be to exclude the very essence of the Mandate."

As we have noted, the most important political result of the Decision was to return the question to the political arena at once.[239] For the more general problems of southern Africa, the major legal issues concern the question of the binding nature and enforcibility of human rights, first, in an area with recognized international status and, second, within national states. On both questions, the impact of the Court's Opinion was negative.

In fact, several of the dissenting Judges asserted, as Applicants had contended, that the action of the nations has already created

55

international legal standards of *national* conduct with respect to human rights.[240] Thus, Judges Koo, Tanaka, Mbanefo and Padilla Nervo all note that an international norm of non-discrimination has been created over the years through treaties, custom, general practice and the quasi-legislative effect of numerous General Assembly resolutions, adopted repeatedly by substantial majorities.[241] Some of these Judges also urged that non-discrimination was now also a binding "general principle" of law.[242] Even if this were not all so, it was argued that special obligations were owed by the Mandatory; that the conduct of the Mandatory in not educating the populace toward self-government and in establishing all rights in the area on a basis of race, color or ethnic origin, was clearly contrary to *this* State's duty as a Mandatory.[243]

On the other hand, Judge Van Wyk of South Africa, in his Separate Opinion, contested the alleged creation of the norm on each count, including the denial that there is any practice of States in accordance with the alleged norm (citing the testimony also of Profs. Possony, van den Haag and Manning). South Africa has repeatedly insisted, as well, that it *is* concerned about human rights and that they *are* protected in South West Africa.[244]

The Court's Opinion itself simply asserted that Ethiopia and Liberia had failed to establish any legal right or interest in the matter. It did reject the notion that "moral" values were given "legal form" in the Mandate System, except as expressly provided in a Mandate Agreement itself, rather than the more general provisions of the Agreement and the Covenant. Thus, certain special rights of missionaries in South West Africa could be protected but the general rights of the inhabitants found no champion even though an explicit international interest existed. For the Court, there appears to be no state which can challenge the administrator of a frankly internationally supervised tutelage designed to benefit the inhabitants. Even members of the defunct League have no legal interest in upholding general "humanitarian" values in the Mandate although a general concern for the welfare of all in the area is expressed in the Agreement itself. Yet the Court's Opinion is itself based on the idea that the Mandate still exists; otherwise, the Court would have lacked jurisdiction in the first instance. This must be taken as a very narrow reading of the legal enforcibility of human rights even when explicitly specified in international contractual agreements.

Presumably, the UN as successor to the League's rights and duties could have sought still another advisory opinion to test its claim as the defender of human rights in general, as well as of the obligations of the Mandate. Both the League and the UN are limited, of course, to advisory opinions; no doubt this was one of the reasons that, in the League period, a Mandatory had to accept the compulsory jurisdiction of the Permanent Court and states were presumably expected to challenge the Mandatory if the need arose. Thus today, under the 1966 Opinion, a legally binding defense of the human rights of a mandated population has proven to be impossible just at a time when the concept of the defense of individuals in national states even against their own governments has found expression in the Nuremburg Principles, the Genocide Convention and numerous other international acts and arrangements, already noted here. A paradox indeed!

Politically, in sum, the Court informed the international community that it would give at most advice on these contentious issues. The job of converting such opinions into decisions, and then making them binding and effective, remains the burden of the UN's political organs without, in this case, the benefit of the clear-cut legal sanctification most governments apparently expected to receive. We have already noted the fury with which the Court's action was received; its repercussions on UN political activity are already being felt; the meaning for the Court's future is less clear.

Whether or not it is possible to find judicially and politically reasonable elements in the Opinion, it is impossible to admire the timorous conduct of the technical majority where the issues, if reached, seemed quite clear. And the technical basis of the Opinion seems to deserve Judge Jessup's comment that it is "completely unfounded in law" and a bit absurd.

On the other hand, even the Supreme Court of the United States, an aggressive law-making court by most standards was also timorous in the field of human rights despite their specification in the Constitution. The great assault on racial discrimination, *Brown* v. *Board of Education*[245] was decided in 1954, some 86 years after the adoption of the Fourteenth Amendment which followed a war intended to settle the question. Nor did the Court intervene in the key political issue of apportionment to defend the political rights of individuals to "fair" representation more nearly on a one man, one vote basis until a few years ago; as recently as 1946, *Colegrove* v. *Green*[246] held that such a question was "political" and hence inappropriate for judicial scrutiny, a view now resolutely rejected by the Court.[247]

Yet in time the Court *has* moved and many students of American constitutional law consider it useful, or perhaps essential, that the Court can be asked to do what the legislative and executive branches, both federal and state, have been politically unable or unwilling to do to meet the needs and desires both of majorities and minorities. This is no place to debate the issue. The limited possibilities for the I.C.J. to adopt such a role effectively in the international community of sovereigns seem obvious. Indeed the Judges themselves come from differing legal traditions, many of which do not comprehend the value of an aggressive law-making court to full in for the failures of other social institutions. Clearly, where the Court must turn for voluntary enforcement of its decisions to the legally defeated sovereigns themselves, or to the politically motivated Security Council, it cannot normally precede the political consensus. Yet the Court is also endangered by lagging behind it, perhaps more so than the U.S. Supreme Court which has an established aura of legitimacy and inviolability, supported by the political ideology of the country so that it can, when attacked, rally great popular emotional support to its defense as President Roosevelt discovered in 1937.[248] Indeed such independent sources of legitimacy are what enable the Supreme Court to be aggressive both in preceding and in deterring the constitutional changes which the other political organs can accomplish. In sum, we can borrow some famous advice for the I.C.J. and say, with Chief Justice Marshall, "[W]e must never forget that it is a *Constitution* we are expounding."[249] But we must also remember the special difficulties for this court in following it *vis-à-vis* the international community.

The South West Africa Cases thus raise several issues for the I.C.J. and for the development of international legal norms which the members of the UN system will eventually have to face. What kind of Constitutional System is appropriate for the international community? What kind of a court should the I.C.J. be, especially when issues of emerging law are concerned as in the field of human rights? And finally, all the operational problems: What kind of a court could it be, considering its heterogeneous composition and its structure, and the revealed propensity of the judges to follow their nations' traditional way of looking at law and life and the record they have produced of deciding issues consistently with their national interests?[250] We do not mean to suggest such constitutional problems are unsuperable, but that this case should remind us that they are becoming pressing.

By promising to "punish" through not reelecting and by other means those judges who vote against their position, the infuriated UN majority is putting pressure on the Court to be responsive to the wishes of the "legislature" and world opinion as reflected at least in the voting majorities at the UN. This too is traditional. How else can a court be induced to respond to the community's wishes? Of course this "legislature," the UN's General Assembly is itself a highly imperfect reflector of the wishes of mankind. It surely does not offer representation on the basis of one *man,* one vote. When African representatives suggest that the 1966 Judgment reflects what is wrong with the whole UN system, they are no doubt right.[251] As such the dilemmas facing the Court deserve some understanding. It is not at all clear, however, that their governments, or the rest of Africa, or the rest of the developing world, or *any* large block of nations would support or be pleased with the results of a more perfect, more perfectly representative world organization, one with the legal and material power to settle effectively even such disputes as beset southern Africa on the basis of agreed norms of equity and human rights.[252] Again we do not mean to imply that some small steps forward would not now appear possible towards a better world constitutional system and a more responsive Court. But it is unreasonable to minimize the difficulties in a world in which even as it is, compulsory jurisdiction is granted grudgingly to this Court, often with serious reservations, by that limited number of states which grants it at all.

In any case, the I.C.J. has revealed its place in the development of emerging law. At present, it has no intention of being a courageous innovator. Particularly in view of the special status of South West Africa, it clearly could have found contractual language and precedents to support the generally expected decision as it did in 1962. It is proper for political questions to be politically decided but it is unseemly for a court to appear ridiculous, to retreat totally when faced by those small portions of great issues to which it can easily find legal answers.

The Law and Human Rights in a Developing World System

Even this brief a survey leads to the conclusion that the conflict between norms of sovereignty and domestic jurisdiction and human rights in a growing, evolving international system is inevitable. In such a system, the meaning and scope of domestic jurisdiction may be identifiable at any one instant but there is no clear-cut, logical, perpetual boundary and its scope has diminished with time.[253] As Mrs. Higgins has written with respect to the UN itself:[254]

> The legal principle of domestic jurisdiction is, for various reasons, singularly susceptible to development by the process of interpretation by political bodies. Article 2(7) is far from unambiguous, and by its very nature the concept of domestic jurisdiction is incapable of capture and crystallization for all time. What is truly domestic today will not be so in five years' time.... Given the mutable and developing nature of the concept ..., a flexible approach is desirable, based on the principle that states must be made responsible to the international community when their actions cause substantial international effects.

She warns, nevertheless, that:

> the interpretation of what may be reserved to the domestic domain must not be so severely limited that the confidence of the member states is forfeited, for this would ultimately discourage participation and goodwill in an Organization that must aim at near-universality of membership if it is to function successfully in its stated aims.

Within the more developed system of United States constitutional practice, the scope of the reserved powers of the states has shifted and lessened with felt necessity over time despite the written Constitution and a system of judicial review to contain the federal legislative and executive arms from self-aggrandizement at the expense of the rights of the states. At the same time, the scope of the Constitution's protection of individual human rights has been steadily broadened against all governments with federal power made available to limit improper state encroachments on individual liberties where needed. The boundaries have depended on what society as a whole is intent upon achieving and cannot leave unregulated or unprotected centrally, and on what standards it seeks to have made uniform, and finally on what matters it can achieve an operational consensus to regulate. As between the governments, federal and state, the division of powers can in fact be moved by reinterpretation by the relevant Supreme Court and/or the legislature and/or the executive, or, as a last, usually unnecessary resort, by amendment of the Constitution itself.[255] The major question respecting the division is when should it be moved, and how, not can it constitutionally be moved in any viable constitutional system.

It is true that even in the Western world there exists a great variety of constitutional practice among the UN's members. The British, without a written constitution, nevertheless enshrine "constitutionally" the inalienable civil and political (human) rights of their people. Yet their courts have rarely believed that it was in their competence to limit Parliament's capacity to make new rules, though statutes tend to be strictly construed for their "legal" meaning, and the courts have not sought new roles, on constitutional grounds, except for the holding action in defending the British citizen's basic rights. The legislature remains the principal if not the exclusive engine of constitutional change. Nevertheless, British scholars are aware that this approach is not directly applicable to the world legal and constitutional system where, lacking an effective legislature, there might well be room for a more aggressive court.[256]

In civil law countries, constitutions tend to combine broad principles and detailed enumerations with an attempt to avoid the American Constitution's indefinite phrases, such as "due process," which seem patently to call for interpretation in accordance with changing times. Courts tend to read narrowly. If it is not in the code, it is not there at all. And the legislature remains the principal organ for constitutional change. In any case, *some* internal institutions for constitutional flexibility and evolution are essential in all modern, complex, dynamic social systems, if they are not to be torn apart completely.

The international legal system, being a "horizontal," decentralized system of sovereigns which consequently lacks an effective legislature, relies primarily for the derivation of obligatory norms on treaties, general and particular, on international custom, once "accepted as law" and on "the general principles of law recognized by civilized nations."[257] The system in fact relies heavily on sovereign self-interpretation of international obligations, on interpretations by international organizations and, to a degree, on interpretations made by tribunals, both national and international.

With respect to "unwritten" law, the I.C.J. has already recognized, in the human rights field, the existence of principles which "are recognized by civilized states as binding on states *even without any conventional obligations*."[258] These "general principles of law" have, in the jurisprudence of the Court, been "used to fill gaps in international law by relying upon private law analogies, based upon legal rules and institutions commonly found in municipal legal systems."[259] We have seen that the Court did not choose to do so with reference to apartheid in the South West Africa Cases Opinion of 1966. Several dissenting Judges argued, in those Cases, that even without the special conditions of a Mandate, under the circumstances of 1966, and in view of the Charter, the Constitution of the I.L.O., the practice of the UN, the numerous human rights covenants, and declarations at the UN and of individual states, there is evidence by now of the existence of a customary international norm and of standards of non-discrimination and non-separation which can be, in a proper case, superior to the claim of domestic jurisdiction, whether a state wills it or not.[260] And indeed, though the specific rights and duties were left to be specified, this conclusion has been said to flow from the constitutional nature of the Charter itself.[261] For some years now, other scholars have made similar statements.[262]

We have observed that, in addition to those fundamental "inalienable" human rights which many now argue exist as part of an unwritten "world constitution," to use the term "constitution" in the British sense, and which must somehow be interpreted and enforced, there is by now also a complex set of written norms in the international community. Of these, the most basic is the Charter which is itself, in a real sense, a constitution, or basic norm. Like other constitutions, the Charter requires interpretation, especially when its provisions conflict in cases that are important to its parties, as well as reinterpretation as circumstances and the world's consensus on norms change. In most of this paper, we have been discussing just such a set of constitutional conflicts, that between the norms of human rights (individual and group self-determination) and state inviolability (domestic jurisdiction, territorial integrity and peaceful settlement), both of which appear in the Charter.

Commenting on this type of constitutional issue and on the relationship of law to political decision-making at the UN in general, Oscar Schachter has noted that:[263]

> ... because principles are general and fundamental they tend to clash with each other in specific cases—thus every principle in the Charter can be paired off with a contrary or opposing principle in the context of a particular situation. ... Even the salient rule against force is "balanced" by the right of self-defence and collective enforcement measures and the most fervent supporters of the principle of self-determination have recognized the opposing claims of the obligation of peaceful settlement and the principle of "territorial integrity." This characteristic opposition of principles is not, as some have suggested, the result of political confusion or defective drafting; on the contrary, *it is a desirable and necessary way of expressing the diverse and competing aims and interest of mankind.* An attempt to eliminate such inconsistencies can only result in an artificial emphasis on some abstractions and a suppression of valid and basic human values.[264] (emphasis added).

The question remains which body or bodies is to undertake the important job of interpretation of the general norms in specific situations as conditions change.[265]

It is now generally understood that in most governments all political decision-making processes, whether by court, legislature or executive, involve just such choices between competing general norms which can be construed as applicable to the specific situation and usually turn out to reflect also competing individual or group interests. Preferably, given our Western political orientation, the choice will accord with the consensus of the community concerned as to relative importance of the relevant general values both in general and at the time and in the particular situations. This gives some weight to the British constitutional view that the principal interpretation should be legislative, at least in societies where overwhelming popular consensus is readily producible. Indeed, most constitutions, whether written or unwritten or both, are, no doubt, given life and interpreted in action primarily by the decisions of the legislative and/or the executive rather than the courts. Nevertheless, for differentiated and vastly more complex societies, like the United States or the world community, it is also recognized that there is more need for an explicit constitutional bargain specifying the overall political constitutional agreement between the parts, the division of authority between central and local government and between all governments and the individual and establishing the framework for the agreed institutions of binding decision-making and judicial review in cases of conflict of norms or interests.[266]

Whether or not its organs were initially designed to achieve flexibility, the UN system requires some minimal constitutional flexibility, some adaptability to change, if it is to survive.[267] Unlike the United States, for example, where an executive, legislature and interpreting judicial branch with well-established roles exist to keep the Constitution in line with the times, the international system has frankly inadequate "legislative" (lawmaking) arrangements. This is the direct result of the sovereign members' jealousy over their sovereignty without which such obvious defects as voting weights in the present Charter system, for example, could be rapidly corrected by technicians so that an improved organization with genuine legislative powers could be created. The community's Court too, as it reminded us in the South West Africa Cases, is, for practical as well as jurisprudential reasons, "reluctant" as a law maker and reviewer of constitutions even when states agree to submit cases to it. This may change as present "court packing" proposals are effectuated and its composition shifts.[269] Even without these, the experience of acute disapproval, if prolonged, and the normal changes in personnel which will occur with time, may well accomplish similar results as they did in the United States in the late 1930's.[268] Yet while the I.C.J. does on occasion give advisory constitutional opinions to the UN when asked, the interpretation and development of the UN constitutional system, which contains these numerous unspecified norms, values and interests, has been predominantly by the political organs.[270]

Unlike most states, at the UN the power to declare rules and recommend action lies with the numerical majority of states but the formal capacity to make decisions, some of which are legally binding at once, rests with the Security Council. The power to *enforce* a UN decision, when it is unpopular with any sovereign, if and when the will exists at all, rests largely with those states which have and are willing to use a plurality of real enforcement power in the matter in question. Thus, a General Assembly "decision" is something substantially less, both in law and practice, than a law-making or constitution-modifying or interpreting decision by a domestic legislature. In most cases, the resolution simply expounds what the numerical majority of states would like the "law" to be in a given case or type of situation.[271] It *is* the intention of the states that, in this system, the emergence of new rules, binding on a sovereign which has not specifically agreed to be bound by them, comes only slowly and with great pangs, if at all,[272] and that they enjoy an uncertain life expectancy. Thus, despite the growing agreement that some basic minimal standards of justice do exist and should be reliably enforcible against all sovereigns, after reviewing the constitutional capacity of the present international institutional system one is tempted to conclude, as the I.C.J. did in July, that "you can't get there from here."

This is of course both a politically and intellectually unacceptable approach. If, for purposes of speculation, we transcend the present and look briefly at where we would be going if we did establish the kind of world constitutional system in which all human rights were effectively internationally guaranteed, we may also be able to highlight the conceptual nature of the constitutional, human and political problems of getting there and explain part of the reluctance of even consciencious "citizens of the world" to take great constitutional leaps into the future right now.

Since this paper is no place to investigate and explore so challenging an issue in detail, we shall for these purposes be frankly ethnocentric. Indeed, the concept of legally enshrined individual human rights is part of Western political and humanistic traditions, and is frankly far less congenial to other political ideologies and traditions, for example, to Communist traditions.[273] Certainly the Communist view of the role and rights of the individual is at the core of the unacceptability to Westerners of *their* institutions and ideology and the reason we insist on being ethnocentric in our long run visions and hopes. Here, we will simply assume that our long-run constitutional goal *vis-à-vis* world human rights and a political system, with the capacity to defend them effectively, is very like that of the founding fathers of the United States. This includes as decentralized a federal system of government for the nations as is possible, considering that we also wish to make war between them not merely officially illegal but unfeasible and *unnecessary,* for the two are clearly linked. This means that we will have a) norms, rules, and effective organs for achieving "fair," binding, definitive conflict *resolution of issues* between the states, something we certainly lack in the present world constitutional order. There will also be, b) a reserved sphere of action left to the states, far smaller than at present, which will not inhibit the achievement and enforcement of a fair resolution of a conflict between them. And c) the actions of such central conflict resolving machinery and the limitations on the actions of the component states' governmental machinery will be consistent with our basic Western humanistic values and standards, and therefore consistent with a set of specified human rights on the order of those specified in the U.S. Constitution and its Amendments and the many recent international conventions and declarations which, in fact, hark back to 1776.

In such a system, the defense of the inscribed human rights would be incumbent both on the national governments and on the international governmental machinery. Presumably if the national governments' treatment of their citizens was consistent with international standards, the need for international intervention to protect these rights would be minimal. Yet familiar as we are with the gaps in the present international system and the limitations on its capacity to grow and adjust to human desires and needs, we must now also face the fact that the establishment of a "better world constitution" with "better" world institutions on the American model would not necessarily leave us without enforcement problems on human rights issues.

The basic dilemmas of constitutional government were indeed remarkably well-comprehended by the remarkable group of men we call the "founding fathers" of the U.S. Constitution.[273a] The analytical core of their constitutional problem and of the problem we face now can be summed up by the fact that, in principle, unless further qualified, the total range of choice of simple voting rules offers the alternatives of "the tyranny of the majority" or "the tyranny of the minority." Without workable specific constitutional institutional bars to such outcomes, a simple majority which can decide any issue, can thereby ignore all the claims of the losing minority including, of course, their claims to human rights, and to a future chance to vote again, or to life itself. In the case of simple minority rule, a minority with the effective power can similarly do anything, however heinous, it desires. If as is more common a qualified majority rule is chosen instead, for example, a required two-thirds majority, (or simple majority in a legislature chosen by some rule other than "1 man 1 vote" designed to have the same effect then a "tyrannous" minority of one-third plus one can block decisions urgently desired by two-thirds less one of the community members, including, of course, all changes in any special privileges accumulated by this minority. In this sense, the veto can be seen to be the "rule of the smallest minority"; it enables the veto bearer to block any action it disapproves for which its consent is needed.[274] No simply voting formula such as the "one man one vote" majority rule proposed by the UN for South Africa is free of this choice among tyrannies.

As we know, the Founding Fathers tended to be more concerned with the tyranny of the majority though even originally the constitutional compromise was designed to cope with both potential tyrannies.[275] Various well known, brilliant, oft-copied strategies were designed for this end, including, *inter alia,* a bicameral federal legislature with special voting weights in the Senate to help protect states and regions from becoming endangered minorities, the separation of powers within the federal government, the division of powers between levels of government, and, especially, the overall strategy of checks and balances. The powers of each major federal decision-making organ were thus made subject to built-in controls by the others. Most important, perhaps, since qualified majority rule remained the choice, the constitutional bargain included a Bill of Rights which limited the rights of the federal majority, acting as the federal government, to deprive any member of the community of certain basic human rights by specifying them as exceptions to majority rule. Unfortunately even this highly sophisticated governmental design did not prevent the existence of a secularly deprived racial minority which grew out of the special circumstances of the "peculiar" institution of servitude existing when the Union was formed which was accepted, though as an aberration, in the constitutional compromise.

Even a civil war, precipitated by the issue, followed by attempts to assure equal treatment of the deprived minority through specific, entrenched constitutional guarantees binding on the states as well failed to obtain equality for all. Given the imperious nature of the local majority's demands, the actual, functioning political system found ways to subvert the constitutional safeguards.

This simply reminds us of the crucial importance of the actual political system and of the actual *constitutional values and aims* of those with the majority of power in any society however ingenious their official constitution. If this majority is not somehow kept loyal to the concept of minority rights, it will find a way to subvert them. We cannot then counsel heavy reliance on constitutional guarantees alone where they are totally artificial, *i.e.,* where no community of values and no habits of mutual accommodation exist or are created. "There is no substitute for political adjustment," that is, for consensus creation, for seeking out mutually acceptable compromises and bargains "as a means of managing relationships among the units which constitute complex human societies . . ."[276]

What can be done where the political process of accommodation fails because the politically dominant group controls the government in part for the purpose of thwarting the constitutional guarantees of the rest of the society? If there had been a world authority with power to intervene in favor of U.S.-deprived minorities on human rights grounds,[277] perhaps we would have finished that particular social revolution earlier. Perhaps, but is it necessarily so? Have we any reason to feel that without great improvement in the solidarity of the human race, international protection of human rights would have produced better results than did our federal system? Historically, considering the decentralization of the international system, the answer has been resoundingly "no," not by the methods thus far devised in this system to protect minorities. We have already noted the bitterly disappointing international experience with internationally imposed entrenched constitutional rights of any importance. These include the Minorities Treaties of the League period and the more contemporary example of a multi-ethnic Cyprus, where indeed the Greek majority, having attained national sovereignty expressly presses the argument in terms of the sanctity of the majority will over the "unfair," "imposed," entrenched rights of an unassimilatable ethnic minority.

To sum up, there is nothing inherently undesirable in adding a superior level of binding federal "checks and balances," another guarantor of the rights of the individual to live and to a "maximum chance," whether he is a member of the majority or the minority. This might be helpful if, but only if, it could *safely* be given the effective capacity to protect human rights, that is, if the superior government itself were designed to perform effectively and yet would not become itself an invincible tyranny of the world majority at any moment or of some world minority against the rest. This is, of course, the familiar challenge of this century. It requires for solution much more than appropriate, even brilliant, constitutional innovations. It requires the making of a genuine moral and political community, one which can and is determined to find a common ground for thrashing out conflict of interest problems and settling them peacefully by mutual political accommodation within a framework of common values, in a setting emphasizing respect for governmental institutions, peaceful acquiescence in the binding nature of decisions appropriately taken by those institutions, and acceptance of constitutional techniques for changing those decisions, as, for example, through regular elections, based on broad representation. In Inis Claude's words.[278]

> The ultimate task is to convert the world into a pluralistic society marked by a high adjustment potential—by the existence of component parts which are susceptible of regulation in their relationships with each other and with the whole, through processes of political accommodation.

We do not seek here to set utopian standards lacking relevance to real world problems. The pressure to establish an international interest in some minimal set of human rights now, one that can be imposed, if necessary on recalcitrant national states including, *e.g.,* the United States, is already a political reality. It has made discussion of these long-run issues relevant and it forces us also to look at "constitutional" changes in progress now.

Lacking a ready made perfect world, with effective institutions and a developed capacity for mutual tolerance of all groups, much less any genuine agreements on values and "fair" governmental institutions, we can nevertheless identify the problems, and indicate the preferred directions with respect to southern Africa. Despite the various institutional incapacities of the international constitutional system, we have found that in fact there is now a wide consensus derived from the Nuremberg Judgment, the UN Charter, some UN decisions, the Genocide and Human Rights Conventions, some of the Opinions of the I.C.J. and the great growth of international interest and innovational activity in this field, and in the writings of experts, that some limited group of particularly offensive actions against humans are presently barred to states. Though the issue is not without doubt, a good legal case can even now be made against the domestic policies of the Republic of South Africa.

At Nuremburg, the Tribunal was often concerned with the *intent* of the defendants. South Africa's intent to perpetuate massive racial discrimination is explicit.[279] In other states, racial and ethnic conflict normally occurs without official approval and is recognized as undesirable. Moreover, this particular tyranny is employed by a racial minority, intent on retaining exclusive political control of the nation for itself, to enchain a racial majority with a minority of political power and thus delimit their political and economic roles and their lives. If this is a "crime against humanity" and intent is a necessary element of the crime, proof is no problem in this case.

The two offensive conditions, intent plus racial discrimination by a controlling minority, are no doubt interrelated. An intentional policy of racial tyranny appears necessary for the maintenance of perpetual exclusive control of a society by a minority race. Thus those of British descent in South Africa, who were once more "liberal" about racial policies, now are generally reported to "understand" the necessity of the government's policies. It is likewise difficult to believe that a small white Rhodesian minority which practices discrimination and which has demonstrated an unwillingness to achieve an ultimate mixed society on the basis of "one man—one vote" could indefinitely avoid the development of a similar conspiratorial tyranny in support of exclusive minority power.

On the basis of our survey, we can conclude that, in the scale of international values, as objectivized by the political organs of the international community, the human right of "peoples" to "self-determination" has for some decades outweighed the right of states to exclusive control of problems within their self-defined domestic jurisdiction. This has, in turn, spawned new human rights problems for the new minorities.

In addition to this development, it now appears that a good case can be made that the deprivation of the human rights of a *racial majority* being subjugated politically, legally, economically and socially *by intent* by a racial minority is internationally unacceptable and illegal even when limited to their own homeland. Indeed this can be viewed as a simple extension of the concept of self-determination itself to apply against resident as well as foreign *racial* tyrannies.

In saying this we leave open for the present the question of the international interest in the defense of many other acknowledged important human rights, for example, all the rights of the minorities within national states. These remain in a less clear-cut status.[280] Even in these instances however Nuremberg demonstrates that at some point the right to undertake heinous, intentional

71

centrally organized and directed tyranny, at least that based on racial, ethnic or religious factors, is also regarded as beyond the present rights of a sovereign even if confined to the homeland. This does not, of course, mean that effective international intervention is now possible. It most assuredly will not be available against a determined Great Power for the foreseeable future.

This limited list of clearly pathological, organized, intentional, discriminatory conduct can be barred to a sovereign on human rights grounds without fear of cutting great inroads into the sphere of true domestic jurisdiction or undermining the integrity of most sovereigns. The lessons of the holocaust which Hitler's fanaticism unleashed and the international political passions which South Africa's policies have produced and the danger of race war these still imply also all speak of international intervention, not to mention the "inalienable rights" of all men. If the states are willing to enforce the elimination of at least these pathological conditions, it seems evident that this small but huge step towards the international protection of human rights can be taken now, even in the present international system and in the context of the present highly imperfect international organizations, without great legal trauma. This will also be without prejudice to the pace at which the world community will be able to take the next step towards international institutions capable of more comprehensive implementation of the defense of the human rights of minorities, majorities and individuals. The real issues are not legal; they are political and organizational.

Whether we accept the issues of southern Africa, including the Republic of South Africa as basically human rights cases requiring intervention within a state, or as extremely explosive decolonialization and human rights cases which can be classed as a present "threat to the peace" as a large number of states now assert, we must still examine more generally the minimal standards of performance to be attached to international interventions within delinquent sovereign states ultimately for human rights reasons. If even these minimal standards seem impossible of achievement, within the context of a UN intervention, then intelligent political policy will have to adapt to these probabilities as it has elsewhere. Despite the Charter ban on war, not all conflicts have been subject to UN containment.[281]

It is always possible to allow the aggrieved parties to pursue "justice" in the traditional way, the "just" war, fought with the help of whatever allies a sovereign can find. This is obviously an undesirable, damaging alternative for the Charter system. Such wars cannot usually in practice be distinguished from all other wars in their effects and they tend to breed more "just" wars. Yet it might be less damaging than an "unjust" UN intervention.

One thing seems clear however, what was "practical politics" in the 1930's is not practical now. It is not politically practical now to say to those states which refuse to ignore such an offense to their brothers and themselves that they should not make war because the Charter bans war, and also tell them at the same time that the UN may not intervene within the sphere of domestic jurisdiction, as currently defined, of a state, however morally defensible such intervention seems to be. The argument that expanding the role of the UN this way might in time lead to unwarranted interference in *their* "internal" affairs is simply not sufficiently persuasive. Genuine, bitter conflicts of the nature of those in southern Africa will not disappear readily. Africa will either have access to effective international settlement institutions or to the traditional institution of self-help and self-help alliances. If it is possible to do so decently, it would seem preferable politically, and it is certainly *constitutionally* feasible, for the present peacekeeping organization to cope with these passionate problems by methods consistent with the Charter ban on all "private" war, "just" or not, and in accordance with the growing pressure for international protection of human rights.

Thus in the end we may agree that this particular deviation, the wilfull denial in southern Africa of a majority's human rights on the basis of skin pigment, being universally abhorred, certain to continue, an unendurable irritant, an exacerbator of race relations elsewhere, a temptation to non-African communist giant states, including an emergent, racist China, and hence a threat to peace in Africa and potentially to world peace, is for humane and political reasons as good a place to attempt an international inter-

73

vention in the name of human rights and the preservation of peace as any. This leaves the questions of what to do and how to do it in this case. It doesn't assure us that the UN can cope effectively with such problems in general or even in this case. How can we take this step with maximum safety for all, including the UN system, and with a maximum gain for world order? What criteria should be applied? What international aims are appropriate for southern Africa in general and for South Africa in particular, given the present facts? These are all difficult normative questions. Rational choice as to specific policy actions requires far more information and foresight than we can summon. We can only attempt to analyze some of the problems and alternatives that seem relevant to southern Africa.

Before attempting this, let us review briefly where our argument has led us. 1. In a federal constitutional system, the sphere of "domestic jurisdiction" is roughly identifiable at any time but it is capable of evolutionary change in almost all constitutional traditions.

2. At the present time, in the hierarchy of international legal and political norms, the "self-determination," decolonization aspects of "human rights" have been regularly found, by the world's shadow approximation to a bicameral legislature, the General Assembly and the Security Council, to be more important than the right of the colonial sovereigns to exclusive control of their relations with their dependent nationals. At the same time, while the UN has discussed a wide range of "domestic" issues and entertained a wide range of petitions and demands by individuals, with the significant exceptions of Spain, southern Africa and, perhaps, some of the refugee situations, the UN has not asserted a right to intervene actively or demanded action by states to defend individuals or groups against other outrages to human rights perpetrated by what it regards as their own legitimate domestic sovereign.[282] In short, in these cases, in general, human rights have been found to be less important in the scale of norms than the traditional right of the sovereign over his domestic affairs. The reasons for this caution are obvious in view of the widespread generality of the offensive conduct, the still primitive, often inchoate nature of central government in many of the new,

74

poorly-integrated states,[283] the primitive state of the international elaboration of the specific legal content of the desired norms themselves,[284] the limited enforcement capacity of the central organs of the international system, the structural and constitutional defects of the system itself, especially as to voting rules, and the strong insistence of all sovereigns on control over their domestic political institutions, free of outside interference for any purpose.

3. Development of an enforcible international interest in the human rights of a citizen within a state is an extension of the present sphere of international concern and a break with the past constitutional division between international organizations and national states. It lacks neither precedent nor authority however. Such constitutional growth is of course legitimate when it is needed, genuinely desired by the society and potentially workable on the usual bases of yielding predictable, roughly equal treatment of all parties.

4. While such change has been achieved in the American constitutional tradition in great measure through judicial reinterpretation, this seems less suited to the international community where the Court's traditional role is more limited and where different legal traditions, many of which do not encompass this kind of judicial review of constitutions and legislation, converge in the I.C.J. Moreover, sovereigns not only have the traditional right but, more important, also usually the power to refuse to be bound by new obligations they do not care to consent to.

5. The cautious 1966 Decision becomes more comprehensible when we remember these inherent limitations on judicial processes in the current international system. Even so, since the issue related to a Mandate for which specific "contractual" obligations were undertaken, it is especially disappointing and discouraging. Instead of avoiding explosions, it has precipitated one.

6. In such a setting, constitutional growth probably has to take place through the "legislature" though the "executive" can help by prodding the nations. The UN decision-making machinery is itself both a transitional, highly imperfect apparatus and also, quite possibly, about the best that could be achieved at present. The strategic fact is that the UN can do no more than an *effective majority*, not merely a *numerical majority*, of its members is will-

75

ing to enable it to do. This is inevitable, considering the actual distribution of enforcement capacity among the members and the distortions of voting weights in the UN, considering the population in various states, for example.

7. The issues vis-à-vis these various regions of southern Africa therefore turn out to be: a) what type of international standards or roles is the UN system able and willing to assert with respect to decolonization problems of the type now represented by the Portuguese territories, Rhodesia and even South West Africa? The latter two, especially, are not free of important issues of "pathological" racial discrimination as well. b) What type of international standards and roles is the UN system able and willing to assert at this time with respect to the human rights of the populations of its members and, of course, of non-members and ex-members (as South Africa may become).

8. Regarding the first set of issues, the Charter itself greatly extended the League's modest interest in the self-determination aspects of the colonial problem. The UN rejects the view that decolonization is a "domestic" concern of the colonial sovereigns. The international roles in expediting decolonization have been varied but in most of this nation-building effort the UN has not used armed force. When troops were necessary, as in the Middle East and the Congo, it was not to evict a colonial overlord but to quiet disorders and to create the semblance of stability and peace in the wake of abrupt colonial departure.[285] As the recent decision of the General Assembly to terminate the South West Africa Mandate shows, the UN can be expected to continue to play an equally determined role in the decolonization process in southern Africa. This will include such "hard core" areas as Rhodesia and the Portuguese territories.

How this will be done is beyond our predictive ability but suggestions as to the peaceful alternatives can be found in the past history of action taken in various cases by the various organs of the UN. But if the Portuguese and the well-organized "Europeans" controlling South West Africa and Rhodesia refuse to accede gracefully to constant prodding, as others have in the past, and if the UN's members will not countenance the continuation of a colonial condition, who will intercede with force to evict

Portugal and South Africa and who will depose the minority government in Rhodesia?

9. With respect to internal human rights, the persistence and insistence with which the UN has "intervened" in South Africa over two decades, the great numerical majority of states in favor of such intervention and the comprehensive approach thus far taken, including the recommendation of a suggested set of domestic political institutions and a drastic reversal in its basic constitution and voting rules, plus the widespread willingness to *recommend* diplomatic and economic sanctions in support of international intervention to achieve these changes, all suggest that the particular type of offense to human rights involved is regarded or is coming to be regarded as illegal or at least is politically unacceptable "pathological" domestic conduct on the part of a sovereign against its own citizens. These discriminatory acts against a racial majority are, like the intentional elimination of a racial, ethnic or religious minority for which Nazi leaders were tried, now considered "of such a heinous character that they clearly violate basic principles of justice." [286] We are left with the key question of what can be and what is likely to be done about this question at this time and under the present world system. But we can conclude that there is no unsuperable constitutional bar to international action on these issues, that the transfer of this narrowly defined an issue to the sphere of international remedy leaves most of the traditional sphere of domestic jurisdiction intact. Although there is a growing interest in a more widespread international concern for domestic human rights which may, in time, lead to much broader norms supporting interventions of some sort, this is likely to continue to be a slow process. The small states which are most active in support of international human rights are also most insistent in demanding legal protection for their sovereignty against all types of interventions, economic, social and political.[287]

10. We have suggested that, given the genuinely non-integrated state of the peoples of the world community, we cannot expect great strides but we cannot stand still. In the international system, where, traditionally, a sovereign's consent is normally required to bind him, such non-consensual development of obliga-

tions must be overwhelmingly important, desired and, preferably, clearly workable. To lend greater specificity to these comments, we suggest the following preliminary partial set of criteria for international actions on human rights as consistent with contemporary thinking on such issues:

a) The new role or sphere of binding regulation should be clearly needed and/or desired by some overwhelming, nearly unanimous majority of the component parts of the federal system *or* of their human constituents and yet not be achievable effectively by them through their individual action without uniform central direction and coercion over all. There are innumerable domestic examples, major and minor, of such demonstrable needs and of growth in response to them.[288]

b) Some general, near universal agreement should be possible or createable as to the appropriate administrative and legal norms and aims and as to their specific content in implementable form which the society as a whole has found so important that their achievement must be centrally assured and uniformly supervised or controlled.

c) It is necessary that these decisions of the central authorities can be enforced with predictability and reliability. This tends to assure equal treatment of sub-jurisdictions, the reduction of the danger of unpredictable, "political" justice and, incidentally, that the central organs, the legislature and the courts, will not be embarrassed in such a way as to diminish their capacity to function in the fields in which they have traditionally been able to achieve reasonably "fair," effective results on generally agreed norms.

If we apply these criteria to the case of human rights, we can see that the *need* is undeniable. Hitler reminded us of the tyranny of the majority the threat of which so concerned our Founding Fathers. We see the same problems daily both at home and abroad. And South Africa poses, in a peculiarly acute form, the problem of a tyranny by a minority.

If we turn to the other criteria, however—the capacity to develop meaningful consensus on the content of "human rights" and the difficult questions of making it operational and enforcible so that some semblance of orderly, predictable, equal justice

78

can be reliably achieved in the present international system—we see again the major obstacles with which the international regulation of human rights within a state must cope.

The need and the difficulties indicate that we cannot give up where our humanity itself demands persistence and that we cannot expect to advance rapidly towards some better world. We should therefore not be dissatisfied to take the maximum present steps which are consistent with our minimal objectives, including not only the development of effective guarantees of human rights but also, unless and until we can genuinely foresee the feasibility of a sounder world organization, the continued survival and growth potential of the UN system.[289] Such an "optimum" choice is of course never easy to define in practice; it has to be based on innumerable guesses as to the real alternatives and their implications and probability; this is what a nation's "decision makers" regularly do for a living.

IV. *PEACE: THE INTERNATIONAL ORGANIZATION FOR PEACEKEEPING AND ENFORCEMENT*

We have observed in Part I that the white minorities in effective control of the various component units we have grouped under the rubric "southern Africa" have each refused to yield to the will of the overwhelming majority of the international community for decolonization and genuine effective racial equality. We have seen that the organized community, acting in concert, and the bulk of its component nations have become increasingly insistent and are unlikely to yield on these issues even if this implied a fight.

We have seen in Parts II and III that analysis of the law raises complex, important conflict issues that are fundamentally imbedded in the present international system; and that the rights of the parties conflict. But even now the law does not bar appropriate, proportional intervention in defense of human rights, including the "communal" rights of self-determination and protection of minorities against genocide; nor does it bar intervention for the protection of human rights, at least when the offenses involved are so intolerable that they are credible "threats to the peace" because they cannot reasonably be prevented from ripen-

79

ing into genuine breaches of the peace. Nor of course does the Charter or the law bar military self-defense at least on the part of legitimate sovereigns; the internationally accepted rights of rebels are considerably less clear.

We may assume that the African and world-wide rage against South Africa is justified on present common conceptions of human, political, social and economic rights. Moreover, South Africa is not among the politically exempt; unlike some states she has no effective veto over the will of the international community. The question remains as to how much the UN, as an impartial international organization of sovereigns, can be safely asked to do about it.

We know that the Charter system bars private "just" wars or military interventions. At some point soon the issue of internationalized or multi-national, open or clandestine interposition by force within southern Africa will probably become unavoidable. To proceed any further in a delineation or evaluation of the alternatives within the present system for *action* within or outside the UN requires that we spend some time on another perenially dominant problem for the UN system, the problem of the uncertain capacity for centrally organized peacekeeping.

Many writers have analyzed the peacekeeping capacities of the international community in the abstract as a model community of sovereigns, of unequal strength but genuine sovereignty. Many have analyzed the evolution of the peacekeeping functions of the actual general international institutions thus far created, the League and the United Nations, on the basis of the purposes, hopes and institutional potentials indicated in their basic Agreements and in the subsequent history of their actual peacekeeping activities. The UN itself has gone through several years of self-analysis which is still in progress, precipitated by the so-called "financial crisis." [290] We would not expect here to come to radically different conclusions on either the implications of logical *a priori* theory or the lessons of experience. As expected, a current reading of these lessons cannot be glowingly sanguine either concerning the future of UN peacekeeping capacity in general or the specific problems in southern Africa. Neither on review does it appear at all hopeless. The UN has had major peacekeeping and warmaking successes as well as failures. Furthermore, one can always hope that the future will be better; that it will represent a genuine structural break with the past because humans are thinking, adapting, problem-solving animals with intellectual and moral aspirations and because we *have* to assume that their problems are not intrinsically insoluble.

International Collective Security

The major significant differences in the improved endurance and flexibility of the UN's collective security system as contrasted with the League have been psychological. The League embodied a "new" approach, a grand conception for the regulation of international relationships. It inspired widespread hopes which were belied by the actual capacity given by its membership to its institutions which, in the security field, were more like than unlike the past.[291] When, after the failure of its initial arrangements for "automatic," instantaneous sovereign cooperation in repelling aggression, it failed to cope with what it could not have expected to cope with, without a revolution in the actual peacekeeping system created, the members proved incapable of sufficient constitutional improvization to save it. The League fell hard.

In fact, the initial system was an obviously naive design for peacekeeping. There can be nothing automatic about the organization of international peacekeeping which requires the evolution of a political consensus, the taking of an international decision and major efforts to achieve coordination in the application of threats and in the making of war, if necessary, and in organizing the subsequent peace. Despite the letter of the Covenant, the members "interpreted" it when the need arose at least sufficiently to avoid the veto retained by each member against all important decisions, including collective measures against itself. Thus, in its major peacekeeping attempt, economic sanctions against Italy in 1935–36, the veto was avoided by taking no votes, a device to which the UN's General Assembly repaired at its nineteenth session to avoid one of its constitutional crises. The League, then, established its operational "command," the Coordination Committee, as an *extra-League entity,* a conference of all States Members other than Italy and Ethiopia![292] This is itself another

81

interesting example of how one might avoid a Security Council veto when absolutely necessary.

A more detailed examination of the cases of League peacekeeping suggests that the organization worked adequately, if not brilliantly, throughout the period when the participating victor states, those with the greatest stake in the maintenance of *status quo* stability, retained a virtual monopoly of force, and ran a traditional concert of victors.[293] Within this period of their dual political hegemony, France and England decided such issues without flinching from making decisions *between* contestants, most of whom were their allies and "clients" of varying degrees of favor, or political outcasts, like Germany.

Inevitably the actual power situation changed; the postwar peace of victory and exhaustion passed. Defeated Germany, and the erstwhile allies, Italy and Japan, all still dissident to the *status quo* international division of power and wealth, were galvanized by dictators and armed themselves by their own regimented efforts. They quickly became powerful enough to challenge Anglo-French political control of international affairs.

The subsequent revelation of the League peacekeeping and enforcement system's overwhelming dependence on a total lack of conflict of powerful interests among the increasingly numerous Big Powers, or as a substitute, on an unwilling and all too soon unable Britain and France to supply enforcement capacity for the defense of the *status quo,* was a blow to confidence from which the League could not recover. In Manchuria, Ethiopia, the Rhineland and elsewhere, the League failed to summon effective capacity to dissuade aggression.

Although the UN was not explicitly tied to a peace treaty, it too, as designed, was essentially a compact of victors. The Charter in fact adopted as its principal over-all purpose the defense of the post-War *status quo* against armed attack with the already recognized exception implying the eventual dissolution of colonial systems.[294] It accepted frankly the sovereignty of its members *as well as their lack of equal power* and also the inherent limitations of collective security processes against Great Powers in an organization lacking an enforcement potential independent of these members' power, if it were to avoid the danger of pitting these

Great Powers against each other. This bias in favor of a few Powers is no doubt in the long run constitutionally unworkable in an organization purportedly banning *all* resort to armed force. But the fact that it was acceptable as a first step is itself indicative of the psychological difference between League and UN to which we referred before. Despite all the glowing talk, the "political" limits of the possible at the time with respect to an internationally organized collective security system were at least recognized and acquiesced in, and so also was the absolute necessity for such an organization for world order. Both these themes have become leitmotifs of the Organization's subsequent performance in this, its main purpose, the maintenance of international peace and security.[295]

Despite the immediate falling out of the victors and the failure to create a UN military force, in this more sophisticated world of revised expectations, the UN has survived several bitter demonstrations of the limited capacities of its truncated peacekeeping equipment, especially where the great powers were directly involved as in Hungary and Viet Nam. It has managed to retain widespread popular loyalty, to innovate new peacemaking roles for itself and even to perform decently in some instances of substantial, demanding enforcement activities.

UN peacekeeping has worked most smoothly when its basic premises were sufficiently relevant to allow it to perform easily, that is, when the two great powers were in fact in agreement on an issue. Many of the UN's peacekeeping successes have been achieved under the umbrella of the Big Two anti-colonial ideological agreement. The battle-scarred lesser "Major" Powers and the few Minor Powers who possessed the vast bulk of such areas could not hope to stem the tide significantly despite official possession by some of a Security Council veto, thus reminding us again of the dangers of relying on formal constitutional safeguards which are not consistent with the prevailing mores or objectives of those with overwhelming power.

Even so, even in decolonization, most of the UN's peacekeeping intervention has been in the role of negotiator and guardian of a colonial settlement and has taken the form of investigator, truce negotiator, armistice line and border patroller, vote observer, interim administrator, trust supervisor and the like *after* a political settlement has been fought out, most often locally by force of arms, no doubt often with outside assistance from some sympathetic nations. The UN has also performed major technical and humanitarian functions related to these peacekeeping activities, such as the care and resettlement of refugees and stateless persons. It has provided technical assistance and special services for needy Members, in especially heavy doses to some of the new post-colonial states which it helped create, legitimatize and defend.

The alternative range, duration, organization and involvement of UN peace enforcement activities in general has obviously varied widely. On occasion only the provision of good offices, sometimes in the person of the Secretary-General was required or possible, or truce negotiations were hosted. The Organization was at times also directly involved in on-the-spot peace enforcement activities such as the supervision of plebiscites and disputed boundaries, often by a relatively small group of "international" experts or "neutrals." It has also been required to provide an extended UN presence in the form of a substantial police force, as with UNEF, engaged largely in interposition in the boundary zones between the national disputants. It has regularly undertaken international intervention into traditionally domestic spheres on invitation. Thus it has undertaken long-term overall political and economic "technical" assistance (as in Libya) or direct administration of an area (as, briefly, in West Irian) or direct supervision of an internationally appointed and responsible administration of an area (as in the Trust Territories, and especially in the reinforced time-limited Trusteeship of Somaliland), and it has undertaken, on "invitation" from the local government, a long-term extensive armed internal pacification effort, combined with extensive political and economic technical assistance, in the Congo. Several of the UN undertakings involved the Organization in more than one of these classifications of peace-keeping-peace-making efforts. And of course extensive UN pressuring (the Middle East) and warmaking (Korea) have also entailed prior and subsequent use of some other peacemaking, peacekeeping activities, as well. Despite the apparently logical contradiction between the two roles of international warmaker and "neutral" peace-maker, peacekeeper, the UN has performed all these roles, some-times in sequence.

There have been "successes" and "set-backs" or "failures" in each category of activity. For example, when the UN has lent its good offices for truce negotiations or observations prematurely, that is, before even a temporary "final" military boundary was evolved, as in Southeast Asia, without any UN intention to inter-vene to create a stable division, the achievements have been illu-sory and indeed the long-range effects of the limited UN partici-pation have not necessarily been impartially beneficial. Truce observation and supervision in the Balkans, Korea, Kashmir, and the Middle East have generally meant just that. Sometimes the armed truce has led to or been part of a stable settlement; some-times several UN truces have had to be arranged as in Kashmir and Palestine where the militarily defeated party to the partition, or the kindred neighboring states who feel intensively involved, remain inconsolable.

There have been several major cases at the UN where a parti-tion failed to remain peaceful without UN efforts: India-Pakis-tan, Palestine and Korea. In the first two, the Organization, with the crucial help of the U.S. and the cooperation of the U.S.S.R., used its pressure to restore the *status quo ante* partition again, and again started policing it. In Korea, where the Communist states were open adversaries, it summoned up warmaking capaci-ties with the same results. Nothing was achieved in improving the political stability, much less the "justice" of the initial positions whatever the merits of the cases internationally.

Most important for the southern Africa issues, it must frankly be noted again that very little has ever been achieved in the way of securing long-run compliance to the unpoliced dimensions of even a UN-negotiated, fostered or guaranteed settlement. Once the assisted, reinstated or new sovereign took over and the cur-tain of "domestic jurisdiction" dropped down, any imposed, un-defended rights have vanished whether they were other nations' national rights, as with Israel and the Suez Canal, or the property rights of foreign owners of capital, or political or individual hu-man rights, including a treaty-promised right of self-determination of minorities. No plebiscite has in fact been arranged in Kashmir, or North Korea or the South Moluccas, or Goa. Where it was expressly provided for after the UN departure, enforcement has and will remain a problem; the future of the Papuans of West Irian seems all but sealed, even after Sukarno's fall from grace.

Similarly, post-World War II treaty-guaranteed rights of minorities in Eastern Europe have never been enforced; the negotiated political federalism of Indonesia, and of Eritrea with Ethiopia, has not been insisted on; there are numerous similar examples of similar fates for the elaborate political bargains negotiated in the process of colonial dissolution. Though initially bitterly fought out to an apparent bargain in often lengthy negotiations and sometimes taking the form of constitutionally entrenched political rights or of special international guarantees of the rights of foreigners or property holders or the like, these too, like the earlier minorities treaties and the various economic "derogations" of the League period, have proved unenforcible and of transitory reliability. Of course specific international administrative or enforcement procedures, backed by a long-term enforcement presence or credible commitment to appear on the scene as needed, has never been included. This seems realistic, since the potentials of such persistent imposed, international intervention in the domestic sphere of a Member is realistically limited at present and indeed would appear to be dangerous to the preservation of international stability and to the survival of the interventionary organization at the present stage of the world system.

The Cyprus case, in which Turkey, Greece and Britain were given rights to attempt to enforce a constitutional structure embodying minority rights in return for a unitary government rather than a partition comes immediately to mind. The entrenched rights of the minority proved intolerable to the majority within a couple of years as did also the right of outside sovereigns to intervene to protect those rights. The issue rests undecided and now constitutes another chronic peacekeeping problem for the UN. Without Turkey, a determined interested sovereign, willing to "threaten the peace" "justly" to champion the rights of the Cypriot-Turks, it would have been decided long since, no doubt, in the standard summary fashion of sovereign states.

Indeed one of the implications of this analysis seems to be that, if "just private wars" are to be effectively disallowed, the existence of their substitute, "just" threats to the peace must be acknowledged. A responsible peace organization which is not yet able to solve the irreducible elements of such conflicts between sovereigns also cannot afford to deny their existence. It would appear to have little choice but to seek, to find ways consistent with "minimal standards of justice" and the political array at the time to contain the "just" threat to the peace. If political agreement on the achievement of these minimal standards proves impossible, containment may prove impossible. Peaceful settlement having failed and "just" containment having proved impossible, the very practical question then again becomes simply: what should the UN role be in each case?

This very summary review of UN experience[296] seems to show that UN efforts for peace and security have tended to yield most stable results when 1) the Big Two were in at least temporary agreement; and/or 2) militarily realistic, politically stable, or temporarily politically best possible, perimeters between the contenders had already been delimited by the interaction of their own power; and/or 3) when no major non-self-enforcing and ultimately (domestically) unacceptable promises have had to be extracted from the parties in the bargaining. In such instances, the UN roles can be viewed as reduced to the *relatively* manageable, *relatively* apolitical ones of facilitating negotiations for a formal settlement and of interposition between the parties, if necessary. Lacking these preconditions, successful UN efforts have been far more contentious and difficult. They have required the hammering out of a general international consensus both on the overall political goals in the case and the operational means and institutions for achieving them, which clearly goes far to determine the actual features of the new *status quo* which the UN was willing to agree to impose. This has been true even when no further military effort was required of the UN, as in the lengthy negotiations within the UN on how to effectuate the disposal of the former

87

Italian colonies. Where an immediate, substantial armed response was required in a situation in which UN action was clearly politically appropriate or necessary as in Korea, Suez and the Congo, the existence of a general consensus on clear-cut, agreed, limited aims became crucial. Certainly in the Congo case the lack of such an effective consensus on operational aims converted the action into an almost intolerable political, administrative and constitutional, and therefore financial burden to the Organization. Even a gifted, dedicated Secretary-General can be expected to find it difficult to pursue unspecified goals (meaning in fact internationally disputed goals) efficiently or effectively.

Military Enforcement

The effective state of peacekeeping/war-making capacity of the UN is related to the issues of southern Africa in two ways: can the present UN be expected to mount and to win a "war" there, if one is necessary to impose UN aims, and can it be expected to win the peace there, that is, is it likely to achieve a political consensus on 1) the overall human rights and other aims of the intervention, and 2) on a "workable" constitutional strategy for achieving them, and 3) on perseverence after an initial military victory, i.e., on maintaining the intervention as long as necessary after the peace to achieve these aims. These issues of effectively organizing the war and the peace by the UN are interrelated and we will discuss them both briefly.

We have noted that, due to the inability of the major powers to agree, the original Charter provision for armed forces, Article 43, was stillborn. The Charter as designed also gave five powers a veto capacity over the Organization's capacity to conduct mandatory enforcement activity while at the same time denying *all* parties, including the veto-bearing powers, the right to use arms except in self-defense against armed attack. The dynamic infeasibility and dangers of honestly applying such an international straitjacket are obvious, not to mention its "undemocratic" biases and hence, in the long run, its inevitable unacceptability.[297]

When the victors, perhaps fortunately for the others, inevitably[298] fell out before they could even begin to try to produce the armed forces required by the original design of the Charter's enforcement system, the system became much more like that of the League. The Organization was now in fact dependent on there being no important conflicts of interest among the states, an unstable position for a peacekeeping organization in a world of conflicting sovereigns. Unlike the League, the UN has remained *unwilling* to yield its principal function. It has therefore been extemporizing with pragmatic substitutes for failure ever since. With the occasional approval, and/or the cautious acquiescence, or the sullen disapproval of the initial Veto Powers, it has been treating the Charter like a constitution and adapting it for *ad hoc* survival through each crisis and even raising various kinds of forces as needed despite the logically untenable problems of imposing peace among sovereigns who retain a monopoly of the capacity to make war. This sophisticated constitutional opportunism, born of a determination to survive (an organizational "will to live"), is the second major difference from the League's experience. It is obviously a dangerous game for the central organization in a dangerous world of recalcitrant sovereigns, but it is better than capitulating to impotence.

The inevitable failure of the original machinery led to the participation of the General Assembly in many of the modest peacekeeping activities we have described. The Uniting For Peace Resolution, proposed by the U.S. to allow the General Assembly to conduct and raise forces for "recommended" peacekeeping operations when the Security Council could not act, legitimized the trend, gave it some potential teeth and also broadened it temporarily to include the potential of United Nations actions against the important interests of Major Powers on the basis of a warmaking General Assembly-directed coalition which would, it would seem, of necessity, have to include some of the war material-supplying Major Powers. This Resolution was supported by a U.S. which was apparently satisfied with the bargain it had made with the General Assembly on Korea, and overconfident of its capacity to control that Assembly in the long run, despite the "undemocratic" design of that body too, and the fact that, looming over the time horizon, were the innumerable offspring of the colonial liquidation which swelled its ranks, each with an equal vote.

Second thoughts developed soon enough. As a result, substantial warmaking by the UN remains very difficult to negotiate, organize and effectuate. The "peacekeeping crisis" is itself intrinsic in the Charter and would be in any constitution negotiated among sovereigns at present. As such, it is a chronic disease but one which the patient has so far ingeniously survived. In short, UN warmaking and enforcement capacity is not non-existent, but it has been used only twice.

Both in the Korean and Congo cases, initial Security Council action was possible.[299] In both cases, for similar reasons, supervision over the conduct of the fighting and the peacemaking was largely or entirely transferred out of the Council. The implications of the two experiences are particularly important for any evaluation of the problems of UN enforcement activities in southern Africa.

For Korea, it is essential to recall that the Soviet Union was boycotting the Security Council over the issue of Chinese representation in June, 1950 when the UN was faced by demonstrable aggression and was presented by a quick-reacting United States with a *fait accompli,* a decision to fight. The Council, freed for the moment from the Soviet veto, could not easily avoid committing the UN to a choice between Big Power protegés of the two opposing camps, one clearly the aggressor, the other cooperating with prior UN nation-building activities. Indeed a UN Commission working for Korea's unification was on the spot at the time and witnessed the aggression.

In part because the largely U.S. intervention was "internationalized" in this way in the UN's name, the conflict was limited to Korea. Internationalizing thus limited the extent of the permissible victory in effect to a more-or-less permanent reimposition of the admittedly imperfect prior *status quo.* These can be viewed as the price to the U.S. for internationalization of the action.[300] The capacity of the UN to impose limits to the U.S.-UN action was no doubt enhanced by the forceful entry of Communist forces as the UN army reached the Yalu River.

In fact, it is likely that, at the time, such externally reinforced pressure to containment was on balance not merely bearable but a domestic political asset. It was an additional set of arguments to

90

reinforce the preferences of the responsible U.S. decision-makers in their pursuit of a politically difficult set of war aims.[301]

In sum, for the U.S., internationalizing the conflict had a value and probably negligible costs; it contained while legitimizing U.S. intervention. Indeed, this is another important example, one of the most important and encouraging to date, of the already noted theoretical concept concerning the process of the "rational" emergence of new, coercive governmental authority, *i.e.*, that the decision of a sovereign to submit important functions to the control or supervision of a higher governmental authority may often be desired by and beneficial to the submitting sovereign, after strictly self-interested rational calculations, even or especially in the case of warmaking in the nuclear age.[302]

From the point of view of the international organization, the major potential dangers of a Korea-type solution to international enforcement problems, as "internationalized" unilateral intervention, are obvious. Indeed they are analogous to some of the dangers to the majority of small states of enforcement as provided for in the Charter. The Organization is dependent on the good will of the single or several disproportionate contributors of its enforcement power (Of course in the case of several Major Powers the likelihood of their inability to cooperate in war itself becomes another source of danger to the peace).

Moreover, it seems quite likely that some other nation providing the military power and serving as UN Command might prove even more determined in its national military commitment and more decisive, even aggressive, in its *national* objectives, or even more under the pressure of the decisive elements of national public opinion, whether in response to an electorate, a Party Presidium, or an ideological rival, and therefore more difficult for the UN to contain, persuade and control, than was the United States in Korea.[303] In addition, any "limited" war that dragged on would no doubt create the normal domestic pressures for escalation from the warring member. In this case, genuine blame instead of convenient acquiescence might well be focused on the UN as the source of the enemy's "privileged sanctuary." Under such circumstances, any Power, no matter how particularly "moral," would be hard for the UN to control. Instead of containment, escalation might indeed result, perhaps more readily.

There are other obvious problems for the Organization implied in the Korea brand of internationalized unilateral military intervention. The decision to make war requires a rapid, long-term, largely irreversible, all-embracing commitment which is inherently unsuited to even well organized legislative decision processes within an ideologically integrated state. Whatever the constitutional formula, the decision to fight normally turns out to be an executive function. The citizens of the United States had in fact little opportunity to reject armed resistance to Communist aggression in Korea. Indeed, though they do have an ultimate veto over the retention in office of their leadership, they had less opportunity than the UN to reject their leaders' decisions, although the commitment made for them was personally far more comprehensive, irreversible and demanding. The UN, a headless "legislature of sovereigns," was presented with U.S. intervention in the name of the UN on a more-or-less take it or leave it basis with the implied threat of gross U.S. dissatisfaction if UN action were not prompt and useful. The difficulty implied is at a *minimum* in instances like Korea, where the act of aggression is clear-cut and the aims of the Organization are those traditional for an international organization and almost self-evident: *i.e.*, the containment of aggression and the return to the already established initial, relatively stable, *status quo* in which a legitimate government exists, asks for aid, and is capable of rallying at least the bulk of the native population to the defense of their native soil despite foreign supported subversion and insurgency. In such cases an almost *"automatic"* definition of the agreed purposes and the limits of the aims of international action, not unlike that assumed by the League Covenant, is potentially possible, and rapid decision even at the gunpoint of the state or states which have elected to do the international intervening may not be morally difficult for the Organization.

In addition of course the mobilizing of effective forces for the conduct of war is unsuited to legislative-type decision-making. It requires hierarchical command, preferably responsible to some responsible executive. Of course we cannot extensively examine these issues here[304] but some comments are unavoidable.

92

Where one state is in fact supplying the bulk of the forces, the problem arises only in relatively minor form. In Korea, the United States ran the war for the UN, supplying the overwhelming bulk of the men, equipment, aircraft, and naval vessels which came from UN sources. The usual problems of even a well motivated coalition, meshing strategy, transport, different types of equipment, ammunition and training, and the like, were therefore minimal. Where a force volunteered by a country was too small or presented particular problems of equipment or training, or was considered a potential political problem (as with the Chinese Nationalists from Formosa), it was simply rejected by the UN Command with no real fear of political repercussions or possible shortages.[305] Where one state plays this dominant a role, technical problems are minimized and many political problems these would engender are minimized as well. The basic political problem for the Organization of controlling the contributors and delimiting the sanctions remains difficult.

In sum, it seems inherent in the nature of this type of operation that, as in Korea, the initiative and the important first reading and interpretation of the "will" and aims of the international organization will tend to be made by the major intervening Power(s), rather than by an international negotiating process seeking a consensus. If more than one Power elects itself to the role, clearly they must agree on all relevant important issues or the dangers to peace are obvious. Then the organization is required to choose between powerful members, as it has in Suez, Korea and the Congo. So long as the organization's control remains inchoate or unspecified and the organization remains in fact dependent in terms of military power on the good behaviour and responsiveness of the enforcing state(s) to international pressures, responsiveness can be expected to prove at best uneven. The need for a clear-cut, relatively "self evident" set of *limited* aims shared by the enforcers and the majority of members is clear. If a UN Command chooses to defy the UN and is not disciplined by the Command's *de facto* Commander-in-Chief at home, as in Korea, a new UN enforcement action backed by at least another Great Power might be the only ultimate corrective device.

The burden of this discussion is that internationalized Great

Power intervention for peacekeeping is likely to be risky for the Organization. It is most likely to be mutually satisfactory for the intervening state(s) and the Organization when the international war is in defense of the classic set of clear-cut, limited international aims enshrined in the League and UN systems. Nevertheless in reviewing Korea from hindsight we probably must conclude that the constitutional improvisation with which the UN was in fact presented worked decently, though, of course, like most other UN peace enforcement issues, the remnants of that fire still smolder and flare a decade and a half later. The UN was lucky. It survived, the conflict was contained; the *status quo* with its defects was preserved. If not improved, it was not worsened. And, incidentally, there were no peacekeeping bills hanging over to be used as a potential [306] weapon to hobble further UN activities by those states which wish to discourage UN peacekeeping and enforcement.

For such "limited," clear-cut cases then, Big Power intervention for raising fighting forces in the name of the majority cannot be dismissed as a warmaking technique despite the obvious dangers. For intervention in the complex problems of southern Africa, the dangers seem especially real.[307]

An alternative to the dangers of uncontrollable Major Power(s) intervention on the UN's behalf for modest UN warmaking, which directly produced the so-called "financial crisis," involved the conscious policy of improvising UN forces tailored to each need from various smaller countries, preferably selected so as to assure the disinterestedness or neutrality of the forces and hence its controllability by the UN Command, however established. Such a force was to be financed by peacekeeping levies voted by the General Assembly as well as by members' contributions. The levies have been ruled obligatory by the I.C.J. but have remained uncollectible from the two major dissident Powers, the Soviet Union and France, which regard General Assembly peacekeeping activities as illegal, and from several other nations as well.[308]

When relatively small forces have been needed for the preservation of an already effectuated truce, as in the Middle East in 1956–57,[309] this improvisation has sufficed thus far. The aim, size, and mission of the UN force, patrolling a border between two angry states to keep down infiltrations and other hostile activity, were relatively easy to agree on; the force, which is still in service, is small, easily supplied and only lightly armed, and its presence accords with the needs of the parties and has been in fact or *de facto* agreed to by them. With the Secretary-General's military designee exercising control over this small multi-national force, few of the problems of Great Power coalitions or unilateral activities seem to have arisen.

On the other hand, the Congo experience revealed some of the limitations of this alternative, ingenious, pragmatic strategy, at least for larger conflicts involving shooting by UN forces. It also served to remind all states of the difficulties and dangers of using the military forces of an international organization of sovereigns to impose an internal, domestic political order, or for any action which might develop into a major conflict for large stakes.[310] The initial conception of the military operation in the Congo was, as in UNEF, the UN force in the Middle East, to exclude the military presence of the Great Powers and other unwanted parties and thus to "insulate the problem area from the impact of extraneous political rivalries."[311] Forces were raised in smaller and "neutral" states. Moreover due to the nature of the undertaking which entailed the establishment and propping up of a *de facto* domestic government, none of the Powers in the great rival blocs acquiesced more than formally in their exclusion from the settlement; China, the USSR and the U.S. had their traditional conflicting ideological political interests to press: Britain, France and Belgium had post colonial economic interests to preserve. Moreover, as a contemporary observer noted, even "The states which accepted the mission to exclude 'extra-Africa' conflicts have not in every case resisted the temptation to inject their own brands of disruptive influence into the chaos . . . ,"[312] for example, by intervening in support of factions in Congo domestic politics. It will be remembered that the internal cause of the chaos itself reflected a still largely divided tribal society,[313] a population too long kept "orderly" and uneducated to any complex modern skills, an uneven geographical distribution of resources and wealth, particularly in mineral-rich Katanga, in which European post-colonial interests were important and aggressive, in sum, a

95

non-integrated nation, unable to produce a domestic political consensus on its own political organization peacefully, headed by an unprepared and largely unarmed leadership, and subject to multifarious, divisive foreign pressures and interventions.

Internal pacification even by invitation proved to be a new, inherently uncongenial role for an international organization, the most dramatically politically interventionary type of peace-making yet attempted; the most divisive for the members and the organization. The problem of interventionary roles for "impartial" organizations of sovereigns has been well summed up:[314]

> "The promotion of law and order in a setting of domestic factionalism is not compatible with the ideal of neutrality and impartiality. It requires that a choice be made among competing prescriptions for law and order and competing candidates for the order-giving function. In this sense, the mission of the United Nations in the Congo is one that invites debate, if not conflict, among member states concerning the direction of policy."

It was said of Napoleon by a cynic that he did not need to be a great general; he fought only against coalitions. The underlying truth in this oft' repeated comment has also been demonstrated, even in this century and even when the alliance was one between a few highly motivated powerful nations with clearly interrelated interests. Obviously parallel problems exist in any effort to weld a multi-national force of any size from a heterogeneous group of small units from many countries using different languages and equipment and trained to differing standards into a militarily effective alliance. Indeed, pure theory suggests that as the members of a coalition increase so also does the likelihood of conflict among them. But the fact that there are many members is also likely to reduce the importance of the participation of any one member if the central command is strong and vigorous. Is this last proviso likely in Secretary-General run military coalitions or in those directed by some other possible device, for example by a committee of sovereigns? This surely depends on the size of the forces necessary and on who leaves the coalition. Large expeditions requiring a heavy Great Power participation are not in logic likely to be free of Great Power influence. The difficulty in keeping such a group together in the field while the diplomats quarrel with each other, with the major military provisioning Powers, with disapproving members and with the local government selected by the UN as "legitimate" over the appropriate international political goals of the mission and the means to attain them is obvious in theory and demonstrated in practice in the Congo.

These problems arise for the Organization's image, both as to its "impartiality" and its capacity for effectiveness, because it is, in fact, choosing a *winning* coalition and a *losing* one from among its sovereign members and imposing its choice in an issue involving the use of force. This—the existence of a winning and a losing coalition even on very important issues—is a typical phenomenon in the legislature of a government. It is a typical phenomenon of the international "balance of power" system in which war is the normal way to separate the winners from the losers on genuinely important issues. But on genuinely important issues it remains a dangerous process for organized sovereign cooperation, precisely because each sovereign portion of the divided house retains its own arms to which it may resort if sufficiently frustrated or threatened. And at minimum, of course, the possibility always exists that a losing sovereign(s) may withdraw from the organization, or especially if they have vetoes, stay in merely to obstruct its future functioning. Indeed this latter seems to have happened more than once at the UN.

The additional strains of this often inevitable resort to a choice of a winning and a losing coalition even on UN warmaking within this organization of sovereigns complicate the already complex position of the Secretary-General, who may well be called upon to manage at least a trinity of not necessarily compatible roles by himself. He thus remains a) the appointed, symbolic embodiment of the conscience of mankind and of peace, and b) the impartial civil servant of the sovereign members, and c) the partisan combat director, perhaps even issuing orders to officers in the field, for the winning coalition of nations within the General Assembly or even the Security Council.

Some of the specific problems we have noted in the Congo mission can be associated primarily with the type of mission faced in the Congo. Before dismissing even these we must recall *again* that this type of intervention by invitation to assist in domestic pacification may well be frequently necessary in the future in a post-colonial world of numerous, vulnerable, emergent states, which remain tempting subjects for subversion and counter-insurgency. Some of the difficulties of the Congo mission may be primarily due to the specific type of military coalition extemporized and to mistakes in its organization which need not be repeated.[315] Many, however, emanate from the inherent contradictions in the concept of major warmaking by an international organization of sovereigns however organized. The duration of the so-called "financing crisis" over very modest sums attests to the reawakened awareness of all the major sovereigns to these contradictions.

Other very important problems may have special characteristics because UN forces are involved but they emanate basically from the intrinsic dangers of any warmaking, especially in the nuclear era, including those of containing the objectives of the military presence and of limiting the war in general. Neither variant of a UN warmaking force so far extemporized has satisfactorily solved these political or technical problems. In principle, the Congo-type of mixed coalition in which financing, supplies, mobility and manpower come from many different national sources seems logically—and morally—preferable on these counts, but at the great price of unwieldiness in both warmaking and peacemaking. Indeed in large wars this may amount to an intolerable price. It is therefore in fact best suited to small engagements again with limited, widely agreed, preferably traditional objectives.

In any case logic, and the Congo experience, and its long aftermath indicate that the UN can do the job. They also suggest that it is naive to expect that any substantial international armed force can exclude the interests of some major or middle power(s) if at least one such state must supply the material or financial resources for the fighting. It may be possible however at least to exclude the added dangers of the military presence of such states. If their resources, arms and transport equipment are needed, keeping out their men can hardly imply successful exclusion of their political presence though this may still be very worth while both as a limitation on their staying power, and on their bargaining power during the mission. Although any absolutely essential member retains an actual veto over continuing to cooperate with a UN peacekeeping coalition manned by others, this variant is likely to provide less decision-making power than actual control of the operation itself. Indeed even for the "essential" Power, the use of such a "veto" may be so self defeating to its own aims as to raise questions of its practical existence. And of course if several competitor Middle and Major Powers are contributing or available to be called on, the independence of the coalition from any one of them is thereby heightened, unless, of course, they can cooperate to impose a "group veto," as in the initial Charter plan, and make it work. In that case, inside or outside the UN nothing but a holocaust could stop them.

We have attempted to suggest the "stable" international framework in which international decisions appear to be made, and we have posited some "reasonable" ends for the UN as an organization in the long-run (roughly, effective survival and safe devolopment as part of a more perfect international system) and some reasonable compromise ends for these difficult specific issues, a stable "fair" (just and humane), preferably peaceful, solution which minimizes the need for future international intervention.

Even so unspecified a set of goals when applied to so bitterly contentious but relatively clear-cut set of issues as those of southern Africa reminded us again of the need for and the reasonable fears aroused by an international organization with effective force. The present balance of force in the decentralized, self-defending system of sovereigns supports the continuance of conditions in southern Africa which are inconsistent with almost any normal specification of these posited minimum aims and the minimum obligations of the UN itself to humanity.

Since we cannot return to the "good old days" of pre-nuclear world wars, we have assumed that we have to make slow progress safely towards a less volatile world, where the need for the use of centralized force will be minimized and the dangers thereof denatured as much as possible. We are further suggesting that, when the use of armed force appears essential for "justice," or other imperious reasons, and therefore, ultimately for the stability of a generally bearable peace which can be maintained, that this should be accomplished preferably by the UN where, at present, the conflict itself can normally be most reliably contained, and where the original ethical justifications of the war need not dissolve in a peace of retribution rather than "justice." We have briefly surveyed the present Organization's improvised attempts to perform this role. Though no one failure or success is definitive, each big crisis that the UN does or does not handle well does affect our prognosis. The present congeries of crises in southern Africa hits at such particularly fundamental and important dilemmas, involving both sovereignty and the racial justice which must be enshrined in a world institution, that their outcome, especially if that outcome is a major failure on the part of the UN, cannot fail to have important impact on our posited goals. In the shorthand of game theory the payoffs are asymetrical; negative payoffs are disproportionately high. A stable, successful resolution of the problem promises to leave the system basically unchanged. It seems rational to choose to avoid failure.

It will be useful to synthesize out and summarize in a preliminary way some general conclusions with regard to the safe, effective use of internationalized force at the present time which seem to have been suggested, *ceteris parebus,* from our review. We will then attempt to apply these abstractions briefly to the major longer run alternative objectives which appear to be open to the UN in southern Africa, and to suggest some of the principal alternative sources of force available to be tapped by the parties if UN action is stymied altogether. The specification and evaluation of strategy and policy moves, the raising of the required forces, the very important "how to do its," on a month to month, or day to day basis, must perforce be left to others.

If the application of armed force appears essential to establish the minimal essentials of justice and peace, when should this be undertaken "legally" for UN members, *i.e.,* by the UN? Under what conditions does it appear safer that it be undertaken "illegally" or "a-legally," by the states? Or, more likely, legally, by an exclusionary regional organization? In the abstract, warmaking *outside* the UN can normally be expected to be preferred by all members for themselves. This is precisely because it relieves them of the need to negotiate concerning their war aims, and thus to limit these to what would be agreeable to the Organization or at least to all of its importantly interested Powers. The advantage for international peace of UN warmaking and peacekeeping is the converse. In addition to the noted, very important legitimatizing effect, warmaking by an international organization does force the winning enforcement coalition to hear and contend with most, if not all, of the powerful interests in a conflict, including all those which might be tempted to explicitly or covertly sabotage the combined effort and threaten its limited nature. In short, the making and maintenance of an *international* consensus on war ends and means becomes a major new element of the war effort itself. It can be expected that the normal net result of this super-imposed political effort will be to impose compromise and limita-tion on the aims of each as the price of containment of the others and of the conflict. If it is successful, it is reasonable to expect that the risk of major armed response or of escalation by those whose interests are being countered by so overwhelming a world coalition will be substantially reduced.

Obviously, important issues will not exist without important disputants. If the internal divisions among the members are so great that inaction would be imposed at the political stage be-cause no compromise is possible which can satisfy the minimal interests of an overwhelming majority, this stalemate may be in-tolerable to some groups of states. If this reinforcing fact does not, in turn, induce the holdout states to modify their bargaining position, then the realistic conclusion is that an international organization of sovereigns cannot cope without great internal stresses with the issue on which its members are severely divided, perhaps sufficiently to fight a war. When this happens, the UN can, in effect, either choose to fail by default in its major role of containing war, or it can arrange a war-making coalition of its own. The key estimating problems in all such calculations of what to do next seem to concern, among others, the relative stra-tegic strength with respect to the issue (the amount of force which can be expected to be allocated by the dissenting state(s) to it) and, even more difficult, the estimation of the determination and likely effectiveness of those apt to become part of the losing Gen-eral Assembly coalition to continue attempting to bar or change from its purposes, etc., a UN war-making/peacekeeping activity. Overlooking for the moment the halfway house of Regional Organization war-making, if the UN abstains from the conflict, it is returned to the traditional organs of war, the alliance systems. We again borrow the language explored by game theorists to look at the implications of reversion to those ancient traditions.

In the unorganized international system of largely self-interested sovereigns, warmakers, especially the crucial supplying and financing powers, have traditionally exhibited a persistent tendency to seek to form a minimal coalition,[316] and often, also, normally whether they be the U.S. or France or China or Russia, they regularly prefer hegemony within it, presumably in order to retain major control of its direction and objectives, and therefore its "pleasures" and its "spoils" of various types. All history has demonstrated the dangers and the endurance of this game among sovereigns. The incentives of all potentially competitive sovereigns not to yield but to continue to contest the game are intrinsic. They are fortified by the potential great stakes, and especially, by the insecurity of survival itself if defeated in a society of ruthless pure egoists.[317] We have noted that the calculation of minimal over-balancing or prevailing coalitions is intrinsically bound to vary with the perspectives, "styles," information, rationality, and commitment of the parties, in a situation in which stochastic elements, chance, and shocks, including even storms at sea which befall "invincible" armadas, have always been clearly important to the final outcome. In sum, it has normally appeared more rational for threatened potential losers in the game of balance of power to attempt constantly to build up balancing alliances and to promise to fight, as a deterrent to aggression and, if necessary, to fight, against the weakening encroachments of even implicitly victorious exclusionary minimal coalitions, in the unorganized system of sovereigns. Moreover, when the implicit losses of accommodation or appeasement appear to be unlimited, and, for that reason, to be no less than those implied by a disastrous, destructive war, this resolve is fortified. "Never capitulate!" appears to be sensible advice even from the technicians' point of view, as relevant as the defense attorney's admonition "Never Plead Guilty!"

Minimal coalitions arranged within the UN have features parallel to minimal coalitions in the unorganized international community of sovereigns especially for the coalition's hegemonous sovereign, if the gains of legitimatizing the conflict are balanced by any net costs of limiting the losses of the defeated and excluded parties. The best of all currently possible worlds for such a sovereign may be such a UN action. This is likely when these UN imposed net costs are low or negative, 1) because the losses of the losing coalition are not limited by the organization or 2) because, as may have been the case in Korea, and will perhaps, hopefully, be a structural feature of the nuclear age, the hegemonous power finds the limitation a convenience, or 3) because the limitation of losses and of conflict are "fictitious," because, for example, they require purely formal, non-enforcible promises on future conduct of the sovereign within his realm. We have already mentioned several types of unenforcible, historically unenforced constitutionally entrenched rights, as in Cyprus, and unenforcible promises of fair compensation for post-liberation nationalization, etc. which have regularly been frankly regarded as "unjust," even unfairly extorted, from the domestic majority in favor of some "unfairly" privileged, often "foreign," minority, rather than as expressions of the rights of every man, whether or not he is in some losing minority. Under the circumstances, for reasons already elaborated in our discussion of the case of non-internationalized conflict, it will be rational in case 1 or 3 above for the state being militarily "sanctioned," when the issue is vital (*i.e.* survival) and when the international organization is demanding unconditional surrender (*i.e.* when the losses and gains of the losers and winners are not going to be effectively limited), to follow the traditional "Never Capitulate" rule. If the UN coalition is a minimal coalition, and other almost balancing coalitions exist (or as is possible in this UN, an over-balancing one in power exists, though it is in the minority in votes) and the interests or the nationals' interests of these states have not been absorbed into the objectives of the winning UN coalition, they will have incentives to subvert the UN action, or if they are highly motivated in the dispute or clearly disproportionately powerful perhaps even to openly make war on it. In such circumstances the UN would be *de facto* dissolved, at least temporarily, into warring coalitions; the possibility would diminish of limiting the war territorially or in permissible weapons technology.

All this has relevance both to the general issues of the future of the international enforcement of collective security and to the future of the UN in southern Africa. To summarize our conclusions on the first of these:

1. The pursuit of a traditional minimal coalition for warmaking is in two out of three cases likely to be unsuited to an organization of sovereigns and dangerous for the survival of that organization and for world peace. It was obviously always a dangerous strategy.

2. For best results, it would appear that the aims of any internationalized peacekeeping coalition should assure the minimal rights (*i.e.* at least the *survival*) of all vitally concerned parties (*i.e.* those who could be credibly believed willing to fight in defense of their interest, immediately or perhaps even in the long run). Where this is impossible, perhaps because contending parties are willing to fight for more than survival or are willing to fight separately rather than acquiesce in the shape of the UN designed peace to be imposed, as for example in the Congo, where many conflicting vested interests, private and national all asserted themselves, internationalized peacekeeping is frankly divisive among sovereigns.

3. Where containment is impossible and active international intervention is nonetheless essential or preferred to the effects of the probable alternative regional or unilateral interventions, the general rule which suggests itself is to attempt to come as close as possible to the ideal implicit in the League and Charter enforcement system compromises, *i.e.* to seek the a) *widest possible* enforcement coalition with, b) the largest possible number of Great Powers (if not the coalition of the whole, at least the maximal rather than the minimal coalition), backed by, c) the widest possible political and moral consensus on the goals of the action consistent with the fundamental compromise on values and issues in the name of which it appears necessary to undertake even a divisive action and, d) to clearly limit these aims, if possible, to assure at least the physical survival of all parties, winners or los-

ers, majority or minority, *i.e.* to assure safety against vengeance or genocide for losers.

4. The rationale seems obvious. Such overwhelming coalitions may be expected in some cases to lower the short run possible gains of some of the winners, but if the winning coalition is visibly overwhelming, it will tend to induce compliance or at least acquiescence of the losing coalition and at least to limit wars of mistaken calculations again, if, and only in so far as their losses are credibly limited and bearable. The long repetitious prevalence of the US-USSR anti-colonial entente despite the British and French veto power which culminated in Suez and is now moving into southern Africa, is again evidence for this position.

5. Such a pursuit of collective security on the basis of the broadest possible coalition and for limited goals can be expected to change the rational response of the losers from "Never Capitulate" to "Wait till next time."

This, of course, is the hope. It also is the way minorities, including the losing coalitions in the legislatures of western states, act and are expected to act within national states, when the will of the required majority is ascertained in legitimate decision processes. Sometimes there is no credible "next time" on that particular issue, even within national states. Thus the imposition of a federal income tax, of central control over the economy and over citizens' welfare, the centralization of the bulk of the military enforcement system in a federal system are irreversible constitution-modifying steps, however achieved. The minimal content of the minimal safeguards for the minority even within such national states comes down to moral and physical survival, *i.e.*, freedom from persecution or genocide. For the losing legislative and voting coalitions in Western-type societies, we can add, they normally retain also the right to continue to participate in the domestic political game, probably on "equal terms," (given its newly adopted basic rules), where the meaning of "on equal terms," itself, depends both on the constitutional and the effective political system, and can change with time.

6. Within the current non-integrated international system the minimum rights of the sovereign (win or lose) if he is not to feel forced to fight to the death must include credible, bearable sur-

vival for the nation but not necessarily in unmodified form; almost all wars bring important imposed modifications. Assured survival makes it possible for the losing sovereign to "wait till next time" and to acquiesce in the overwhelming power of the majority's will.

7. We have seen that UN action has seemed most facile in instances of narrow or specific delimited aims of a traditional type, probably not requiring any major interventions within the normal domain of the sovereign, preferably limited to interpositions between sovereigns. These are more likely both to require small forces and to be consistent with the ready attainment of the preferred UN-wide consensus. Nevertheless the UN has managed to repulse aggression (Suez, Korea) and even to achieve at least a temporary internal pacification (Congo). It has been "gifted" and lucky, on the whole, in achieving internationalized war with containment.

8. It is fantasy or escapism to expect to "return" to the initial Charter system or to its watered down variant, a group veto without a force. This is *tantamount to insisting that there be no forceful collective security.*

9. The "return" to a regional organizational solution as a substitute for general organization peacekeeping is often, in fact, also an attempt to find another variant for achieving an uncontrolled, uncontained minimal coalition. In these cases it can be expected to retain the usual special risks of a minimal coalition of sovereigns whenever it excludes vitally interested parties. In any case, the actions of the hegemonous Power are normally more difficult, *not less difficult* for the *other members* of the regional organization to control. The hegemonous Power has normally eliminated its competitors by the strategy of "going regional."

10. *If* the Great Powers are willing to settle for less than nearly full control over each enforcement action in which they participate, even within the UN, extensive peacekeeping operations on the basis of the largest possible coalition with the broadest participation seem feasible.

11. We have repeatedly stressed what can be regarded as two *prima facie* rules for UN enforcement actions at the present time,

both of which suffer from the same very serious defect: they are
not necessarily self-enforcing. For completely egocentric sovereigns with short run horizons, they have to be consciously reinforced. Possibly the ideology of brotherhood can do what the
"idea" of a European civilization has often been credited with doing for 19th century Europe. The first, it will be remembered, is
the necessity of limiting the aims of "internationalized" enforcement actions and, therefore, also hopefully, their size. The absolute
minimum constraint on the gains of the winners seems to be the
survival in some reasonable form of the sovereigns. The second
is that interventions into the normal domestic sphere of a sovereign, being an aberration, should be minimized. Where they are
absolutely necessary, these should again be aimed to produce
limited losses which are consistent with the overwhelmingly important objectives which justify them and self-enforcing solutions which will obviate further such interventions. This happens
to be of particular interest to the most likely present political
subjects of intervention, the relatively poor and weak, who work
most assiduously for the international legal restriction of intervention. Like all *prima facie* "rules," these may not apply well
to some specific cases. We have suggested that though they are
not self-enforcing, they both would tend to be the normal results
of adhering as closely as possible to the traditional strategy of
international enforcement procedures, that is of seeking the widest possible coalition for "internationalized" enforcement actions,
in order to minimize the disruptive effect of essential coalition
making within international organizations of sovereigns. This is
important since it has the virtue that it can be viewed as a self-
enforcing, long-run national strategy even for egocentric sovereigns cooperating in a collective security organization.

12. UN efforts alone cannot assure a limited war. If a UN action, in whatever form, is to remain limited, the UN Command's
adversary, even if it is a nuclear Power (as South Africa may be
in time) must reciprocate the willingness not to escalate or gen-
eralize the conflict even if it views its objectives as overwhelmingly important to its survival. The constrained state must also
accept containment even if the UN is intervening to change its
internal political system. This also reinforces the logic and in-

ventives supporting the use of the broadest possible peacekeeping coalition our two *prima facie* rules.

13. In sum, however imposed, effective limitation on the sought after control of and gains from war seems essential to a stable growing system of collective security among sovereigns in contrast to pursuit of war in the unorganized international jungle of self-interested coalitions, in which the choice to fight is normally rational for both sides. At the present time it is also clearly preferred to an integrated federal government on a world scale with centralized preponderant enforcement powers, which might easily become a tyranny of the whole against each in turn, which is the classic problem of government.

Applying some of this discussion to the possibility of UN military action in southern Africa, let us assume, as we have indeed been doing at times, that the white population will somehow be effectively driven back to take its stand in the Republic of South Africa. In view of the genuine conceptual problems and of what has happened elsewhere we can assume the South African strategy will remain "Never capitulate" to the imposition of a non-white dominated, majoritarian government.

We have already noted that the military weakness of the African states and their internal problems and internecine disputes are probably one of the major factors in their mounting frustration and their demands that the Major Powers (*e.g.*, the U.K. in Rhodesia) and the UN collectively take strong measures.[318] With respect to the Republic of South Africa proper, any forceful action at present would presumably be facing one of the most advanced military establishments in Africa with military and police forces, including reserves, but without full-scale mobilization, on the order of 250,000 men.[319] It has now a first class, modernized air force[320] and is apparently developing an aircraft-building capacity. Its navy is "rivaled in strength and size only by that of the United Arab Republic."[321] There are at least rumors that South Africa has entered the missile field, that it is developing potent poison gases, and that it is making efforts to develop a nuclear capability.[322] Simply to enforce a naval and air blockade in support, let us say, of obligatory economic sanctions and without South African armed resistance, it has been suggested that

50–60 warships, including 3–5 aircraft carriers, and perhaps 300 aircraft would be needed at a cost of perhaps $30 million a month.[323] It has been estimated that to actually mount a military program against the Republic would, depending of course very much on unpredictable factors including the possibility of internal uprisings, the local morale and the like, require several hundred aircraft, perhaps six divisions of troops and a hundred or more naval vessels and transports. Based on past estimates of similar actions, the author concluded that the UN could expect 19,000 to 38,000 killed and wounded.[324] It is perhaps this sort of analysis, taken together with the UN "financial crisis" of the last several years, which led Secretary-General U Thant to say, in June, 1963, that: "The idea that conventional military methods —or, to put it bluntly, war—can be used by or on behalf of the United Nations to counter aggression and secure the peace, seems now to be rather impractical."[325]

In fact, after we recover from our natural revulsion, these admittedly rough estimates suggest a modest war effort, somewhat more demanding but on the order of magnitude of Korea. They remind us that South Africa can be no match for a determined world community. They do also indicate that, for the short-run at least, military measures (and even a policed "economic blockade") could only be sustained with the participation of one or more dedicated Middle or Major Powers. Obviously, where some Major Power believes its vital interests are at stake, such estimates would not necessarily be a serious deterrent. In Korea, for example, the United States put over a quarter of a million men in the field at one time sustaining over 111,000 overall total casualties, including 18,000 killed in action.[326] In Viet-Nam, without UN sanctification, the United States has already committed well over 325,000 men with another 100,000 expected to be there by spring, 1967, for a total nearly twice that of the present South African military and police force, at a roughly estimated cost of $1 billion a month for the war alone (which would be 33½ times as much as the estimated cost of imposing a blockade in support of obligatory economic sanctions on South Africa), all this out of a total U.S. defense budget now over $60 billion.[327]

For the African states the key question clearly is which Major or Middle Powers would be their best ally either outside the UN or in a Security Council or Assembly action aimed at South Africa, either as major direct participant or as indirect financer of UN intervention, and on what terms. Considering our limitations, such questions remain so highly speculative and so demanding that for illustrative purposes only we will confine ourselves to presenting a suggestive list of some apparently feasible alternative coalitions inside and outside the UN, which could presumably rely on the African states to furnish the bulk of the fighting men:

A PARTIAL LIST OF POSSIBLE ENFORCEMENT COALITIONS TO SUPPORT
AFRICAN EFFORTS AGAINST THE WHITE SOUTHERN
AFRICAN GOVERNMENTS

I.   *Some Possible Coalitions for Unofficial Insurgency Outside the UN*
     a) Africa plus China
     b) Africa plus China and Communist bloc countries

II. *Some Possible Coalitions Outside the UN with OAU Sanctification*
     a) Africa plus U.S. or/and U.S.S.R. with possible parallel Chinese-aided insurgency

III. *Some Possible Coalitions Inside the UN*
     a) General Assembly Coalitions:
        1) Africa plus U.S.S.R. with possible Chinese-aided insurgency
        2) Africa plus U.S., U.S.S.R., other states; with possible Chinese-aided insurgency
        3) Africa plus U.S. and perhaps U.K. and others, perhaps with Communist-fed insurgency
     b) Security Council Coalition—all Veto Powers assisting or acquiescing in a UN action. (This assumes that the French government does not veto on the grounds of domestic jurisdiction, in which case this could become a General Assembly coalition).

We cannot survey here these alternatives and prospects; there are also many others. The political situation itself modifies old possibilities and generates new ones regularly. The game of coalition comes naturally to organized human collectivities. A few general comments on the candidates are nevertheless in point.

Is there an acceptable basis for an alliance of African men and Soviet financing of the UNEF-ONUC type for a UN intervention in South Africa if Britain or others were to veto Security Council action? The possibility of such operations by the veto-free Assembly exists, but seems unlikely. The Soviet Union (and France) has long insisted on the legal incompetence of the Assembly in peacekeeping. Furthermore, this coalition would certainly compromise the future of the UN. Russia, a large white state with a long common border with China, may need the UN, sooner or later, or even the West more directly, for its own security. Most important, however, while objecting to the probity of UN interventionary actions, Russia regularly intervenes for its own "peaceful" competitive purposes. The genuine discipline implied in officially internationalizing a quarrel is even less congenial to its style and admitted long-run revolutionary aims than it is to the United States. The Russians prefer secure hegemony or at least completely controlled access to their aid. Their dislike for genuine multilateralism is well known.[328] Since the African States may also prefer to lock out other UN Powers' interests, a "minimal coalition" of this type is more likely to be run outside the organization. It could lead to pressure for U.S. and U.K. intervention on the "wrong" side if it engendered mass racial slaughter.

The Chinese intention to prevent or hinder any non-Chinese Communist national pacification, and the development of any effective national consciousness and, indeed, to disrupt all peacemaking, anywhere, is clearly opposed to the needs of Africa and responsible African political leaders. However, Chinese anti-white policy strikes a responsive chord in Africa. Despite Chinese mistakes in Africa, the states do share a common, bitter past of humiliations and deprivations at the hands of white nations. The existence of this enormous common emotional basis for Chinese-African cooperation cannot be overlooked as a threat to the UN and perhaps to the integrity of the African States' own independence.

Paradoxically, one major hope for avoiding durable mergers of "hate" nations is the prevalence of racial intolerances among them. But the most important factor is that this combination probably cannot yet prevail, at least until the Chinese nuclear arsenal multiplies.

In the longer run, if the South African issue lingers on, this non-UN racist coalition, quite probably with USSR participation, with regrets, would if anything seem likely; it would also seem to imply the hazard of widespread racial violence.

It may prove possible for the Africans to avoid choosing between ideological systems or partners entirely, in order to get the most from all aid sources to achieve a maximal coalition in their favor via the UN or possibly the OAU. While the UN offers valuable services on its own, it is also a means of keeping both the Communist systems and the Western Powers in line and competing for African good will. In logic, as we have stressed, the small states have a stake in the UN's survival, perhaps the greatest stake of any group.

If we ask whose interests these possible extra-Security Council coalitions might exclude, the answers would seem to be a) the white South Africans and perhaps other South African minorities; b) the United Kingdom; c) the other major foreign investors in the area; d) those who fear the imposition of a potentially racially unstable peace. This suggests the major problems for the Africans in relying on a UN coalition if, as is likely, the General Assembly will not produce an enforcement coalition entirely excluding these interests.

Great Britain faces not merely the possibility of a major loss of overseas assets but ultimately of course a major threat to British lives in Africa. While not identical, American interests parallel Britain. If British cooperation is desired, even in a naval blockade, the other states cannot avoid taking present British needs into consideration. They may seek alternative sources of borrowed power within the UN but unless they accommodate on most of these issues with the British they will probably face American recalcitrance as well. We have already noted that the USSR may also be an unlikely *intra*-UN military ally.

In sum in instances where it suits the parties, UN-led or deputized military intervention may prove technically and financially feasible, even as a largely US-supported project along Congo or Korean lines, or possibly as a largely Soviet project or even as a Security Council-led operation if a broad UN consensus is achieved. Any of these could rely principally on manpower from "neutral" and African sources. The new states have a great stake in the UN and, of course, in their newly won sovereignty. They presumably want their own independent chance above all. They are the likely victims of both Communist and non-Communist intervention and subversion. They are the more likely to require the various types of UN peacekeeping and nation-building and other services. They have disproportionate voting strength in the General Assembly and can therefore retain considerable control over its activities in their region. Given their genuine military and economic dependence, there are good logical reasons for suggesting that they could better control the terms and promote the adequacy and reliability of any large dependence on Great Power help by channeling it via the UN rather than outside it or even via the OAU. The U.S. shares with the rest of the UN a great stake in a stable long-run solution in southern Africa. This, among other things, would obviate the dangers to the African states themselves and to peace of their "borrowing" Chinese or mixed Communist power "informally" or via the OAU. The alternatives to U.S. aid via the UN—*i.e.,* invited unilateral intervention or intervention by regional political alliances into strategic contested areas, such as Southeast Asia, represent reversion to older, more dangerous forms of alliances than even a General Assembly enforcement coalition. They also have a way of proving far more expensive in blood and treasure, and may prove less successful militarily or less controllable, especially on these issues, than even an awkwardly articulated, internationally legitimized UN operations. These are not predictions; they represent an effort to see some of the dimensions of some of the future alternative roles of the UN in peacekeeping and warmaking in southern Africa.

In southern Africa the peace is unstable in the long run. Ultimately the issues as to the UN's appropriate and, indeed, likely role in enforcement, peacemaking or peacekeeping seems to hinge on the capacity of the members to forge the necessary, broad, preferably near-universal consensus on acceptable objectives. Are the African states able and willing to compromise? When the chips are down, will Great Britain be willing? If not, to what extent and under what conditions, if any, would the U.S.

pursue its long standing independence of British overseas policy in the UN into southern Africa?

V. *SOUTHERN AFRICA*

We venture, on the basis of the materials presented in this study, to comment briefly on the future of our broad themes "race," "peace" and "law" in southern Africa. Of the areas surveyed, Portuguese Africa, as we have suggested, seems likely, in the foreseeable future, to become independent. Portuguese control is an anachronism; local "freedom" forces exist and have been reported active again in Angola after a hiatus;[329] friendly sanctuaries for dissidents exist in neighboring states;[330] and opposition has even developed at home to the Salazar regime's expensive policy of resisting decolonization,[331] a right now acquiesced in as such by almost every other nation and sanctified by the UN. No nation outside southern Africa can be expected to come to her active support.

Likewise, Rhodesia is even now under direct "attack," so far only by use of threat and pressure weapons: diplomatic pressures via several political fronts, and economic sanctions by Britain and the UN. At the same time, it is receiving economic aid and moral support from Portugal and, especially, South Africa. While internal native opposition is divided and apparently impotent for the present, again, in time, the overwhelmingly disproportionate population figures make it clear that the majority will some day prevail. Unlike the Republic, the small white Rhodesia even now relies in part on "native" troops. In the long run access is assured for men and supplies from contiguous African states to feed native insurrections against the white rebel government. Perhaps at some time a division may be attempted, perhaps with the smaller, white-controlled area becoming part of the Republic of South Africa.

South West Africa is already under review by a UN Committee, charged with implementing its independence. Will South Africa yield, or will there, eventually, be UN or UN-supported military measures used to liberate this area long of international concern?

Some immediate actions and pressures seem possible. The UN can urge total compliance with the arms embargo on South Africa, and serve notice to international capital and immigrants that, moving to South Africa, they are risking their survival. It can ask states to bar such moves or at least make clear policy statements that they are very risky politically and that under no circumstances will "the flag" follow trade and investment and that there can be no guarantee even of personal safety, etc. It can impose mandatory general economic measures. There are numerous pressures which the U.S. and other nations could use and the UN could call for to demonstrate clearly to the white South African population, even those among the Afrikaners who have been most obdurate, their completely outcaste state, and the determination of the UN to honor its obligations to their former Mandate. It would likewise seem to be in the interests of all governments, including the British under certain circumstances, to stress the same message diplomatically.[332]

If the eventuality that even military measures will be used if necessary is made clear, there is still some room for hope for that happy phenomenon, a "cheap" victory for the UN in South West Africa along the lines of the Greek retreat before international pressure in the League period[333] and of Suez in 1956–57. It is possible that firm pressures, plus clear, credible threat of more precise, extensive interventions, perhaps something like an ultimatum including a timetable for stair-step increases in international enforcement procedures *starting* with various economic measures,[334] may bring South Africa into line.

The potentials for succeeding in inducing collapse of a determined society by use of the "economic weapon" *alone* are normally minimal, and especially does this seem true for the Republic of South Africa. As Professor Hance has concluded: "Indeed, South Africa could probably hold out against a complete boycott and embargo reasonably well for several years, possibly longer."[335] Furthermore the whole of the long southern African coastline would require policing. These measures are very expensive for their yield and difficult to maintain in the long run. Their major attraction is that they are normally bloodless for the sanctioning states, though, if severe and prolonged, hardship may be implied for the sanctioned population, especially the poor, including in this case the natives who remained city dwellers. This does not mean that economic measures could not be potentially useful in the unusual political climate of southern Africa essentially as a *short term interim threat* weapon, with some economic nuisance value as well. The complex problems of military planning and the gathering together of international forces could be dealt with in this interim as specified in the timetable for action. The possibility of still further increasing white solidarity, a normal effect of international pressures, including economic sanctions, appears small. Southern Africa is girded to challenge the world's opinion. The use of a program of increasingly serious credible threats including ultimately, if necessary, actual military preparations for intervention might be persuasive not only because of the broad consensus within the UN that South West Africa represents an international responsibility that must be honored, but also, ironically, because experience has demonstrated that UN military interventions are difficult for the Organization to control.

We have seen that limiting the military sanctions to their original objectives has been a problem even in the somewhat less emotionally charged cases of Korea and the Congo. Once it had to be utilized it would no doubt also prove difficult to limit any broad, extensive military intervention to South West African boundaries in the current political setting. South African leaders have given some indication that they are aware of this fact. But having "won" their case at the I.C.J., they are reported "defiant" and "determined to fight" for South West Africa.[336] Will they have the capacity to back down enough to exit with sufficient grace to allow some promise of subsequent political survival for the Government at home?

In any case such a program of increasing threats to liberate South West Africa, by arms if necessary, would seem much less potentially persuasive to South Africa (and so far much less acceptable to those states which would in fact have to provide much of the required naval enforcement forces for a blockade) if the constitutional or political future of the Republic itself were directly tied to this issue, especially on the basis of the present UN majority's demands for a unitary one-man one-vote South Africa. This is in part why some western governments have urged a step-by-step approach to the issues and the areas of Southern Africa.

Whatever the precise developments, when South West Africa becomes free or is freed, a vast range of UN experience is relevant to aid the new, inchoate, national state. There is the possibility of some form of *temporary* direct UN administration, as proposed in the Assembly in 1966, for which there are precedents as recent as West Irian. There are many other nation-building precedents: Libya, the nation-building side of the Congo, and the many other cases which might be urged to support immediate independence aided by UN massive assistance, a shadow administration, medical, sanitary and other services, etc. until a more viable state existed. The great desirability of avoiding the creation of the makings of another Congo-type internal pacification experience strongly suggests that careful study of the alternatives is required and also suggests the need for a direct administration to provide careful, rapid preparation for independence, possibly with a fixed time-table. For history indicates that, with the support of the other African states, the local population could be expected to soon demand the status of independent sovereign, however bitter the remaining internal divisions.

The Republic of South Africa

South Africa is a deliberately polarized society. What interchange there has been between the races, and there is great economic interchange at least, has been on the basis of exploited and exploiter. It is not well designed to increase mutual tolerance, much less "fraternity." Though the Afrikaners did not invent ethnocentricity, and, indeed, have not confined their over-riding cultural intolerances to non-whites, it was intrinsically compatible with the religion they brought with them, in addition to being enormously convenient in all ways. For them, genuine integration is not a comprehensible possibility. The English in South Africa, though apparently not ideological segregationists, are nevertheless at present not much more capable of rising to the actual economic redistributions and other even greater personal dangers that an imposed free, multi-racial society would have to entail. Indeed, what peoples ever have been? "Dr. Verwoerd says we would rather be poor and white than rich and mixed. I believe that most South Africans will opt for the latter once the time of decision comes." This hopeful statement was made by a South African, Helen Suzman, but she was for years the sole surviving legislative member of her once promising Progressive Party.

The deprived and abused non-white South African majority remain in fact both exploited and personally stigmatized from birth till death, whatever the varying Afrikaner rationalizations. Can they, when they become the majority, be reasonably expected to bring love and understanding, long-run patience and a willingness to compromise to the intolerable and unforgettable? Experience in economic exploitation has reportedly left them more "acculturated" than many fellow Africans, but not more than many others, for example, the Moslems of French North Africa who have not proved to be equal to the demands of long-term saint-like self-control, much less of "fair" sharing in a world in which "fair" seems inherently impossible, and even starvation persists.

The white population of the Republic knows all this. They have created a police state; they have built themselves an arsenal against the world and they have held out against its bitterest condemnations. At present their military control appears unchallengeable by those most affected by their offenses, the non-white majority at home and their fellow African states.

The Republic of South Africa presents, as we have noted, a quite different case from the others. It is a sovereign state whose *internal* policies are now considered not only reprehensible and intolerable but unlawful as well, in accordance with contemporary norms concerning the "minimum standards for justice" by most of the nations of the world. For South Africa, the UN has, by large majorities, overridden arguments based on "domestic" jurisdiction, and has gone further in its specification of what it would like this Member's domestic political constitution to look like than in any other instance with the possible exception of Spain. It has specified Western institutions as the desiderata, including, as an ultimate goal, a "fair," one-man, one-vote majority rule arrangement for South Africa. Bantu Chief Lutuli specified these conditions in his Nobel Lecture in 1961.[337]

Neither the African states nor the UN as a body has been willing to search for other possibly more politically acceptable solutions, such as a partition. The demand is for a "democratic," unified "non-racial" South Africa. Would this yield a stable, viable, oppression-free nation, or would it lead to the replacement of an intransigent white supremacy by an anti-white supremacy?[338] Is there reason to feel that "entrenched" minority rights would offer better hope in South Africa than in Cyprus? Internal constitutional guarantees by an international organization, even if they can be initially arranged, have always remained unenforcible, and therefore dependent on the grace of the sovereign, the politically effective "majority." To impose them, and actually defend them would require an uncongenial permanent or long-run commitment by the UN to intervene internally and, if necessary, to sanction the sovereign repeatedly on behalf of a white minority. Even in relatively well-integrated federal nations like the United States, the capacity of the central government, even with clear-cut authority and genuine police power, to impose constitutionally entrenched minority rights locally is limited. We can only judge by experience. We are led to conclude that the UN cannot logically call for both a peaceful, stable "democratic" South African solution and insist on a unitary state or an undefended internationally undefensible federalism with entrenched human rights obligations to all.

Yet all partition, even a partition draconically favoring the non-whites and leaving the whites "poor," in Verwoerd's terms, if they would so choose, has been consistently summarily dismissed in the UN and its study groups. Nor has genuine attention been afforded to effective devices for the defense of the human rights of other large South African minority groups—the Indians, the Coloureds, the Chinese—despite the record of the mistreatment of similar groups in other sovereign nations. Under these circumstances, unless the white South Africans' will to survive has been overestimated by the experts, all the cumulative UN pressures have little chance of success by themselves in reforming the Constitution of the Republic. In contrast with South West

Africa, international diplomatic sanctions and partial or even complete economic measures, even if backed by a credible threat of a military intervention, offer little hope for a "cheap" South African success for the UN. For their survival, the well-organized, determined white South Africans can be expected to fight; and they do not rely on "native" troops.

We have seen that to overthrow this government for these stakes, which amount in the eyes of the defenders to total capitulation and suicide, would probably require a large military expedition. We have already suggested why, in logic, such an undertaking by the UN for such extensive disruptive politically interventionary purposes is dangerous to the future of the Organization and why safety requires at minimum a very broad consensus among the members as to the need for the unusual action in the name of overriding human rights or peace, and also, indeed, especially a consensus as to the broad outlines of the specific aims of the action, *i.e.*, the new and fairer stable peace which is to be imposed in this extraordinary way. We have argued that, in view of the historical record and the contemporary political facts, it would seem that only a solution which can be self-enforcing in the present international system is appropriate, and to this we can add that only such an outcome would seem to have a reasonable chance of being ultimately acceptable to a Britain bound by ties of blood, history and investment in South Africa, even if we assume that the last two are in the long run less important than the first. Only a solution which promises to be racially stable is likely to look safe to Britain[339] or the United States[340] and perhaps, even to a white Soviet Union, at least in its "heart of hearts," indeed, to all who are focusing their concern on limiting the likelihood of race war.

Aside from the present mutual unwillingness on the part of all parties to yield a sacred inch (which is an understandable bargaining pose—if that is what it is), there are several obvious emotionally sound reasons why partitions are not popular. In an Africa and Asia in which all countries are continually threatening to disintegrate, integration, not partition, is, in principle, the generally strongly preferred bias. In the case of South Africa this antipathy to all partition has been reinforced by the identification of partition with apartheid. The formation of Bantustans which are, in fact, unviable, disparate, impoverished native ghettos cannot provide the basis for a policy of workably "fair" partition. No doubt this is the type of partition the white South Africans would prefer. Indeed the present Bantustan policy probably does not even provide the basis for a functioning federal system in a state where all other personal legal disabilities and stigmas and bars to movement, and the memory of them, were removed.

As Verwoerd's statement reminds us, the idea of partition is not new to white South Africans.[341] Afrikaners themselves have produced other more realistic partition plans.[342] No doubt even more "realistic," "fairer" ones could be produced.

There are genuine technical, political, economic and humanitarian problems in the designing and administrating of any partition. What is a "fair" partition?[343] Once the basic political agreements were achieved this would become a difficult but clearly not unmanageable, essentially technical set of questions.[344] For many reasons, to an outsider the rational move for a white South Africa that will not accept racial integration would be a *fait accompli*—seizing the best time soon for establishing a potentially stable, general settlement on the future of southern Africa, by carving out a partition for itself.

We have quite possibly found one of the principal sources of the obdurate unwillingness to consider this alternative. It is obvious that white South Africa would not willingly elect to undergo a brutally "fair" partition though it is repeatedly reported they might very well accept such an outcome rather than a unitary state in the face of imminent disaster. This returns us to a familiar problem. Assuming it is designed, how and by whom is a "fair" partition going to be imposed? Though there have been several major partitions, the UN has *not* intervened by force within states, once recognized as such, to enforce a separation between dissident ethnic, religious, or language groups nor has it, *except* perhaps in the Congo with respect to Katanga, intervened to force a dividing area to be or to become unitary. It did not successfully impose its proposed partition plan in the Holy Land: while the Arabs refused to yield an inch, a different, more favorable partition was achieved by the Israelis on the basis of military self-help.[345]

A strategic reluctance is perhaps understandable on the part of the African states to acquiesce beforehand for the voiceless majority of another state in the *de facto* outcome of a *fait accompli,* even if accompanied by very likely unequal military contest. The alternative bargaining strategy of being "reasonable," of cooperating with the international design of a "fair" partition— or of at least offering to consider all reasonable alternatives including one-man, one-vote *or* one-man, one-share, would seem to offer at least public relations advantages. Indeed since at this writing a *de facto* partition seems the likely long-run outcome of any South Africa bloodbath the *best* alternatives and strategies for achieving forms of this alternative with help would seem important for the Africans to explore.

Partition is no panacea. In rich southern Africa, it could leave two viable if unloving neighbors. Considering the ancient bitterness in South Africa, it might well need regular border policing, as elsewhere. While unappealing, this type of interposition, limited to the peripheries, is at least congenial to the capacities and resources of the UN, it is consistent with the logic of collective security by this Organization now, and it is a role the UN has performed adequately on several occasions.

The other major possible alternative solution, sometimes discussed which, indeed, was the traditional solution for Europe's oppressed, for several hundred years, is a mass population transfer of the white population or of the other major population groups out of South Africa. This faces several major difficulties. Although South Africa, in some ways, presents a situation much akin to the colonial areas, it is not one. In addition to its political unacceptability to the parties, with a few exceptions for Indians and some of British descent, neither the whites nor the Bantu nor the coloured have any other place to go back to. There are 3½ million white people. Perhaps some of the continental areas of white immigrations (Canada, Australia, etc.) would take some of them. But they are almost all native Africans and all experts suggest that they cannot be expected to accommodate to dispersion; that they can be expected to fight for their homes, their culture, their nation. As for the others: where are the welcoming areas for large non-white immigration in "non-racial" societies?

Thus, mass transfer is not a current separate alternative. It would probably be part of either of the other alternatives. Again there seems no reason to doubt that the UN could take an important role in humanizing this and minimizing the personal tragedies which would, even so, be great. A rich South Africa could afford to support most or all of the financial costs.[346]

Indeed, UN failures on this score in the Middle East have been due, in part, at least to the political desire of the intractable neighboring states to perpetuate, for decades if necessary, the personal disasters of the victims of partition for their own political purposes, another example in favor of planning ahead for likely partitions rather than looking backward in anger or sorrow. Other UN and international transfers and refugee programs have worked decently. There seems no necessary basis for a similar problem arising in any South African transfer and resettlement program, and memories of the India-Pakistan partition riots must suggest this as perhaps the most worthwhile UN undertaking possible for troubled South Africa.

In all, the historical cases and the current setting indicate some criteria for a workable, internationally supported approach to peacekeeping problems in general and to southern African problems in particular. They suggest that a solution should preferably require minimal long-run UN internal supervisory participation and that what it does require should be preferably of a nature traditionally suitable to an international organization in its relations with its sovereign members. It should thus not call for any avoidable prolonged or repeated internal interventions in the state or states which are the result of a settlement. After a preferably limited intervention in a short humanitarian transitional role for population transfers, and similar measures, if these are unavoidable, it should emphasize financial aid and humanitarian economic, and political technical assistance, election supervision, etc., with military interventions concentrated preferably on such minimal intrusion as border policing. Most important, its guarantees should preferably be to support the integrity of resultant state(s) and should not run to individuals whenever it is likely that the Organization cannot look forward with any assurance to defending them.

We have also suggested that all experience inside and outside the UN suggest that, if the UN is to negotiate and guarantee a settlement for South Africa proper, it cannot offer much hope even of a tendentiously stable solution for anything but a reasonably "fair" partition. Hope may, of course, belie history. We have not suggested that the UN intervene internally in the Republic to impose any generally unwanted political settlement. If the major South African ethnic groups feel they can lead the rest of us on the road to the brotherhood the world desperately needs to march down this seems clearly the most morally desirable solution. We do hope that, when the UN intervenes in South Africa, as it will have to at some stage(s) no doubt, and if it does so in the name of human and legal rights or stable peace, rather than as conqueror, it give the numerical minorities some independent choice in their own destiny, independent of the preference of the would-be majority. The reasons are analytically analogous to those which unfortunately justify the retention of national sovereignty as the cornerstone of the present system and explain the difficulty of modifying the "undemocratic" equal voting rights of the UN itself which votes on a nation rather than on a population (one-man, one-vote worldwide) basis.

For the UN to intervene within the normally domestic sphere of a state to impose genocide or to switch tyrannies may reflect a certain jungle justice but it is an inappropriate role for an Organization for the preservation of peace among imperfect sovereigns, with higher aspirations. It is unhealthy for the future possibilities of a useful, responsible, "impartial" reliance on this UN as well as for its evolutionary growth into a more perfect union.

From the days of Hammurabi through the Christian era, from the Peace of Westphalia to the present, representatives of nations have been struggling to defend effectively the human rights of the lonely, helpless individual in the face of the overwhelming organized coercive powers of the community in which he finds himself. The year 1968, the International Year of Human Rights, is the symbolic culmination of this long pursuit. There are no genuine legal or constitutional bars to bringing such basic, "inalienable" human rights to all the various peoples of southern Africa. Whether or not the various groups of members of the United Nations can summon the will, the political flexibility and wisdom, the self-restraint and the force to lead and to control the deliverance of the majority of human beings in southern Africa from a racial tyranny, some sources of power will be found to arm and provision the soldiers who will carry the banners of "Freedom" in southern Africa. Whether they will also be constrained to espouse "justice" and "human dignity" for all may depend largely on whether the nations will allow the UN to devise the capacity to cope effectively with the demands of this great crisis of conflicting wills before it gets out of hand.

The stablity of the peace has already been definitely broken. In polarized South Africa, tragedy looks irreversible.

FOOTNOTES

1 Southern Africa is here used to include the Republic of South Africa, South West Africa, Southern Rhodesia, Zambia, the Portuguese territories of Angola and Mozambique and Botswana (formerly Bechuanaland), Lesotho (formerly Basuto-land) and Swaziliand, still a British colony, entirely surrounded by the Republic of South Africa. Botswana became independent as of September 30, 1966 and Lesotho became independent on October 4, 1966. Both are now UN members. None of these three areas figure prominently in this study nor does Portuguese Guinea.

For UN studies on conditions in Botswana, Lesotho and Swaziliand, see *e.g.*, Report of the Special Committee on the Situation with regard to the Implementation of the Declaration on the Granting of Independence to Colonial Countries and Peoples (hereinafter known as the Committee of 24), A/6300/ Add. 5, 19 Sept. 1966 (all documents cited in this form are UN documents). See also A/AC.109/L.273 and Adds.; *New York Times*, Feb. 14, 1966 and Oct. 5, 1966; Brit. Info. Serv., R. F. P. 5751/66 (July, 1966) on Lesotho and R. F. P. 5748/66 (June, 1966) on Botswana. For a recent summary, see "Issues Before the 21st General Assembly," *Int'l Conciliation*, No. 559 Sept. 1966, pp. 58–60 (hereinafter cited as *Issues, 1966*).

In the fall of 1966, the General Assembly warned the Republic of South Africa that any "encroachment" on these areas would constitute "aggression." See *UN Press Release* WS/261, 30 Sept. 1966, pp. 1–2.

2 For Pres. Johnson's comment, see *New York Times*, May 27, 1966, p. 16 (text). His remarks extended to white supremacy in general, Rhodesian as well as South African style.

3 See *infra* Sections on Rhodesia and South West Africa.

4 See, among many, statements at the UN by representatives of Japan (*UN Press Release* WS/261, 30 Sept. 1966, p. 18) and Saudi Arabia (*ibid*, WS/264, 21 Oct. 1966, p. 3).

5 For a discussion of some of the possible alternative futures for southern Africa, see the essays in Leiss, ed., *Apartheid and United Nations Collective Measures* (Carnegie Endowment, 1965). On the interconnection of the areas, see statement of the Liberian representative, *UN Press Release* WS/263, 14 Oct. 1966, p. 6.

6 See statement of Abdul Rahman Pazhwak of Afghanistan, President of the 21st General Assembly, *UN Press Release* WS/260, 23 Sept. 1966, p. 2.

7 For an account of the remaining "hard core" colonial areas, see *Issues, 1966*, pp. 55–91, esp. chart pp. 86–87.

8 It can reasonably be said that one of the principal functions of government is to mediate between the conflicting demands of cherished norms and of the interest groups which press them. See Claude, *Power and International Relations*, Chapter 7. He defines government as "the function of promoting order through political management of inter-group relations." (p. 271).

9 See Schachter, "The Relation of Law, Politics and Action in the United Nations," 1963 *Recueil des Cours*, Vol. II, pp. 171–200; reprinted in Falk & Mendlovitz, eds. *The Strategy of World Order*, Vol. 3, 94 ff. (1966).

10 See *infra* note 82.

11 See the comments of Secretary-General U Thant, in February, 1964, *U.N. Press Release* SG/SN/3/Rev.1, 4 Feb. 1964.

12 For comment on the sameness and the diversities, see Drew Middleton, *New York Times*, May 12, 1966.

13 In general, see Wohlgemuth, "The Portuguese Territories and the United Nations," *Intl. Concil.*, No. 545 (Nov. 1963); Duffy, *Portugal's African Territories: Present Realities* (Carnegie Endowment, 1962).

14 See, e.g., Gen. Ass. Res. 1542 (XV). And see Sec. Counc. Res. 163, 9 June 1961.

15 See Duffy, *op. cit.* p. 7.

16 Conditions in Angola were primarily at issue. See U.N. Doc. S/4835. The Reso-

lution was adopted on June 9, 1961, by 9 to 0, with 2 abstentions (France and the U.K.). See 5 Whiteman, *Digest of International Law* (U.S. State Dept.) 80, (hereinafter cited as *Whiteman*).

17 Res. 1603 (XV), Apr. 20, 1961.

18 On conditions in Portuguese Africa, see A/6000/Add.3, Part I, 11 Oct. 1965, and Part II, 18 Nov. 1965 (on foreign economic interests); A/AC.109/L.266 and Corr. 1 (Secretariat Working Paper) and A/AC.109/168, 13 June 1966. (Portuguese Rejoinder). Portugal has denounced the Secretariat study as "racist" *ibid.* See also Portuguese letter of 17 Oct. 1966, A/6476, 18 Oct. 1966.

19 On the military struggle, arms from the Communist countries, etc., see *New York Times,* Oct. 2, 1966, p. E3 which also gives a brief account of events from 1961 to date. In the fall of 1966, Portugal and the Democratic Republic of Congo exchanged charges at the UN about support for guerilla forces. See *UN Press Releases* WS/262, 7 Oct. 1966, p. 13, WS/263, 14 Oct. 1966, and WS/264, 21 Oct. 1966, pp. 17–18 and *New York Times,* Sept. 25 and 27, 1966.

20 In 1965, it was estimated that Portugal's defense outlay in the three areas amounted to over $262 million or 42% of the national budget. See *New York Times,* March 20, 1966. On Portuguese successes, see also *New York Times,* Oct. 2, 1966, p. E3.
On generally "booming" conditions in the colonies, especially in Angola, see *New York Times,* March 20, 1966.

21 See A/AC. 109/L.266, 1 April 1966. Portugal has also been barred from the International Conferences on Public Education and from the World Congress of Ministers of Education on the Eradication of Illiteracy. The question of her membership has also been raised in the I.L.O., the I.T.U. and the International Sugar Conference. Portugal has noted that exclusion from such activities as those of the WHO simply compromises the health of those in Portuguese Africa. See A/AC. 109/168, 13 June 1966.

22 See G.A. Res. 2107 (XX) 21 Dec. 1965 and 2108 (XX) 21 Dec. 1965, and U.N. Docs. A/AC.109/L.293 (7 June 1966) and A/6076 (26 Oct. 1965).

23 See Council Res. 218 (1965), 23 Nov. 1965. There were 4 abstentions.

24 Gen. Ass. Res. 2107 (XX), 21 Dec. 1965. The resolution was adopted by 66–26–15. For a summary of UN pressure through resolutions, etc., see A/AC.109/187, 29 June 1966 (Ctee. of 24).

25 For continued demands along these lines, see action of the Ctee. of 24 on June 22, 1966, GA/COL/429, 430.

26 See S/7385, 30 June 1966. With the exception of the bar on Portuguese overflights, the measures taken by the African states appear to have had little effect.

27 See S/4760, 7 March 1961, S/4821, 3 June 1961.

28 On the Rhodesian statistical background, see *British Record,* No. 19, Supp., Nov. 24, 1965.

29 On Rhodesia in history, see Anglin, "Unilateral Independence in Southern Rhodesia," 19 *Int'l Journal* 551 ff (1963–64); Spiro, "The Rhodesias and Nyasaland," in Carter, ed., *Five African States* (1963). On the UN developments in 1965–66, see *Issues, 1966,* pp. 67–77.
On the rule of law in Southern Rhodesia before UDI, see Ezijiofor, *Protection of Human Rights under the Law* 234–244 (1964) (hereafter cited as *Ezijiofor*).
In general, see Boyd, "The Rhodesian Tangle," 2 *Vista,* No. 1, July-Aug. 1966, pp. 33–39; *Time,* Aug. 26, 1966, pp. 18–25; Barton, "A Look at Rhodesia," 1 *Vista,* No. 4, Jan.-Feb., 1966, pp. 29–35.

30 G.A. Res. 1747 (XVI), 28 June 1962. The General Assembly earlier asked its Special Ctee. to determine whether or not Southern Rhodesia had attained independence. See G.A. Res. 1745 (XVI), 23 Feb. 1962.

31 For discussion, see S/7382, pp. 133ff. The vetoed resolution is in S/5425/Rev.1.

32 See G.A. Res. 2024 (XX) and Sec. Council Res. 216 (1965). No state to date has recognized the Smith regime.

33 U.N. Doc. S/PV. 1257 (12 Nov. 1965) p. 12.

34 Sec. Counc. Res. 217 (1965) U.N. Doc. S/PV. 1257, 12 Nov. 1965, p. 12. Some international organizations such as GATT, ILO, UNESCO, and WHO, have suspended official communications with Southern Rhodesia, and all experts serving under the auspices of the United Nations Development Programme have been withdrawn to Zambia.

35 See *New York Times*, Feb. 1, 1966 (editorial).

36 On demands for the use of force, see among many, Draft Sec. Council Resolution of 11 May 1966 (S/7285/Add.1) which failed at the 1285th meeting (23 May 1966) by 6–1–8; debates in the Fourth Ctee. in 1966, GA/T/1573–1580; *U.N. Press Releases* WS/261 (30 Sept. 1966), p. 22 (Nigeria); WS/263 (14 Oct. 1966), p. 3 (India), p. 10 (Gabon), p. 12 (Iraq); WS/264, p. 3 (Zambia), p. 4 (Mali), p. 6 (Madagascar), p. 7 (Congo), p. 10 (Ceylon), p. 11 (Somali Rep.). On African feeling about Rhodesia generally, see Hargreaves, "Pan-Africanism After Rhodesia," *The World Today*, Feb., 1966, pp. 57–63.

In answer to suggestions from Africa that the British will never use force against a "white" area, Boyd, *op. cit.* points to the American colonies and to Cyprus and Ireland in this century. There is undoubtedly little feeling in the U.K. for violence against Rhodesia however. Boyd, *op. cit.*; A. LeJeune, *Dallas Morning News*, Sept. 20, 1966, p. 2D. See also *New York Times*, Sept. 15, 1966.

37 See Barton, *op. cit. supra* n. 29 at 35; Brit. Info. Serv., Nov. 12, 1965, No. T.83, p. 15.

38 Southern Rhodesia: Documents Relating to the Negotiations between the United Kingdom and Southern Rhodesian Governments, November 1963–November 1965, Cmnd. 2807 (London: HMSO, Nov. 1965), pp. 99–100 and BIS Docs. T.69, 11 Oct. 1965, and T.2, 25 Jan. 1966.

39 Sec. Counc. Res. 221 (1966) 9 Apr. 1966. Southern Rhodesia, in response, severed most of its remaining ties with the U.K.

In discussing this move, France found no threat to the peace but did not interpose a veto (S/PV.1277, p. 51) while the U.S. called it a "grave" step but supported it (S/PV. 1276, pp. 47–50). For Arthur Krock's comment, that it is an internal matter and a "perversion" of the Charter, see *New York Times*, Apr. 13, 1966. See generally Carey, "The U.N. and Human Rights: Who Should Do What?", *Bull of the Sect. of Int'l & Comp. L.*, Am. Bar Assoc., July 1966, p. 9 at 11–14.

40 The country is only partially industrialized and relies primarily on coal, which is abundant, and not on oil for 75% of its power. Its needs from the outside world are relatively limited and can apparently be supplied by South Africa which has adopted a most friendly "business as usual" policy.

On the irritant but not major effects of the sanctions, see Report of a UN expert, *UN Press Release* WS/231, 4 March, 1966, pp. 3–4; and *New York Times*, May 27, 1966, Aug. 9, 1966, Aug. 10, 1966 (Anthony Lewis), Sept. 24, 1966 (P. M. Smith), Sept. 25, 1966 (P. M. Smith), Oct. 2, 3, 1966.

On British application of the sanctions and sanctions generally, see *The Economist*, Dec. 11, 1965, Feb. 19, 1966, March 19, 1966, April 9, 1966. On South African aid to Rhodesia, see *e.g., The Economist*, Feb. 26, 1966. On Rhodesian counter-sanctions, see also *New York Times*, Nov. 19, 1965. In 1964, half of Rhodesia's exports (about $210 million) were to the U.K. and the Commonwealth. See generally *New York Times*, Dec. 19, 1965, p. 4E.

On the effects of sanctions and Rhodesian counter-measures on Zambia, see *e.g., New York Times*, Dec. 17, 1965, March 20, 1966, Sept. 7, 1966. After an initial impact, the economy has straightened out but Rhodesia's place in trade has been gradually taken over by South Africa which may in time cause similar difficulties. See 18 *Int'l Financial New Survey* (IMF), No. 41, Oct. 14, 1966, p. 341.

On conditions in Rhodesia generally, see also *New York Times,* Jan. 5, 1966, Feb. 12, 1966, March 25, 1966 (Middleton), July 22, 1966.

For UN reports on conditions in Rhodesia, see A/6300/Add. 1, Parts I and II, 7 Oct. 1966 (in general and on foreign economic and other interests). For attacks on foreign interests, see also A/AC. 109/SC.2/SR.24, 2 June 1966 (Ctee. of 24, meeting of May 9, 1966).

41 See, *e.g.,* Anthony Lewis, *New York Times,* Aug. 12, 1966 and Aug. 14, 1966, p. E3 and *ibid,* Apr. 10, 1966, p. E1; Sept. 15, 1966.

42 On dealing with invaders, see *New York Times,* April 30, 1966. On the crushing of early dissention, see *New York Times,* Nov. 21, 1966, p. 3E, Nov. 30, 1965. On internal divisions among native leaders, see Barton, *op. cit. supra* n. 29, at 29–35; Fellows, "The Other—and First—Rhodesians," *New York Times Mag.,* Nov. 21, 1965, p. 36. The local chiefs have been given broad independence and reportedly support the present regime. See *New York Times,* Dec. 4, 1965, p. 2E.

43 On censorship, see *New York Times,* Feb. 9, 1966.

44 See *New York Times,* Aug. 10, 1966 (A. Lewis). In early October, 1966, a U.K. Commission noted that the Smith regime was *unwilling* to assure the natives' rights firmly by constitutional process.

45 See, *e.g.,* on the pressures by the "Anti-Colonial Committee" (the Committee of 24), A/AC.109/158, 21 Apr. 1966; A/AC.109/167, 7 June, 1966; A/AC.109/188, 29 June, 1966. On more drastic Security Council resolutions, see S/7285, 10 May 1966, S/7285/Add.1, 11 May 1966, S/7285/Add.2, 12 May, 1966. Nine African states —Algeria, Congo (Brazzaville), Ghana, Guinea, Mali, Mauritania, Sudan, Tanzania, and the United Arab Republic—broke diplomatic relations with the U.K. Ghana and Sudan have re-established their relations with the U.K.

46 For the Commonwealth communiqué, see *New York Times,* Sept. 15, 1966. On a similar statement at the UN, see *UN Press Release* WS/263, 14 Oct. 1966, p. 8 and see *British Record,* No. 15, Sept. 26, 1966, pp. 2–3. On dissention at the meeting, and Zambia's departure when mandatory sanctions and force were ruled out for the present, see *New York Times,* Sept. 14–16, 1966.

47 On these costs, see studies cited *infra,* n. 111.

48 See the last section of this paper and Taubenfeld & Taubenfeld, "The Economic Weapon . . . ," 1964 *Proc. Amer. Soc. Int'l L.* 183 ff.

49 See survey article, *Dallas Morning News,* Nov. 6, 1966, p. 19A.

50 See also *New York Times,* Nov. 21, 1965, p. E3, March 1, 1966.

51 See, *e.g.,* Steward, *The Sacred Trust* (1963) 17 and *passim* and Statement by Smithers, U.K. Representative, March 22, 1961, reprinted in Whiteman, Vol. 1, pp. 707–708.

52 See, *e.g.,* 9 *Journal of Comp. Legis.* 111 (1927), 3rd Series.

For an account of South Africa's policies in the mandate,, see Bradford, "The Origin of the League of Nations' Class 'C' Mandate for South West Africa and Fulfillment of the Sacred Trust, 1919–1939," unpub. diss., Yale, 1965.

53 For summary, see Intl. Com. of Jurists, *South Africa and the Rule of Law* 83– 90 (1960) and sources cited. See also 24 *Brit. Y.B. Int'l L.* 386 (1947).

54 On conditions in South West Africa, political, legal, economic and social, see *e.g.,* A/AC. 109/PET.535/Add.1, 27 Sept. 1966 (esp. on labor); A/6000/Add.2, 28 Sept. 1965 (Ctee of 24); A/6300/Add.2, 20 Sept. 1966 (Ctee of 24). See also Dissenting Opinion of Judge Mbanefo in I.C.J., South West Africa Cases, Second Phase, Judgment of 18 July 1966.

For the South African view of conditions in South West Africa, see statement of de Villiers at the General Assembly on 26 Sept. 1966, in A/PV 1417 (26 Sept. 1966) and the Separate Opinion of Judge Van Wyk (South Africa) in I.C.J., South West Africa Cases, Second Phase, Judgment of 18 July 1966.

55 See sources cited in last footnote.

56 On the Odendaal Study, see A/6300/Add.2, pp. 16–18; Mason, "Separate Devel-

opment and South West Africa: Some Aspects of the Odendaal Report," 5 *Race* (London), No. 4, 83–97 (1964).

57 International Status of South-West Africa, Advisory Opinion July 11, 1950, *I.C.J. Reports* (1950) 128 ff. The majority view was also that of the U.S. Government on both issues. See 1 *Whiteman* 715–720.

58 In the matter of Voting Procedure on Questions Relating to Reports and Petitions concerning the Territory of South-West Africa, Advisory Opinion, June 7, 1955, *I.C.J. Reports* (1955), the Court stated, unanimously that decisions of the General Assembly with respect to South West Africa were "important questions" within the meaning of Article 18(2) of the Charter. This called for decision by a two-thirds vote, not a unanimous decision as might have been needed in the League Council nor a simple majority as is the case for other questions in the General Assembly. In 1956, in Admissibility of Hearings of Petitioners by the Committee on South-West Africa, Advisory Opinion, June 1, 1956, *I.C.J. Reports* (1956) 23 ff., the Court, by 8 to 6, stated that oral hearings by petitioners from the Territory were permissible although the League had no such procedures (in contrast to the Trusteeship Council of the UN which did).

59 In the final submissions, some of these claims were expressed as follows:

"(3) Respondent, by laws and regulations, and official methods and measures, which are set out in the pleadings herein, has practiced apartheid, i.e., has distinguished as to race, colour, national or tribal origin in establishing the rights and duties of the inhabitants of the Territory; that such practice is in violation of its obligations as stated in Article 2 of the Mandate and Article 22 of the Covenant of the League of Nations; and that Respondent has the duty forthwith to cease the practice of apartheid in the Territory.

(4) Respondent, by virtue of economic, political, social and educational policies applied within the Territory, by means of laws and regulations, and official methods and measures, which are set out in the pleadings herein, has, in the light of applicable international standards or international norm, or both, failed to promote to the utmost the material and moral well-being and social progress of the inhabitants of the Territory; that its failure to do so is in violation of its obligations as stated in Article 2 of the Mandate and Article 22 of the Covenant; and that Respondent has the duty forthwith to cease its violations as aforesaid and to take all practicable action to fulfil its duties under such Articles."

Note that even in dissenting opinions in the 1966 Judgments, one of the allegations, that concerning military bases, was taken as not well founded.

60 For comment, see Landis, "South West Africa in the International Court: Act II, Scene I," 49 *Cornell L.Q.* 179 (1964); Ballinger, "The International Court of Justice and the South West Africa Cases: Judgment of 21st December, 1962, "81 *S.Af.L.J.*, Part I, 35 (1964); Barton, "Apartheid and the World Court," 1 *Vista*, No. 6, May-June, 1966, 42 ff.

61 The decision is now in print. For a brief account of the case, see Gross, 45 *Foreign Affairs* 36 (Oct. 1966); "Issues Before the 21st General Assembly," *Intl. Concil.* No. 559 (Sept. 1966); 60–67. For a recent South African statement on the decision, see A/6480, 20 Oct. 1966.

For background, see also Nordau, "The South West Africa Case," *The World Today*, No. 3 (Mar. 1966) 122–130; "The World Court's Ticklish Case," *The Nation*, No. 14 (Apr. 4, 1966) 389–393.

62 Joining President Spender (Australia) in the procedural majority were Judges Fitzmaurice (United Kingdom), Gros (France), Morelli (Italy), Spiropoulos (Greece), van Wyk (ad hoc judge appointed by South Africa), and Winiarski (Poland). Dissenting were Judges Forster (Senegal), Jessup (United States), Koo (Republic of China, Vice President of the ICJ), Koretsky (USSR), Padilla Nervo (Mexico), Mbanefo (Nigeria, ad hoc judge appointed by applicants), and Tanaka (Japan).

Not participating were Judges Ammoun (Lebanon), Zafrulla Kahn (Pakistan), and Bustamante y Rivero (Peru).

[63] *UN Press Release* WS/261, 30 Sept. 1966, p. 22 (Nigeria).

[64] See, *e.g.*, *UN Press Release* WS/251, 22 July 1966, pp. 3–4.

[65] As evidence of African ire, an appropriation of $72,500 for salaries and clerical expenses of the Court was blocked in the fall of 1966, even though the monies had already been spent. See *New York Times*, Oct. 11, 1966. Kenya proposed that a way be sought to disqualify the majority judges. See *UN Press Release* WS/261, 30 Sept. 1966, p. 18.

[66] See statement of the representative of Cameroon, *UN Press Release* WS/260, 23 Sept. 1966, p. 5. Several states have demanded the reorganization at least of the Court on more "equitable" geographic lines. See, *e.g.*, *UN Press Releases* 261, 30 Sept. 1966, pp. 18 (Kenya), 19 (Ethiopia), 22 (Burundi) and No. 263, 14 Oct. 1966, p. 13 (Sudan).

[67] See, e.g., Wainhouse, *Remnants of Empire* 52–57 (1964). On a program for UN aid in training refugees from South West Africa, see Secretary-General's report, A/6463.

[68] Res. 2074 (XX), 17 Dec. 1965. The resolution was adopted by a vote of 85–2–19. The Security Council also called for an arms embargo in Resolution 181 (1963), 7 Aug. 1963; it reaffirmed that call in Resolution 191 (1964), 18 June, 1964. For South Africa's protest of Res. 2074 (XX), see Letter of 21 Dec. 1965, A/6219.

The Committee of 24, in a resolution closely patterned on the twentieth Assembly's, further condemned "the activities of the financial interests operating in South West Africa which exploit the human and material resources and impede the progress of the Territory and the right of the people to freedom and independence." apparently referring to the continuing capital inflow from Western states. In addition, the Committee condemned "large-scale settlement of foreign immigrants" designed to "suppress and circumvent the political and economic rights of the indigenous people." See A/AC.109/177, 13 June 1966. The Assembly had also asked for sanctions measures in 1963. See Res. 1899 (XVIII). The Ctee. of 24 constantly refers back to this resolution. See, e.g., *UN Press Release* WS/246, 17 June 1966, pp. 3–4.

[69] See statements of Amb. Goldberg, Sept. 12 and Oct. 12, 1966, *New York Times*, Sept. 23, 1966 and Oct. 13, 1966.

On earlier cautious U.S. views as to the right to modify the Mandate without the Mandatory's consent on grounds of breach of the Mandatory's obligations or change in conditions, see 1 Whiteman 719–720. See Wright, *Mandates Under the League of Nations* (1930) 440–441, for an early comment on this point.

The dissenting Judges in 1966 were clear that the Mandate persisted. See, *e.g.*, Judge Jessup's Opinion. The Court's Opinion does not reach the point.

[70] See also *New York Times*, Oct. 28, 1966. Malawi also abstained.

[71] See *New York Times*, Oct. 28, 1966; *ibid*, Oct. 29, 1966; and *ibid*, Oct. 30, 1966, p. 2E.

[72] See *New York Times*, Oct. 13, 1966.

[73] We do not here give more than the briefest survey of South Africa, South African policies and the UN's interest. For detailed studies, see, among many, Legum & Legum, *South Africa: Crisis for the West* (1964); Leiss, ed., *Apartheid and United Nations Collective Measures: An Analysis* (1965); Walker, *The History of Southern Africa* (3rd ed., 1957); Segal, ed., *Sanctions Against South Africa* (1964); Houghton, *The South African Economy* (1964) Marquard, *The Peoples and Policies of South Africa* (3rd ed. 1962); Lewin, *Politics and Law in South Africa; Essays on Race Relations* (1963); Dale, "South Africa and the International Community," 18 *World Politics* 297 (1966), an excellent review article; Nielsen, *African Battleline: American Policy Choices in Southern Africa* (1965); Leiss, "American Policy and

the Future of Southern Africa," 19 *World Politics* 151 (1966), a review article. For a brief account, especially of apartheid, see *Wall Street Journal*, July 13, 1966.

74 For some indication of U.S. interest in the area and in apartheid, see *e.g.*, Hearings on U.S.-South African Relations before the Subcommittee on Africa of the House Committee on Foreign Affairs, Part III, April 26 to May 24, 1966, p. 393–512 (the Hearings were denounced as "intervention" by South Africa, *New York Times*, Dec. 31, 1965).

75 "It is clear . . . that what the government is offering the . . . Africans in full and final settlement of their right to political self-determination is the possibility to control a little over one-eighth of the whole country in which there is room for little more than one-third of the black population; the remainder would be expected to live as alien migrant workers in the seven-eighths of the country reserved for whites." Legum & Legum, *op. cit.* n. 73, p. 73

76 *Wall Street Journal*, July 13, 1966.

77 For a review of the law, see Hahlo & Kahn, *The Union of South Africa: The Development of Its Laws and Constitution* (1960); Hahlo & Maisels, "The Rule of Law in South Africa," 52 *Va. L.R.* 1–31 (1966). Written by South Africans, these deal extensively with race and law in South Africa in a dispassionate narrative which is perhaps all the more shocking for its calm acceptance, though with some questioning, of separation, permanent discrimination and imposed inferiority, banning and repression without trial, permanent insecurity as to work and place to live for the majority in the country, etc.

Also noted are the fears of White South Africa of a loss of homeland, of "savage and sinister" Black racialism and the possibility of mass slaughter of the whites. In the words of Hahlo & Maisels (p. 30), "Martyrdom does not come easily to the man-in-the-street."

For other chilling surveys of the law in South Africa, see Int'l Comm. of Jurists, *South Africa and the Rule of Law* (1960), and *Bulletin*, No. 27, 1966, pp. 28 ff.

For U.N. surveys of apartheid and restrictive laws, see, *e.g.*, Report of the Special Ctee. on Apartheid: A/5692 (25 March 1964), A/5707(25 May, 1964), S/6073 (30 Nov. 1964), S/6454, A/AC.115/L.18/Add.1 (7 July 1966), on repressive laws in 1964–65; A/AC.115/L.184 (3 Oct. 1966) on repressive laws in 1965–66; A/AC.115/L.185 (4 Oct. 1966) on build-up of the armed forces; A/AC.115/L.183 (measures since 10 August 1966).

78 See Cowan, "Constitution-making for a Democracy," Supplement to *Optima* (1960).

79 On labor and Bantu unions, see also *The World Today*, Feb. 1965, pp. 65 ff. and *New York Times*, April 10, 1966.

80 See *Bull. of the Int'l Comm. of Jurists*, No. 27, Sept. 1966, p. 35; *New York Times*, April 4, 1966; A/AC.115/SR. 71 (2 June 1966).

81 See Legum & Legum, *op. cit. supra* n. 73 at 213.

82 Cited in Legum & Legum, pp. 6–7. It is not "a class but a caste system in which all the whites are Brahmins and all the rest Untoucheables . . ." *Ibid.*

83 *The Economist*, Aug. 7, 1965, p. v.

84 Mr. de Villiers, statement at the UN on 26 Sept. 1966, A/PV. 1417 (26 Sept. 1966) and see *UN Press Release*, GA/SHC/1220, 4 Oct. 1966.

85 On the effectiveness of South African military forces, the only important such force in Africa south of the Sahara, see *The Economist*, Aug. 7, 1965, p. VI.

On police sweeps through areas and the treatment of all Bantu men as "suspected criminals," see *New York Times*, Jan. 23, 1966, p. 4E.

86 For attacks on western (i.e. UK, US and French) investment in South Africa especially, but in other areas of southern Africa as well, and for documentation, see A/AC.115/L.133, 6 June 1965 (report on investments by the Ctee. on Apartheid) and see A/AC. 115/L.56 Rev. 2, 22 Aug. 1966 ("Foreign Investment in the Republic

of South Africa," report by the Secretariat); and *New York Times,* Oct. 26, 1966 (comments of Mr. Achkar), *Wall Street Journal,* July 13, 1966. U.S. investment is on the order of $650 million and annual U.S.-S.Af. trade is at about $400 million. On the fury of Black African states at the continuing trade and investment, at loans from the West and even from the IBRD and the IMF to South Africa and South African firms, see *New York Times,* March 2 and May 12, 1966 and *UN Press Release* WS/253, 5 Aug. 1966, p. 6. On the boom, see *The Economist,* Aug. 7, 1965, esp. p. xxi.

87 On the unifying effect, see "Why South Africa is the West's Business," *The Economist,* Aug. 7, 1965, pp. xii. See this article generally for a survey of South Africa.

88 See *New York Times,* April 3, 1966, p. E9. The main opposition party, the Union Party, went so far as to try to outdo the Afrikaners by suggesting open aid to Rhodesia. See *New York Times,* March 14, 1966. On the opposition parties, see "Minority of One" (re Mrs. Suzman), *New York Times Mag.,* March 20, 1966, p. 34; Gordiner, "Why Did Bram Fischer Choose Jail?", *ibid.,* Aug. 14, 1966, p. 30.

89 See *New York Times,* Sept. 20, 26 and 27, 1966.

90 See *New York Times,* Feb. 10, 1966 (on the Republican Party).

91 See *New York Times,* Sept. 14 (editorial), 15, 18, 1966.

92 See sources cited *supra* note 73.

93 See, e.g., *U.N. Journal,* No. 54, Suppl. A-A/P.V/50, p. 349. The United States, the U.K., Sweden and some other states supported the suggestion of an I.C.J. opinion. *Ibid,* pp. 350–353.

94 *U.N. Journal, Ibid.* p. 356.

95 Panama, *U.N. Journal, ibid.,* p. 370; China, *ibid,* p. 363.

96 For a summary of the resolutions, see Carnegie Endowment, *Synopses of United Nations Cases,* p. 5 (1966) and see I *Repertory of UN Practice,* Arts. 1–22 of the Charter (1955) 67–75, Arts. 1–54 of the Charter, Supp. No. 1 (1958) 29–32; I *ibid* Arts. 1–8, Supp. No. 2 (1964) 126–129. See also 5 *Whiteman* 336–343.

97 For summary of action to date, see Carnegie Endowment, *Synopses of United Nations Cases* 27–28 (1966); "Issues Before the 21st General Assembly," *Intl. Concil.,* No. 559 (Sept. 1966), 113–119. See also 5 *Whiteman* 364–377.

98 For a survey of South Africa's responses to U.N. demands, see A/AC.115/L.103 (Index of Dec. 21, 1964).

99 Discussion took place in the Ad Hoc Political Committee and in Plenary Meetings (G.A.O.R., 7th sess., *passim).*

100 Res. 616A (VII) and see Res. 615 (VII).

101 See G.A.O.R., 8th Sess., Suppl. No. 16.

102 See, e.g., Moskowitz, *Human Rights and World Order* 37–43 (1959). For a list of various ineffectual measures adopted over the years by the United Naitons and the Organization of African Unity and Conference of Non-Aligned Countries, see U.N. Doc. S/6210 Annex VI.

103 Sec. Counc. Res. 134 (1 April 1960).

104 Res. 1598 (XV). See also G.A. Res. 1663 (XVI).

105 Res. 1761 (XVII).

106 See *infra* for a discussion of South Africa and economic sanctions.

107 Sec. Counc. Res. 181 (7 Aug. 1963).

108 See S/5471 (4 Dec. 1963). For other resolutions in 1963, see G.A. Res. 1978A (XVIII) and 1978B (XVIII), 1881 (XVIII), and Sec. Counc. Res. in S/5386.

109 The Report is in S/5658 (20 April 1964). It has been separately printed as *A New Course in South Africa,* U.N. Sales No. 64. I. 13. The experts were Mrs. Alva Myrdal, Sir Edward Asafu-Adjaye, Sir Hugh Foot, Mr. Dey Ould Sidi Baba, and Mr. Josip Djerja (resigned in March 1964).

110 See S/6210 (2 March 1965). The Committee was established by Sec. Council Res. S/5773 (18 June 1964).

111 The Security Council adopted the Report but with only 6 votes in favor (including the U.K.).

For other studies of the potential efficacy of economic measures against South Africa, see Hance, "Efforts to Alter the Future: Economic Action," in Leiss, *op. cit. supra* note 73, 95 ff; *Atlas*, Jan. 1965, pp. 22 ff (the cases for and against sanctions); and Segal, *op. cit. supra* n. 73, esp. 62–84 (legal aspects), 107–119 (strategic implications), 120–134 (trade), 135–152 (petroleum), 153–166 (gold), 167–185 (the impact on the U.K.), 186–196 (the impact on the U.S.), 204–233 (the impact on the High Commission Territories).

On military measures, see Chapter 7 in Leiss, *op. cit.*

For the author's general views on the lack of efficacy of economic measures alone against a determined, prepared state which considers that its vital interests are at stake, see Taubenfeld & Taubenfeld, "The Economic Weapon: The League and the United Nations," *1964 Proc. Am. Soc. Int'l L.*, 183 ff.

112 On Oct. 9, 1966, the *New York Times* reported that enough oil was in stock for one year's ordinary use or 2 years with rationing; that special tax concessions were available for resource discoverers; that oil fields elsewhere were being purchased; and that special relations with Angola, a petroleum producer, were in effect (p. 15). It has also been recently reported that 10 oil companies, *eight of which are from the U.S.*, have been given concessions to prospect for oil and gas on the South African continental shelf. See *Dallas Morning News*, Oct. 22, 1966, p. 3D (Oil News).

113 See Res. 2054A and B (XX) 15 Dec. 1965. On events in 1965 generally, see "Issues Before the 21st General Assembly," *Int'l Concil.* No. 559 (Sept. 1966) 114–119.

114 For replies of governments, see U.N. Doc. A/6356 (S/7387) (29 June 1966). See also UN Docs. A/6226 (6 Apr. 1966). p. 3; A/AC.115/SR. 72 (6 May 1966), esp. p. 4; A/AC. 115/SR. 70 (29 June 1966), para. 20. The Soviet Union accepted. See *UN Press Release* WS/248, 1 July 1966.

115 On the U.K., see UN Doc. A/SPC/SR.472 (6 Dec. 1965) p. 10 and see sources on sanctions cited *supra* note 73.

116 E.g., France. See U.N. Doc. A/SPC/107 (3 Dec. 1965) p. 2.

117 E.g., U.K. and U.S. For other responses to the embargo resolutions, see Secretariat summary in A/AC.115/L.143, (13 July 1965).

118 See, e.g., the Resolution of June, 1964. S.C. Res. 191 (1964).

119 See, e.g., A/6356 (S/7387), 29 June 1966, which, *inter alia*, warns the major Western powers that, if they fail to act, other states "may be obliged to ... seriously consider other appropriate and decisive measures. ..."

120 See G. A. Res. 2054B (XX) 15 Dec. 1965.

121 The Report of the Seminar, with 30 recommendations, several of which were objected to by the Western representatives present, is in A/6412 (13 Sept. 1966).

122 For recent confirmation of the "scriptural justification for apartheid," see *New York Times*, Oct. 30, 1966, p. 11.

It is also said in a more secular vein that the highest law is the security of the state. See *ibid*, April 30, 1966. Of course this is a not unusual view of states.

123 See, *e.g.*, the statements by the representatives of Congo (Brazzaville) and Guinea to the effect that solutions to African problems can only come from action by the Africans themselves, with the UN's aid. *UN Press Release* WS/263, 14 Oct. 1966, p. 7 and WS/264, 21 Oct. 1966, p. 4.

124 For recent calls for non-intervention and non-interference in domestic matters, see statements by the representatives of some of the same states noted in the last footnote: Madagascar *(UN Press Release* WS/264, 21 Oct. 1966, p. 6), U.S.S.R., *(ibid,* WS/261, Sept. 1966, p. 4) and Guinea *(ibid,* WS/263, 14 Oct. 1966, p. 7). Upper Volta, as an example, has said that her foreign policy is based on, *inter alia*, the concept of independence of states, while noting, in the same statement,

that she supports the "freedom fighters" in all of southern Africa. See *UN Press Release* WS/261, 30 Sept. 1966, p. 16.

125 G. A. Res. 2131 (XX). The vote was 109–0–1 (U.K.). For comment, see *New York Times*, Dec. 21, 1966.

126 We cannot here discuss the meaning of sovereignty at length. The suggested definition is meant to conjure up the feeling of inviolability under usual conditions. The sovereign is normally thought of as exercising "the supreme lawgiving and law enforcing authority" within its territory. Morgenthau, *Politics Among Nations* 318 (3rd ed., 1965).

There are numerous exceptions to sovereign control—the rights of diplomats, the rights of foreigners to at least "national" treatment—in general, the obligations of international law. All of this is the subject of extensive analysis and documentation. For surveys of the sources and for information, see *e.g.*, Bishop, *International Law* (2d ed., 1962), Chap. 4 (territory and territorial authority), Chap. 6 (Jurisdiction and immunities from jurisdiction); 1 *Whiteman*, 233–282; Metzger, "The Nature and Extent of Legal Limitations Upon a Nation's Freedom of Action," reprinted in *International Law, Trade and Finance* 1–16 (1962); Morgenthau, *op. cit.* Chapter 19 ("Sovereignty"). The last two named offer sophisticated legal and political treatment of the overall dilemma of sovereignty and international controls.

127 No attempt can be made here even to survey the literature on the issue of the meaning of "intervention." The concept as it relates to the subject at hand is expounded briefly *infra*. On "intervention" generally, see *e.g.*, 5 *Whiteman*, 321–702; Thomas and Thomas, *Non-Intervention: The Law and Its Import in the Americas* (1956); Oppenheim, *International Law* 304–320 (8th ed., Lauterpacht, ed., 1955).

128 *The Law of Nations and Principles of Natural Law*, Bk. II, pp. 115–116 (Fenwick transl., 1916, Carnegie Inst. of Washington).

129 Brierly, "The Sovereign State Today," 61 *Jurid. Rev.*, 3, 5 (1949).

130 7 Cranch 116, 136 (1812).

131 Morgenthau, *Politics Among Nations*, 313–314.

132 See, *e.g.*, Metzger, *op. cit. supra* n. 126; Schachter, *op. cit. supra* n. 9.

133 *Ibid.*, p. 325.

134 See, *e.g.*, Kunz, "The United Nations Declaration of Human Rights," 43 *Am. J. Int'l L.* 316 ff (1949). For the contrary view see, *e.g.*, Lauterpacht, *International Law and Human Rights* 166–173 (1948).

See also, *e.g.*, Preuss, "Article 2(7) of the Charter of the United Nations and Matters of Domestic Jurisdiction," 74 *Recueil des Cours* 553.

135 See generally Wright, "Is Discussion Intervention," 50 *Am. J. Int'l L.* 102–110 (1956); Waldock, "The Plea of Domestic Jurisdiction Before International Tribunals," 31 *Brit. Y. B. Int'l L.* 96 (1954); Shapiro, "Domestic Jurisdiction in the Covenant and the Charter," 33 *Grot. Soc. Transacs.* 195–211 (1947);

Of course some matters of domestic concern, *e.g.*, nationality laws, are also of major international concern. See P.C.I.J., Nationality Decrees in Tunis and Morocco, *P.C.I.J. Reports*, Series B, No. 4, 1923.

136 The question of domestic jurisdiction has been specifically raised in, *inter alia*, the following UN cases in addition to those discussed in the text: Question of convening conferences of representatives of Non-Self-Governing Territories (1946); Question of the establishment of committees on information transmitted under Art. 73(e) (1st–7th sessions); Question of the competence of the General Assembly to determine the territories to which Art. 73(e) applies (3rd–10th sessions); threats to the political independence and territorial integrity of Greece—death sentences pronounced by Greek tribunals (2d–6th sessions); Morocco (6th–8th sessions); Tunisia (7th–8th sessions); the Greek question (I, II and III, 1st–2nd and 5th sessions); Indonesia (2nd–5th sessions); Anglo-Iranian Oil Co. Question (6th session); Cyprus

(9th sess.); West Irian (9th–10th sessions and thereafter); U.N. personnel as prisoners in Korea (9th session).

137 On the Spanish case, see *e.g.*, 5 *Whiteman* 333–336, 381–382.

138 See *De Jure Belli ac Pacis* (Campbell trans., 1814), Bk. II, Chap. XXV, §8 and Chap. XX, §40. See also Stowell, *Intervention in International Law* 53 (1921). On humanitarian intervention, see also Ganji, *International Protection of Human Rights* (1962), Chapter I (hereinafter cited as *Ganji*).

139 *The Law of Nations and Principles of Natural Law*, Bk. II, pp. 115–116 (Fenwick, trans., 1916—Carnegie Inst. of Washington).

140 Treaties as disparate as that of Westphalia of 1648 and that of Paris of 1898, ending the Spanish-American War (Molloy, *Treaties, Conventions, International Acts, etc. between the U.S.A. and Other Powers, 1776–1909*, Vol. 2, p. 1690, Arts. 9 and 10) contain such provisions. See also *Ganji*, Chapters II, III.

141 On the League and Mandates, see Green, *The United Nations and Human Rights* (1956), Chapter I (hereinafter cited as *"Green"*); 1 *Whiteman* 598 ff.

142 On Wilson's Fourteen Points, and the "Principle of Self-Determination," as viewed in 1918–1919, see 5 *Whiteman* 41–44 and sources cited.

143 Pres. Wilson stated that: "Nothing . . . is more likely to disturb the peace of the world, than the treatment which might in certain circumstances be meted out to the minorities." Cited by de Azcarate, *League of Nations and National Minorities* 167 (1945).

144 Arrangements included treaties between the Allies and Poland, Czechoslovakia, Romania, Greece and the Kingdom of the Serbs, Croats and Slovenes (Yugoslavia); the peace treaties with Austria, Bulgaria, Hungary and Turkey; a special Convention between Germany and Poland; the Convention on the Memel Territory; and Declarations on admission to the League by Albania, Finland, Lithuania, Latvia and Estonia. On these arrangements, see League of Nations, *Inf. Bull.*, 1927. 2: Protection of Linguistic, Racial and Religious Minorities by the League of Nations; Provisions Contained in the Various International Instruments at Present in Force and see *Ganji*, Chapter II.

145 See League of Nations, *Report on the Decisions of the Council, 1920–1925*, L. N. Doc. A 10, 1923, p. 41.

146 See *e.g.*, Robinson, *Were the Minorities Treaties a Failure?* (1943); De Azcarate, *League of Nations and National Minorities* (1945); *Ganji* 73–77.

147 See Kaeckenbeeck, *International Experiment of Upper Silesia* (1942). See also Steiner & Gross v. Polish State, Arbitral Tribunal, *Annual Digest* (1927–1928) Case No. 188.

Note that the Treaty of Versailles had permitted nationals of the *victors* to bring certain claims against Germany before Mixed Arbitral Tribunals. Treaty of Versailles, Arts. 298(E), 304 (a). See also the Case Concerning the Jurisdiction of the Courts of Danzig, P. C. I. J., Series B, No. 15 (1928–1930).

Even before the League of Nations period, states at times conferred rights on individuals to assert claims even against states. In 1907, individuals were given the right to bring claims even against their own states before the Central American Court of Justice. In the ten years of its existence, the Court heard five such cases but rejected all of them. It ceased functioning in 1918. See Bishop, *op cit.*, 268–269.

148 Note that oppressed *majorities* within a state had no claim to the League's aid.

It is true that the League's reperesentative in Danzig exercised a restraining influence for several years and the experience, in all its implications, should not be forgotten. For a brief account, see Jessup & Taubenfeld, *Controls for Outer Space* 59–63 (1959) and sources cited.

149 Consult Liska, *International Equilibrium* (1957).

150 Lauterpacht wrote: "it would therefore appear that to the extent to which the Charter incorporates obligations to respect the fundamental human rights and

freedoms, it amounts to recognition of individuals as subjects of international law."
International Law and Human Rights 35 (1950). See also, *ibid* 145–165.

On earlier precedents, see *e.g.,* the American Declaration of Independence and the Constitution; the "Declaration of the Rights of Man," adopted in 1929 by the Institute of International Law, 1929 *Annuaire,* Vol. 35(2), pp. 298–300; 35 *Am. J. Int'l L. Supp.* 662–665 (1941); the "Atlantic Charter" of 1941 (see Churchill, *The Second World War,* Vol. III, pp. 384–400; 35 *Am. J. Int'l L. Supp.* 191–192 (1941) and 36 *ibid* 191 (1942).

On the United Nations and human rights, the literature is again voluminous. Among many, see Robinson, *Human Rights and the Charter of the U.N.; Ezejiofor, passim;* United Nations, *The Impact of the Universal Declaration on Human Rights* (1951); Coyle, *The United Nations* (rev. ed., 1965), Chapter 5; *Green, passim; Ganji,* Chapters IV–VI; Holcomb, *Human Rights in the Modern World* (1948); Moskowitz, *Human Rights and World Order* (1958); Carey, "The UN and Human Rights; Who Should Do What?" Sect. of Intl. & Comp. Law, A.B.A., *Bull.,* July, 1966, 9–29 (cited as Carey); McDougal and Bebr, "Human Rights in the United Nations," 58 *Am. J. Int'l L.* 603–641 (1964) (and see sources cited p. 603, n. 1); Green, *The Position of the Individual in International Law* (1960); Gross, *The United Nations/Structure for Peace,* Chapter 6 (1962); Neal, *International Conciliation,* No. 489 (1953); Henkin, "The United Nations and Human Rights," 19 *Int'l Org.* 504–517 (1965); Humphrey, "The United Nations and Human Rights," 11 *Howard L. J.* 373 ff. (1965).

On the rejection of the human rights provisions of the Charter as self-executing in the United States, see Fujii v. California, 242 Pac.2d 617, 621–622 (1952). On a Canadian view that the Charter provisions are binding on Canada but perhaps unenforcible internally as not part of the law of the land, compare Re Drummond Wren, [1945] O. R. 778; Re Noble & Wolf (1948), Annual Digest Case, No. 100, p. 302

151 At the organizational meeting in San Francisco in 1945, General Smuts of South Africa, among others, urged that the Charter should contain "a declaration of human rights" including concepts of "justice and decency" and "fundamental freedoms and rights of man . . ." See Sixth Plenary Session, May, 1945.

152 Article 1 (3)

153 Article 13 (1)(b).

154 Articles 62(2), 68.

155 See *Ezejiofor* 78–83. The Commission can survey complaints but has no power to act.

156 Article 76 (c). On the Trusteeship System, see 1 *Whiteman* 731 ff.

157 Kunz, "The United Nations Declaration of Human Rights," 43 *Am. J. Int'l L.* 316, 317 (1949); Kelsen, *The Law of the United Nations* 99–101 (1950). Drost, *Human Rights and Legal Rights* 28–31 (1951).

158 Kelsen, *The Law of the United Nations* 29, 30–31 (1950). See also Schwartzenberger, *Power Politics* 629–633 (1951); Hudson, "Integrity of International Instruments," 42 *Am. J. Int'l L.* 105–108 (1948);

159 Jessup, *A Modern Law of Nations* 91 (1948). See also Wright, "National Courts and Human Rights—The Fujii Case," 45 *Am. J. Int'l L.* 62–82 (1951); McDougal and Leighton, "Rights of Man in World Community . . . ," 14 *Law & Contemp. Prob.* 490 (Sum.-Aut., 1949) and see in general the symposium of which this is a part; Lauterpacht, *International Law and Human Rights* 145–165 (1950).

160 The long standing, closely parallel work of the International Labour Organization in the field of human rights must also be noted in such fields as slavery, forced labor, equal conditions of employment, etc. On its work, see Jenks, *Human Rights and International Labour Standards* (1960). On forced labor, see also on the concept and work of the ILO and other agencies, Moskowitz, *Human Rights and World Order* 43–47 (1958).

161 In 1950, a European Convention on Human Rights was concluded within the framework of the Council of Europe setting out a comprehensive list of rights and freedoms. There is a Court in existence; a Commission to deal with human rights complaints in the first instance; and a growing body of case law. See Eur. Comm. of Human Rights, *Documents and Decisions* 1955–1957 (1959), Introduction; Robertson, *Human Rights in Europe* (1963); *Ezijiofor*, Chapter 4.

In the Americas, an American Declaration of the Rights and Duties of Man has been adopted and an Inter-American Commission on Human Rights has been established.

On human rights in inter-American law, esp. the Charter of the O.A.S., Art.5(j) and the American Declaration of the Rights and Duties of Man (1948), see 5 Whiteman, 230–236; Thomas & Thomas, "The Inter-American Commission on Human Rights," 20 *Southwestern L.J.* 282–309 (1966); Pan American Union, *Human Rights in the American States* (1960); Sandifer, "Human Rights in the Inter-American System," 11 Howard L.J. 508 ff. (1965). The Commission issues Reports both on its work at each session and on special situations, *e.g.*, Human Rights in Haiti (19 Nov. 1963), Political Prisoners and their Relatives in Cuba (17 May 1963), Human Rights in Cuba (May 1, 1962) and the Dominican Republic (May 22, 1962) etc. See also *Ezijiofor*, 137–145. There have also been proposals for a Commonwealth Court of Human Rights, an African Convention on Human Rights, etc. See *Ezijiofor*, 145–147.

162 Italy, Art. 15; Romania, Art. 3(1); Bulgaria, Art. 2; Hungary, Art. 2(1); Finland, Art. 6.

163 See also *infra* pp. 50–1 and see *e.g.*, I.C.J., Advisory Opinion, Interpretation of Peace Treaties, *I.C.J. Rep.* (1950) 65.

164 UN Charter, Art. 76.

165 Approved by the General Assembly on Dec. 2, 1950. See G.A.O.R., 5th sess., Supp. 10 (A/1295) pp. 5–11.

166 Chapter XI.

167 See for summary, *Issues, 1966,* pp. 91 ff. On the creation of the post of High Commissioner for Human Rights, to be debated in the fall of 1966, see *ibid* 92–94.

168 Saudi Arabia was absent. On the Declaration, see among many, *Green* 24 ff.; *Ganji*, Chapters V, VI; McDougal & Bebr, *op. cit. passim*. For a report of a Soviet attack on Article 14 of the Declaration as a "maximum attack" on sovereignty, see 20 *Dep. St. Bull.* 690 (1949).

169 See, *e.g.*, Lauterpacht, *International Law and Human Rights*, 408.

170 G. A.O.R., 3rd sess., Pt. I (1948), 3rd Ctee., p. 32.

171 See, *e.g.*, G.A.O.R., 3rd sess., Pt. I (1948), Plenary, pp. 923–930 (Vyshinsky).

172 For a comparison of law in the Republic of South Africa with the terms of the Declaration, see Int'l Comm. of Jurists, *op. cit. supra* n. 77.

173 On the draft covenants, see sources cited *supra* n. 150. and 5 *Whiteman* 68 ff. For a recent review of developments, see *Issues, 1966,* p. 98. On progress in drafting the implementing clauses, see *UN Press Release*, WS/265, 28 Oct. 1966, pp. 8–9.

174 See, *e.g.*, statement of Charles Malik of Lebanon, G.A.O.R., 3rd sess., Part I (1948), Plenary, p. 860. See also Tchirkovitch, "La Déclaration Universelle des Droits de l'Homme et sa Portée Internationale," 53 *Revue Gén. du Droit Int. Pub.* 359, esp. 376 ff. (3rd ser., 1949).

175 See Conventions on the Suppression of the Traffic in Persons and in the Exploitation of Prostitution of 1949; on the Nationality of Married Women of 1957, Res. 1040 (XI); on the Political Rights of Married Women of 1952, Res. 640 (VII); on Marriage of 1962, Res. 1763A (XVII).

176 See Convention Relating to the Status of Refugees of 1951 and related arrangements and the provision by the UN of a High Commissioner for Refugees who has been very active since. See Coyle, 88–89; *Issues, 1966,* pp. 109–113.

177 In 1948, a UN conference also drafted three conventions on news: on the

138

gathering and sending of news, on the right of governments to demand correction of news stories claimed to be false and on freedom of information. The second came into force on August 24, 1962. Others are not completed.

[178] G.A. Res. 2106 (XX), 21 Dec. 1965.

[179] See *Issues, 1965*, pp. 92–94; *Issues, 1966*, pp. 106–109.

[180] Some 38 states had signed by late October, 1966 but only a few had ratified it by that time. On the U.S. signing on 28 Sept. 1966, see L/1722 and U.S. Mission, Press Release No. 4920, Sept. 28, 1966. The U.S., at the time of signature (doubtless with the Bricker Amendment controversy still in mind) notified all states that:

"The Constitution of the United States contains provisions for the protection of individual rights, such as the right of free speech, and nothing in the Convention shall be deemed to require or to authorize legislation or other action by the United States of America incompatible with the provisions of the Constitution of the United States of America."

[181] See *Issues, 1966*, pp. 103–106; Carey, 27–29. Other conventions being drafted include those on polygamy and other similar practices and on asylum. See, *e.g.*, G.A.O.R., 17 sess., 1962, Annexes, Agenda Item 46 (A/5359, para. 6).

[182] Declarations issued include that on the Rights of the Child, unanimously adopted by the Assembly on Nov. 20, 1959 and those in preparation include one on the Elimination of Discrimination Against Women (see ESCOR, 41st sess., 1966, Supp. No. 7, E/4175, Chapter XVI, pp. 103–106). One on Youth was adopted by the Assembly in 1965 (G.A. Res. 2037 (XX), 7 Dec. 1965).

[183] Recommendations include, among others, that of 1947 on granting women political rights with men (G.A. Res. 56 (I)); of 1951 on securing the observance of human rights and fundamental freedoms at home and in trust territories and dependencies (G.A. Res. 540 (VI)); of 1950 on refraining from jamming radio signals from abroad as a denial of the right of freedom of information (G.A. Res. 424 (V)); and that of 1965 on Consent to Marriage, Minimum Age for Marriage and Registration of Marriage (G.A. Res. 2018 (XX)).

[184] Other UN action includes the granting of fellowships and scholarships in the field of human rights, the organization of seminars on such subjects as the "Protection of human rights in criminal law and procedure," "The status of women in family life" and on "Apartheid" in the summer of 1966. For the report on that seminar's activities and conclusions, see A/6412 (13 Sept. 1966).

[185] See *Carey*, 23–26.

[186] *Issues, 1966*, p. 96.

[187] It has, of course, ratified some treaties dealing with human rights, for example, the humanitarian conventions of 1949 on prisoners of war, etc. See *Carey*, 26–29.

[188] See 28 *Dept. State Bull.* 579, 581 (1953).

[189] See Abram, "The Quest for Human Dignity," 2 *Vista*, No. 2, Sept.-Oct. 1966, 35 at 39–41. As noted elsewhere herein, the U.S.S.R. has nevertheless made reservations to any compulsory jurisdiction under these treaties whenever possible.

[190] See, *e.g.*, Emerson, "Self-Determination," *1966 Proc. Am. Soc. Int'l L.* 135 ff; 5 *Whiteman* 41–44 and sources cited.

[191] By 1966, the I.L.O. had produced 124 conventions and made 125 formal recommendations, many of which were relevant to colonial as well as metropolitan areas.

[192] On the special problems of the protection of minorities, see Kunz, "The Present Status of the International Law for the Protection of Minorities," 48 *Am. J. Int'l L.* 282, 284 (1954).

[193] See, *e.g.*, U.N. *Repertory of Practice*, Arts. 1–22 (1955) 115–122; 5 *Whiteman* 384–392.

[194] On Algeria and French claims that Algeria was part of Metropolitan France,

see U.N. *Repertory*, Arts. 1–54 Supp. No. 1 (1958) 48–50, 53–54; 5 *Whiteman* 47–54, 405–409;

195 On the relation between Art. 2(7) and self-determination, see generally I *Repertory of Practice of United Nations Organs*, Articles 1–22 of the Charter (1955) 104–106, 148 and I *ibid*, Articles 1–54 of the Charter, Supp. No. 1 (1958) 64–66; 5 *Whiteman* 38–87. For illuminating discussion, see Bowett, "Self-Determination and Political Rights in the Developing Countries," *1966 Proc. Am. Soc. Int'l L.* 129–135, and Emerson, "Self-Determination," *ibid*, 135–141.

196 Bowett, *op. cit.*, p. 132.

197 G. A. Res. 1514 (XV). (emphasis added)

198 See U.N. Doc. A/PV. 947. For U.S. reasons, see 44 *Dept. State Bull.* 21–27 (Jan. 2, 1961).

199 The full name is the Special Committee on the Situation with Regard to the Implementation of the Declaration on the Granting of Independence to Colonial Countries and Peoples. The Committee was established by G.A. Res. 1514. For 1966 the Members were Afghanistan, Australia, Bulgaria, Chile, Denmark, Ethiopa, India, Iran, Iraq, Italy, Ivory Coast, Madagascar, Mali, Poland, Sierra Leone, Syria, Tanzania, Tunisia, USSR, United Kingdom, United States, Uruguay, Venezuela and Yugoslavia.

For information on the remaining areas and UN action, *Issues, 1966*, pp. 55–91.

200 See U.N. Doc. A/AC.109/188, 29 June 1966. Uruguay and the U.K. did not attend these meetings. On the U.K.'s reasons, see U.N. Doc. A/AC.109/159, 9 May 1966. The resolution referred to was vigorously opposed by the United States.

201 See, *e.g.*, Bowett, *op. cit. passim*, esp. p. 129.

202 See, *e.g.*, Eagleton, "Self-Determination in the United Nations," 47 *Am. J. Int'l L.* 88–93 (1953). See also 5 *Whiteman* 384–392 and UN *Repertory of Practice*, Arts. 1–22 (1955), pp. 115–122. Thus also, the Ewes, long of interest to the UN, have no special claim in Ghana or Togo. See Emerson, *op. cit.* p. 138.

203 For resumé, see S/7382, pp. 115–116. On Dec. 18, 1961, the U.S.S.R. vetoed a draft resolution (S/5033) calling for a cessation of hostilities and an Indian withdrawal (Sec. Counc., 988th meeting).

204 See statement of Amb. Stevenson, U.N. Doc. A/4985, Nov. 25, 1961, pp 6–8, reprinted in 5 *Whiteman* 57–58.

205 See 5 *Whiteman* 82–83; see statement of Lord Hume, 16th General Assembly, Sept. 27, 1961, cited in 5 Whiteman 46, noting that the rule of freedom seems to be only "valid" for Asia and Africa, not Europe or the "Russian empire" where it happened to be relevant initially. The "right of self-determination" has shifted, geographically, to the south.

206 See Ginsbergs, "'Wars of National Liberation' and the Modern Law of Nations—the Soviet Thesis," 29 *Law & Contemp. Prob.* 910–942 (1964); Bowett, *op. cit.* p. 133. And see the arguments at the Mexico City meeting in 1964 of the U.N. Special Committee on Principles of International Law concerning Friendly Relations and Cooperation among States, reviewed by McWhinney in 60 *Am. J. Int'l L.* 1–33 (1966); *Issues, 1966*, pp. 188–193.

207 In general, see *Issues, 1966*, pp. 109–111. On the tragedy of Nigeria, and the attacks based on tribal affiliation, see *e.g.*, *New York Times*, July 14, p. E3; Oct. 3, 1966; Oct. 9, 1966, p. E3. On inter-tribal strife and unrest in Uganda, see *ibid*, May 9, 1966.

In the past few years, two-thirds of the new states have suffered coups or attempted coups. See Matthews, "Forecast for Africa: More Plots, More Coups," *New York Times Mag.*, April 10, 1966 and see *New York Times*, Feb. 28, 1966.

208 See *Issues, 1966*, pp. 109–111.

209 See, *e.g.*, "'India for the Hindus' Says the Jan Sangh," *New York Times Mag.*, Aug. 14, 1966, pp. 20 ff. and see *New York Times*, March 14, 1966 (language riots).

210 See, *e.g.*, King, "The Great Purge in Indonesia," *New York Times Mag.*, May 8, 1966, p. 25 ff. and *e.g., New York Times*, Jan. 13, 1966.

211 When the I.L.O. reported that Burundi's policy towards labor unions, jailings and mass executions was brutal, Burundi promptly argued that this was "flagrant intervention" and "improper interference" in "internal affairs," for example. See Abram, *op. cit. supra* n. 189 at 37 and *UN Press Release* SOC/HR/178.

See Carey, 22–23.

212 We have already noted, for example, reports that conditions in Ghana and Nigeria had strengthened the white Rhodesian government's will to resist. See *supra.*

213 Most of the new governments offer one party rule. Several have rules for internal security very reminiscent of those they criticize in South Africa. Several, such as Ghana and Malawi, have preventive detention laws. See Matthews, *op. cit. supra* n. 207 at 19. Legal proceedings are often primitive. Thus, for example, on Oct. 28, 1966, Zanzibar announced the creation of a "secret court, from which defense counsel and public prosecutors will be barred, to try political offenders, people held in preventive detention and those who steal or damage government property." The court "will establish its own trial procedures and will not be bound by principles or procedures as laid down in law for Tanzania or elsewhere. The court will have the power to impose the death penalty, and only Sheik Karume may grant a reprieve. There will be no appeal to any other court." *New York Times*, Oct. 29, 1966.

214 Resolution 154 (III) D.

215 While the delegate was serving in Moscow as Chilean Ambassador, his son married a Soviet woman. An application for her to leave the country was refused by Soviet authorities.

216 See, for the debate, G.A.O.R., 3rd sess., Part I, 1948, Sixth Committee, (*e.g.* pp. 722, 745). See generally, 5 *Whiteman* 349–352.

217 See G.A.O.R., 3rd sess., Part II, 1949, Plenary Session, p. 55.

218 See A/C. 6/315.

219 See UN *Yearbook 1948/49*, pp. 316–327; *ibid*, 1950, pp. 385–397 and Resolutions 272 (III), 294 (IV) and 38 (V). See generally 5 *Whiteman* 352–356, 397–398.

220 For a summary of UN action in 1959, 1961 and 1965, see Carnegie Endowment, *Synopsis of U.N. Cases* 42 (1966). The U.S.S.R., Albania, Bulgaria, Cuba, Poland, Hungary and Romania were joined by Congo (Brazzaville) and Guinea in asserting that Article 2(7) prevented action. See A/PV. 1401, 1403. Other states reaffirmed the UN's right of discussion and action. See, *e.g.*, A/PV. 1403, pp. 46, 52–53 (Malaysia).

221 Henkin, "The United Nations and Human Rights," 19 *Int'l Org.* 504 at 506 (1965). For similar comments on human rights as the business of the UN, see A/PV. 1401, p. 3 (New Zealand) and UN *Press Release* L/1582 (Chile).

222 McDougal and Bebr, "Human Rights in the United Nations," 58 *Am. J. Int'l L.* 603 (1964).

223 See Hyde, *International Law* 250, n. 6 (2d ed., 1945).

224 See Green, *The Position of the Individual in International Law* 7 (1960). See also Janowsky and Fagen, *International Aspects of German Racial Policies*, Chapter 1 (1937). Lest we think that this sort of approach is gone, we must note that that doctrine of the sacredness and non-reviewability of foreign acts of state in general remains basic to American and British judicial policy even now. See Underhill v. Hernandez, 168 U.S. 250 (1897); the "Bernstein" cases (163 F.2d 246, 2d Cir., 1947, cert. den., 332 U.S. 772 (1947); 173 F.2d 71, 2d Cir., 1949; the "Tate" letter of April 13, 1949 (reprinted in Bishop, *International Law*, 215 (2d ed., 1962); 210 F.2d 246, 2d Cir. (1954), relating to Nazi decrees; the "Sabbatino" cases (193 F. Supp. 375 (S.D.N.Y. 1961), aff'd 307 F.2d 845 (2d Cir. 1962), rev'd 376 U.S. 398 (1964), et seq.) and the Congressional action which followed, esp. the amendment to the Foreign

Assistance Act of 1964, approved Oct. 7, 1964, in Section 301(d)(4). The literature is voluminous.

225 Article 6. For comment see, *e.g.*, Schwelb, "Crimes Against Humanity," 23 *Brit. Y. B. Int'l L.* 176 ff. (1946). On Nuremburg, see generally Woetzel, *The Nuremburg Trials in International Law* (1960).

226 On piracy, see Geneva Convention on the High Seas, Art. 19; Johnson, "Piracy in Modern International Law," 43 *Grot. Soc. Transac.* 63 (1957); *In Re Piracy Jure Gentium* [1934] A.C. 586. On coining, see United States v. Arjona, 102 U.S. 479 (1887). On "ordinary" war crimes, see Lauterpacht, 63 *L.Q.R.* 443 (1947). See generally, Bishop, *op. cit.*; Ezejiofor, *Protection of Human Rights Under the Law* 19 ff. (1964).

227 *E.g.*, does international law prohibit acts and impose sanctions or does it simply authorize any and all states to act in certain ways with respect to certain activities?

228 In addition to the doctrinal barriers imposed by the sovereignty concept to any formalized international intervention between a state and its citizens, we have noted the long-standing reluctance on the part of states and scholars to consider an individual human being as a "subject" of international law having cognizable rights of any sort under that law. In a classic statement, Oppenheim noted that: "Since the Law of Nations is based on the common consent of individual states, and not of individual human beings, states solely and exclusively are the subjects of International Law. . . . An individual human being . . . is never directly a subject of International Law." *International Law*, paras. 13, 18 ff. (1903). Both doctrines reflect a conservative view of the international system which has in recent centuries been basically realistic and reasonable in that sense. States alone have real power to enforce international law on themselves and their subjects and to face each other as equals. At the same time, others have argued that, even in a basic logical sense the law can only deal with the humans who compose the societies in the international community. See, *e.g.*, Scelle, *Précis de droit des gens*, Vol. I, pp. 42–44 (1932); Kelsen, *General Theory of Law and State* 34 (1945). In general, see Bishop, *International Law* 265–283 (2d ed., 1962). Furthermore, as we shall argue, this is a static concept of what is realistic and practical. The law of a growing international community, in which both judicial access (as in Europe) to individuals and even modest central enforcement powers can develop, can grow along with these. What is practical central law-making changes with changes in the structure of power and the development of central functions and institutions capable of undertaking them effectively; thus the present central governments in Europe grew out of the politically decentralized middle ages to assert the sovereignty of the center. For what remains a leading exposition of the need to bring the individual into international law more directly, see Jessup, *A Modern Law of Nations* (1948).

229 See *U.N. Yearbook*, 1946, p. 254.

230 See A/PV. 178, 179.

231 The United States signed the Convention but has not ratified it. The Soviet Union ratified it but with reservations. See A/1372; I. C. J., Reservations to the Convention on Genocide, *I. C. J. Reports 1951*, p. 15. For comment, see *Carey*, 27.

232 It was contemplated that nations would make genocide a crime under their own laws and that a permanent international criminal tribunal would in time be set up. The reasons for lack of international interest in establishing an international code of crimes and a tribunal are implicit in the discussion throughout this paper; there is no agreement on what such a list should contain, who should define the "crimes," who should bring the charges, and who should enforce the decisions. The questions are of course, intrinsically soluble by technicians on the basis of a compromise consistent with the present states' preference for the retention of what might be called "judicial sovereignty," when their desire to see these acts con-

trolled is sufficient. Crimes tribunals to date, including that at Nuremburg, have been those of the victors in a war. However West German courts have, for many years now, been following the trail set at Nuremburg.

233 See, *e.g.*, A/AC.109/L.300 and Rev. 1 (15 June 1966).

234 Metzger, *International Law, Trade and Finance* 7 (1962).

On the use of "natural rights" concepts in early U.S. constitutional practice, see Corwin, *Liberty Against Government,* esp. p. 66 (1948) and see Calder v. Bull, 3 U.S. (3 Dall.) 386, 1 L.Ed. 648 (1798).

234a Metzger, *ibid*, pp. 6–7.

235 As an example, while the Soviet Union has ratified the Genocide Convention and other human rights treaties as well, it has made a reservation to compulsory jurisdiction under the treaty in each case where that was at all possible. See *e.g., Carey,* 27 and Carey, "Implementing Human Rights Conventions—The Soviet View," 53 *Ky. L. Rev.* 115 (1964).

236 On the continuing effectiveness of the 1950 Opinion, see the various Dissenting Opinions of 1966, *passim,* including that of Judge Jessup.

And see A/AC.109/L.325, 8 Sept. 1966, para. 10.

237 *I.C.J. Reports,* 1950, 143–144 and *I.C.J. Reports,* 1956, p. 28 (Advisory Opinion of June, 1956).

238 *I.C.J. Reports,* 1962, p. 334.

239 For additional discussion of the Opinion, see Report of the Sub-Committee on South West Africa of the Ctee. of 24, A/AC.109/L.325, 8 Sept. 1966.

240 Cf. the Dissents of Judges Jessup, Koo, Tanaka and Padilla Nervo, and see the Judgment of 1962, *I.C.J. Reports,* 1962, *e.g.,* p. 343.

241 See their various opinions. On the effect of resolutions, etc., see, *e.g.,* Sloan, "The Binding Force of a Recommendation of the General Assembly of the United Nations," 1948 *Brit. Y. B. Int'l L.* 1–34; Lande, "The Changing Effectiveness of General Assembly Resolutions," *1964 Proc. Am. Soc. Intl. L.,* 162–173. See also Higgins, *Development of International Law Through the Political Organs of the United Nations, passim* (1963) and Jenks, *The Common Law of Mankind,* 121 (1958).

242 See Opinions of Tanaka, Mbanefo, Padilla Nervo. See generally Rosenne, *The International Court of Justice,* Vol. II, p. 610 (1965).

243 See opinions of Tanaka, Mbanefo and Padilla Nervo.

The duties, allegedly violated, include the practice of apartheid (the failure to promote to the utmost the material and moral well-being and social progress of the inhabitants of the territory), the failure to transmit petitions from the inhabitants of the territory to the United Nations; the failure to submit annual reports to the General Assembly of the United Nations; the establishment of military bases within the territory; the attempt substantially to modify the terms of the Mandate without the consent of the United Nations. Not all were taken as proved, even by the dissenters.

Specific allegations of illegality were attached to such acts as: general conferral of Union citizenship upon inhabitants of the Territory; inclusion of representatives from South West Africa in the Union Parliament; administrative separation of the Eastern Caprivi Zipfel from the Union; the vesting of South West Africa Native Reserve Land in the South Africa Native Trust and the transfer of administration of "Native" affairs to the Union's Minister of Bantu Administration and Development.

244 For amplification of the South African position, see also the memorandum addressed to the General Assembly on 19 Oct. 1966, UN Doc. A/6480, 20 Oct. 1966.

245 347 U.S. 483, 98 L.Ed. 873, 64 S.Ct. 686 (1954).

246 328 U.S. 549, 90 L.Ed. 1432, 66 S.Ct. 1198 (1946).

247 See Baker v. Carr, 369 U.S. 186 (1962); Gomillion v. Lightfoot, 364 U.S. 339 (1961); Gray v. Sanders, 372 U.S. 368 (1963).

Note that in a half dozen cases in 1964, the Court has gone so far as to forbid the states to adopt a replica of the federal bicameral compromise which permits the Senate to be elected on a basis of states, not "one man, one vote." In the states, all legislators must be elected by all the voters. See, *e.g.*, Reynolds v. Sims, 377 U.S. 533 (1964); WMCA, Inc. v. Lomengo, 377 US 633 (1964); Lucas v. the Forty-fourth General Assembly, 377 U.S. 713 (1964); Maryland Committee v. Tawes, 377 U.S. 656 (1964); Davis v. Mann, 377 U.S. 695 (1964); Roman v. Sincock, 377 U.S. 695 (1964).

248 See, *e.g.*, 1 Freund, Sutherland, Howe and Brown, *Constitutional Law, Cases and Other Problems* 243–244 (2d ed., 1961).

249 McCulloch v. Maryland, 17 U.S. (4 Wheat.) 316, 4 L. Ed. 579 (1819).

250 In his evident disgust with the Court's Opinion, the representative of Kenya, at the General Assembly, called for the election of judges "whose decisions would [not] be influenced by the policies of their Governments or by ideological considerations . . ." (*UN Press Release* WS/261, 30 Sept. 1966, p. 18). Could he have meant judges whose prejudices and preferences would accord with his own views of what the law is and *ought* to be? It is not only Communist philosophy which rejects the idea that any judge can be totally "neutral." It is also not at all clear that "justice" would be advanced by any such judges if they did exist.

251 See statements cited *supra* notes 63–66 and 250.

252 Note that on a worldwide basis, a vote based solely on "one man, one vote," for example, would give *all* of Africa together about half the votes of India alone and not much more than the votes allocated to the United States or the Soviet Union.

253 For a penetrating analysis of the issues of growth and development through the UN, see Schachter, "The Relation of Law, Politics and Action in the United Nations," 1963 *Recueil des Cours* 171–200. An excellent review of international law developments is in Lissitzyn, *International Law Today and Tomorrow* (1965).

254 Higgins, *Development of International Law Through the Political Organs of the United Nations* 61–62 (1963).

255 This is basically an American viewpoint. Other forms of constitutional structure might suggest different means of system evolution in which courts play little or no part. But constitutional systems must provide for some source of flexibility and among other things permit growth of the government's role when this is desired.

256 As Judge Sir Gerald Fitzmaurice has written:

> Domestic courts can, if they wish, plead with some plausibility as a ground for not going beyond what is barely necessary for a decision that a national legislature exists which can, by legislative action, remedy any gaps or obscurities in the law. In the international field there is at present nothing comparable to a legislature, and the operation of the so-called law-making treaty is both uncertain and leaves many loose ends. The international community is therefore peculiarly dependent on its international tribunals for the development and clarification of the law, and for lending to it an authority more substantial and less precarious than can be drawn from the often uncertain and divergent practices of States, or even from the opinion of individual publicists, whatever their repute.

Fitzmaurice, "Hersch Lauterpacht, The Scholar as Judge," 57 *Brit. Y. B. Int'l L.* 14–15 (1961).

257 See Statute of the I.C.J., Art. 38. For comment on "sources" of international law, see Bishop, *International Law* 22–56 (2d ed., 1962) and sources cited.

258 Advisory Opinion, Reservations to the Convention on the Prevention and Punishment of Genocide, *I.C.J. Reports 1951*, p. 23. Emphasis added.

259 See Gross, Address to the I.C.J., reprinted in 3 Falk & Mendlovitz, *The Strategy of World Order*, 79 at 88 (1966).

260 See especially the Opinion of Judge Tanaka and that of Judge Padilla Nervo.

261 *Ibid.*

262 Years before, Judge Spiropoulos had said: "As the obligation to respect human rights was placed upon Member States by the Charter, it followed that any violation of human rights was a violation of the provisions of the Charter." (G.A. O.R., 3rd Session, 6th Committee, 138th Meeting, 7 December 1948, p. 765.) See also Jessup, *A Modern Law of Nations* 91 (1947); Jenks: "The principle of non-discrimination has been recognized internationally in most solemn form." See also the comments of the delegates from Trinidad and Tobago and from New Zealand, A/C.3/SR.1347, 23 Nov. 1965, pp. 5–6 and 15, citing with approval such conclusions of Lauterpacht and René Cassin.

263 Schachter, "The Relation of Law, Politics and Actions in the United Nations," *Recueil des Cours*, Vol. II, 171–200 (1963) reprinted in 3 Falk and Mendlovitz, *op. cit. supra* n. 9, p. 94 at 114.

264 Schachter, "Dag Hammarskjold and the Relation of Law to Politics" 56 *Am. J. Int'l L.* (1962) pp. 1, 3–5. And for a philosophical discussion of the conception of polarity—see M. R. Cohen, *Reason & Nature* (N.Y. 1931) p. 165 (citation from quoted text).

265 Note the reluctance to accept UN "legislative" interpretation of such Judges as Spender even before the South West Africa Cases which demonstrated a similar reluctance for a major I.C.J. role. In a Separate Opinion in the Case of Certain Expenses of the United Nations, he wrote: ". . . I am unable to regard any usage or practice followed by any organ of the United Nations which has been determined by a majority therein against the will of a minority as having any legal relevance or probative value." See *I.C.J. Reports* 1962, p. 197.

266 On the political rationale of the structure embodied in the Constitution of the United States, see notes and cases in Lockhart et al., *Constitutional Law*, esp. Chapters 1–4, 9 (1964).

267 It has of course shown flexibility in its peacekeeping and armed forces arrangements.

268 See Jackson, *The Struggle for Judicial Supremacy* (1941).

269 At the fall UN meeting, Judges Spender, Winiarski and Spiropoulos, who were part of the I.C.J. "majority" in the 1966 South West Africa opinion were not reelected to the Court (nor was Judge Koo). The new Judges include men from Nigeria (Onyeama) and the Philippines (Bengzon), shifting the balance a bit more towards the newer states. See *UN Press Release* WS/266, 4 Nov. 1966, p. 4.

270 See Schachter, *op. cit. supra* n. 9; Higgins, *op. cit. supra* n. 254.

271 On "law-making" by the General Assembly, see sources cited in notes 270 and 254. On the dangers of "declamatory" resolutions in the Assembly, adopted without "serious regard for the means, the costs or the consequences of their implementation," see New Zealand statement, *UN Press Release* WS/364, 21 Oct. 1966, p.11.

272 See the comment of Judge Spender, *supra* n. 265.

273 Note that the Soviet Union, while ratifying human rights conventions, has taken pains to make them unenforcible as to themselves where possible (see *supra* n. 189) and opposed, *e.g.*, the Declaration on Human Rights as a challenge to sovereignty (*supra* n. 168, 171).

273a There is a voluminous literature on the subject of the designing of the U.S. Constitution, and on the theory of Democratic Government. For a review of some of the issues and their history see Dahl, *A Preface to Democratic Theory* (1956). For a recent dialogue on the current theory, see 60 *Amer. Pol. Sci. Rev.* 285–305 and 391–392 (Profs. Walker and Dahl) (1966).

274 Thus the veto in the Security Council allows any veto Power to bar a UN-ordered enforcement action. This is a far more powerful veto than sovereigns have traditionally had in the international community; although each nation's consent was always required for its own participation in an enforcement action, it normally could not bar an action desired by others so long as they could form an effective coalition without it. General Assembly enforcement under the Uniting For

Peace Resolution retains this right of non-participation in more traditional form. No one power can block all others who want to act from acting but, in fact, as the long peacekeeping crisis reminds us, each nation has a *de facto* veto over its own participation in the UN enforcement coalition and, thus far, over its own financial contributions to the actions as well.

275 The roles of the Supreme Court and the President, as developed, serve as a "check" on the conservative bias of the overall choice for the legislature of a regionally qualified majority rule. As noted, the Court has now barred the states from using the conservative constitutional compromise on legislative representation itself on the ground that, while it was an acceptable constitutional bargain for establishing a safer federal system of large, varied component states, it was nevertheless a compromise with democratic principles.

276 Inis Claude, *Power and International Relations* (1962).

277 U.S. reluctance to ratify human rights conventions is based in part on our awareness of imperfect conduct at home which the federal government itself has often had little success in correcting. For comment, see Abram, "The Quest for Human Dignity," 2 *Vista*, No. 2, Sept.-Oct. 1966, p. 35 at 39–41.

278 Claude, *op. cit. supra* n. 276 at p. 284.

279 Intent to commit an illegal act or to participate in an illegal conspiracy is often required to "convict" defendants in certain similar difficult internal feuds, as in some U.S. anti-trust actions. Explicit intent seems particularly important for international illegal acts in a world in which informal de facto discrimination is endemic.

280 See generally Buergenthal, "The United Nations and the Development of Rules Relating to Human Rights," *1965 Proc. Amer. Soc. Int'l L.* 132–136.

281 As an analogy, note again the Goa experiece, *op. cit. supra* n. 203.

282 As we noted earlier, the UN has discussed human rights within other countries—the Soviet Union, Tibet, the Eastern European countries etc.—but has not recommended international action.

283 Here we use "government" roughly as Inis Claude, among others, uses the term to mean "the function of promoting order through political management of inter-group relations" by effective consensus-making and binding compromise, in contrast to inter-group confrontation and violence." *Op. cit. supra* n. 276 at p. 271.

284 There have been numerous attempts at international legal definition-making in recent years. See for example, the efforts to expound several of the basic tenets of the Charter cited herein and reviewed in *Issues, 1966,* pp. 188–193.

285 Technically, this statement is too broad. The initial Security Council action in the Congo had as one of its objectives to replace and oversee the withdrawal of Belgian forces which, after a withdrawal, had been returned on a stated humanitarian mission for a limited period.

286 Woetzel, *The Nuremberg Trials in International Law* 183 (1960). Metzger has noted the relevance of the "crimes against humanity" part of the Nuremberg Judgment, which punished acts by Germans against Germans which were "lawful" under German law when committed (*i.e.,* the organized wholesale murder of German Jews) to the "activities of the South African Government in recent years in carrying out the 'apartheid' policy." He suggests that a similar judgement against them "would enjoy similar worldwide support." Metzger, *International Law, Trade and Finance* 5–7 (1962). See also his statement cited earlier for the various legal grounds which can be adduced even by a Positivist for action in support of "the basic principles of justice."

287 See Part II of this paper and see R. Taubenfeld, "Economic Aggression," Working Paper included as part of Thomas & Thomas et al, *The Law of Indirect Aggression and Subversion,* U.S. Arms Control and Disarmament Agency (1966).

288 These include, among many, the compulsory mass immunization of school

children against disease, minimum wage and hours laws, the setting of labor standards, the achievement of full employment policy by manipulation of the central government's economic control instruments, etc., etc.

289 For relevant survey and observations, see *Carey* 9–29.

290 See, *e.g.*, on the financial side, Report of the Advisory Committee on Administrative and Budgetary Questions concerning report of the *Ad Hoc* Committee of Experts to Examine the Finances of the United Nations and the Specialized Agencies, A/6475. On financing, including the financing of peacekeeping operations, see Stoessinger and Associates, *Financing the United Nations System* (1964).

291 In the League, as in the pre-League world, each Member had a vote and a veto as befitted sovereigns. This was not stressed since the enforcement system against aggression was to be instantaneous and automatically applied by all Members individually. All states were expected to recognize their own paramount stake in world order and peaceful conflict resolution and to rally automatically to the defense of the inviolability of a comrade sovereign. Whatever the possibly conflicting merits of the case, whatever other political or ethical dimensions were involved, whatever the need for change, Members were apparently expected to put the inviolability of the *status quo* above all else when another Member undertook to make a change by force. The Covenant, like the Charter, stressed international order over "justice," not "democracy" but peace, change if any by unresisted evolution, growth of private (national) power by self help, not by majority rule. This stress was (and is) inevitable for a world political organization with a universal veto, with a deliberating body effectively confined to study, negotiation and persuasion rather than to enforcible decision-making, with a voluntary court and with no genuine executive structure.

292 The authors have in preparation a study which includes this period. The literature is voluminous.

293 For details, see Taubenfeld & Taubenfeld, "Peace, the U.N. and Southern Africa," a study paper prepared for the Carnegie Endowment's study of apartheid in 1964–65. (unpublished). Parts of the remainder of the current study have drawn on that paper.

294 All Non-Self-Governing Territories, as well as the Trust Territories (successor to the Mandates) were the interest of the UN as we have noted in Part III, above.

295 Amb. Goldberg, response to a question, speech at Dallas, Texas, Oct. 25, 1966.

296 This sketch draws on the more extensive papers prepared by the authors for the Carnegie Endowment study cited earlier. For the cases, see the *UN Yearbooks*, various years. A summary of the action in each is contained in the Carnegie Endowment Summary, *op. cit. supra* n. 96. Each is the subject of an extensive literature. For an earlier comprehensive treatment, see Goodrich and Simons, *The United Nations and the Maintenance of International Peace and Security* (1955).

297 Under this system, not only Big Power conflicts but any conflict which threatened or breached the peace in which any of the Five were interested (*i.e. all* important international conflicts) was subject to the veto unless the UN devised some way to avoid the veto or to find veto-free forces. On the other hand, the Charter-required peace of the *status quo* could not itself be reliably imposed because of the same veto unless any undesired change was dangerous to all Five so that they could and would agree. In short, all dangerously destabilizing changes in favor of any one, including any one of the Five, could not be opposed militarily either by the UN or the others by the terms of the Charter. This clearly left strong national arms and arms races, and less easily stymied extra UN alliance systems, for "balancing" and "deterring," essential. They can be expected to remain so until it becomes possible to establish clearly overwhelming central forces in support of an agreed, effective system of final conflict resolution, which is itself reliably workable, to assure safety with minimum justice for all. We cannot ignore the need for these

147

presently non-existant emotional and constitutional prerequisites. No rational sovereign would. We can concentrate on trying to build them; and therefore on trying to avoid organized international action which tends to undermine faith in either the reliability or the "fairness" of the center.

298 See Riker, *The Theory of Political Coalitions* (1962), for some of the reasons in *a priori* theory for regarding such a large coalition of would be *prima donna* states as unstable.

299 Once again, we offer here only a brief sketch of these important episodes. The literature is again voluminous. Among many, on Korea, see Goodrich, *Korea: A Study of United States Policy in the United Nations* (1956) and Hoyt, "The United States Reaction to the Korean Attack," 55 Am. J. Int'l L. 45 (1961).

300 For the nations which are willing to fight or which are, in their own view, unable to avoid a fight, the question of the cost of "internationalization" of the conflict always arises. The ultimate price as usual depends on the final bargaining power (including the "style" and determination) of the parties and this has many components. In this case the most important would normally appear to be militarily revealed balance of credible enforcement power, and the political power and relative tractability of the major contesting parties in the international organization. If this sounds non-operational, it probably is. Different estimates by opponents on these types of issues are, after all, among the major reasons why wars are fought.

We discuss some of the implicit alternative costs (and benefits) of internationalization to the recognized implicit "winners" in the text. It should also be noted that, for the implicit or explicit losers, or potential future losers, "realistic" compromise with the initial *status quo* has normally been expected from international organizations. Thus in the League period the victims, China and Ethiopa, were expected by the League decision-makers to yield in part to the demands of the aggressors, Japan and Italy, and to be "reasonable.' In the UN period, North Korea and South Korea and Israel have been forced back to an "unstable" *status quo* which the UN has undertaken to maintain and police. Should the Republic of South Africa request international *support* as a victim of "aggression," for example or for peacemaking and peacekeeping at the end of some non-UN-struggle which ended in a *de facto* partition, it too would have to be sufficiently flexible to be able to pay for such much needed services, that is, it would have to negotiate with an Organization including other sovereigns with antagonistic, strongly held, powerfully backed points of view and a willingness to fight repeatedly if necessary, for their vision of minimum justice. Furthermore, South Africa's bargaining position as a powerful international political outcast in need of international guarantees can be expected to be far worse even than Israel's since it has earned strong, repeated, near-universal moral and official disapproval.

301 We have noted that internationalizing the Korean conflict provided the U.S. administration with a persuasive argument in "domestic" politics against escalation. President Truman, after all, did recall Gen. McArthur essentially for insubordination to the concepts of limited aims and containment. See, *e.g.,* Truman, *Years of Trial and Hope* (Memoirs, Vol. 2, 1956), *passim.*

Subsequent developments in other places in Asia where the U.S. has become involved in unilateral, non-internationalized, though legitimately invited intervention (notably Viet Nam), indicate that the Korean territorial solution was indeed a good bargain for the United States even though it retained the major burden of containment of Communist aggression. This perhaps explains U.S. enthusiasm for the Uniting for Peace program.

This experience is increasingly important as indirect aggression becomes the prevalent form of conflict as well. It has become increasingly difficult and costly to disprove Mao's thesis that any disciplined local Communist insurgency can defeat U.S. intervention to prop up satellite "central" governments. When military action is essential the symbolic (and real) differences of intervention in the name of the

UN against or to obviate or to contain Communist imperialist indirect intervention cannot be discounted. This would apply also to southern Africa where Communist participation again seems likely in time. The real issue of course is whether Korea-type interposition would be offered and whether it would appear desirable to or even acceptable to the UN majority.

302 The international legal regulation of some aspects of warmaking is, of course, not new. This international *political* control of some aspects of warmaking is so new that it still exists only irregularly. For a "contractarian" approach to the emergence of government see Buchanan and Tullock *The Calculus of Consent* (1962); see also Baumol, *Welfare Economics and the Theory of the State* (1952). For a "contractarian" approach to some of the conceptual obstacles to organizing viable, very large human societies see Olson, *The Logic of Collective Action* (1965).

303 Several recent historical-empirical studies of the international behavior of states have stressed the dominance of domestic political pressures. See for example, Rosencrance, *Action and Reaction in World Politics* (1963).

304 There are many studies of the problems of a "UN force." See, *e.g.*, Bloomfield, ed. *International Military Forces* (1964); Burns and Heathcote, *Peace-Keeping by UN Forces—From Suez to the Congo* (1963); Bowett, *United Nations Forces* (1964).

305 See Goodrich and Simons, *The United Nations and the Maintenance of Peace and Security*, Chapters XVI and XVII (1955) for these matters in the Korean experience and, generally, see Goodrich, *op. cit. supra* n. 299, *passim*.

306 We use the word potential, because if other states are genuinely interested in encouraging and supporting UN peacekeeping, they can continue to do so, and, indeed, they need not allow the miniscule (relatively) debts of the UN to thwart any small part of its activities. See Taubenfeld and Taubenfeld, cited *infra* n. 308.

307 In Cyprus, the U.K., the former colonial Power, provided the initial UN forces. This case, which still plagues it, does not involve combat by the UN forces and is not further discussed here. For a survey of developments including the police force, UNFICYP, see Issues, 1966, pp. 50–54 and Issues, 1965, pp. 45–51.

308 For the I.C.J. Opinion, see "Certain Expenses of the United Nations," *I.C.J. Reports*, 1962, p. 151. On the financing problem, see Stoessinger and Associates, *op. cit. supra* n. 290; Taubenfeld & Taubenfeld, "Independent Revenue for the United Nations," 18 *Int'l Org.* 241–267 (1964); Padelford, "Financial Crisis and the Future of the United Nations," 15 *World Politics* 531–568 (1963).

309 We do not here discuss this United Nations Emergency Force (UNEF) in detail. It was and is a lightly armed "border watcher," a force aimed solely at interposition between hostile states. On UNEF, se Rosner, *The United Nations Emergency Force* (1963); Hammarskjöld, "United Nations Emergency Force," A/3943 (9 Oct. 1958.

310 On the Congo operation, see *e.g.*, Nicholas, "An Appraisal," in Bloomfield, *op. cit. supra*, n. 304, 105 ff. There are numerous other studies.

311 Claude, "The United Nations and the Use of Force," *Int'l Org.*, No. 532, March, 1961.

312 *Ibid.*

313 See Sheehan, "It's Still the Heart of Darkness," *New York Times Mag.*, Oct. 30, 1966, pp.31 ff.

314 Claude, *ibid.*

315 There are for example some well-to-do "neutral" states which could supply both arms and men for small forces and which have been or are now willing to designate specific forces for assignment to the UN. This seems a helpful initiative. If they were determined, the small and "neutral" powers could also bear more of the financial burden too though they probably could not supply the material or the transport for any large engagement. Furthermore the theory of relying primarily on "neutral" small nation manpower for pacification and peacekeeping assumes the availability of *acceptably* impartial outside manpower sources. Africa,

one of the two areas potentially in greatest need of internal pacification operations proved to be a somewhat undependable source of neutral manpower for the Congo operation. Claude, *op. cit. supra* n. 311, at p. 58. On the other hand, the fact that racism is already endemic complicates the recruiting of "impartial" forces for African service from elsewhere within the UN. This leaves the African states, and perhaps a few "acceptable" Asian and Latin American states, with a special need not only to be willing to serve and to absorb the more obvious lessons of the Congo performance, but to surpass the past performances of other, more experienced, richer, better organized nations in the art of self-controlled military cooperation. This is certainly not impossible.

316 See in particular, Riker, *op. cit. supra* n. 298. The exploration of the hypothesis that self-interested political actors tend to form a minimal size winning coalition is one of the major elements of his study. Though he tends to stress internal political examples, actually the concept seems even more relevant to international interactions where the actors are relatively freer of those felt interdependences which make sharing with other members of the same community a positive component of a payoff.

317 Some models of the Balance of Power system assume that in some contexts, for example, in 18th and 19th century Europe, the felt interdependence of the sovereigns generally imposed "rules of the game" limiting the permissible extent of conflict, at least to assure the survival of the other major members. This is what we are suggesting to be a normal outcome of international organization war-making. These limitations, attributed variously to a feeling of common European citizenship, and/or enlightened self-interest plus the existence of an enlightened "balancing," (enforcing) power (Great Britain), etc., did not extend their influence outside Europe even for these states.

Conflicts over empire remained "total wars" for total (overseas) aims, even down to the Spanish American and Boer Wars and the two World Wars. Even in Europe a carelessly weak sovereign, like Poland, was not spared. Hitler definitely breached this European "code." See Kaplan, *System and Process in International Politics* 1957. See also Rosencrance, *op. cit.* who examines the colonial interplay. Both Riker and Morgenthau comment that the important limitations on the players came from *outside* the system and were imposed somehow as constraints. Morgenthau argues that an international morality exists. Among his examples he explores the "German" problem which, for Germany's rivals, was that since 1870, Germany is "by virtue of size and quality of population the most powerful nation in Europe." He points to Clemenceau's complaint that there are "twenty million Germans too many" and notes that this is a technically soluble problem. The fact that it was not treated as such, he contends, "reveals the same moral limitations . . . which we did not find in Hitler." Nor was it in classical times, as for example the Romans vis-à vis the Carthaginians, pp. 236–237. This may be true but this particular example suggests the risk of relying on moral limitations in the international system. The underlying "German Problem" could be traced to its large, centrally located resource base which in time Germany could regularly repopulate. The Europeans seem to have found a solution to their "German Problem" after all, while the possible "compensation" to the West Germans of a truly politically united Europe still hangs in the balance.

318 On Africa's weakness in armed strength, see also study of the British Institute of Strategic Studies, reported in *New York Times*, Nov. 6, 1966, p. 122.

319 These estimates for a South African campaign rely almost completely on material developed in Leiss, ed., *Apartheid and United Nations Collective Measures* (1965), Chapter 7. See also sources cited therein, esp. at p. 139, n. 9.

320 A much debated sale by the U.K. of Buccaneer bombers to South Africa at the time the Security Council recommended an embargo on arms sales is credited with much of the improvement. Ibid., p. 140, and see p. 140, n. 12.

321 *Ibid.*

322 *Ibid.,* p. 142.

323 *Ibid.,* p. 148 and see pp. 166–167.

324 *Ibid.,* p. 150.

325 Cited in Bloomfield, ed., *International Military Forces* 260 (1964).

326 Of total forces, the U.S. supplied 50.32% of the ground force, 85.89% of the naval force and 93.38% of the airforce. The figures for the Republic of Korea were, respectively, 40.10%, 7.45% and 5.65%. Total maximum troop involvement by 1952 was about 450,000 of which the U.S. supplied 250,000; Korea supplied 150,000 and other UN members about 50,000. See *New York Times,* May 1 and July 10, 1952; *The United States in World Affairs,* 1951, p. 82 and *ibid,* 1952, p. 190, n. 26; Goodrich and Simons, *op. cit. supra* n. 296, at 460; Goodrich, *op. cit. supra* n. 299 at 116–118.

327 For facts, figures and estimates, see *New York Times,* Oct. 1, 1966, Oct. 3, 1966 and Oct. 10, 1966 (Secy. McNamara). There are now also some 35,000 U.S. servicemen in Thailand in support of these operations. See *Dallas Morning News,* Nov. 17, 1966.

328 Stalin is reported not to have trusted or used even those multilateral organizations he set up for his own purposes in the years in which he could have dominated them. See Korbonski, "Comecon," *Int'l Conciliation,* No. 549, Sept., 1964.

329 See *New York Times,* Nov. 7, 1966.

330 See *supra* n. 19 on disputes this fall with the Congo.

331 See *Dallas Morning News,* Nov. 11, 1966, p. 1A.

332 For some further suggestions of pressure devices, see McKay, Chapter 3, in Leiss, *op. cit. supra* n. 73.

333 See generally de Fiedorowicz, "Historical Survey of the Application of Sanctions,' 22 *Trans. Grot. Soc.* 117ff. (1937).

334 See Taubenfeld and Taubenfeld, "The Economic Weapon . . . ," *1964 Am. Soc.Int'l.L.Proc.* 183.

335 Hance, chapter 6, in Leiss, *op. cit. supra* n. 73 at p. 130. See also UN and other experts cited above at n. 110, 111.

336 See, for example, *New York Times,* Nov. 6, 1966, p. 122.

337 For the declaration of Chief Lutuli, see S/5658, 20 April 1964, p. 42.

338 On the recognition of the dangers of a possible new tyranny by the majority, by others as well as the White South Africans, see remarks of the Australian representative, *UN Press Release* WS/261, 30 Sept. 1966, p. 11 ("Neither a minority nor a majority should be oppressed.").

339 One cannot but face the likelihood that for Great Britain at this time all the multiple aspects of any solution to the southern African problems promises to be especially burdensome. Britain at present probably cannot afford to support a war—incidentally aimed at the safety of a major share of her overseas assets. The feasibility of British cooperation with the UN may well have to be supported by international mutual assistance arrangements in addition to the intelligent self-discipline on the part of the major gainers, the expectant new majority rulers of South Africa and their supporters. On the present need to share out the burden of sanctions, see *UN Press Release* WS/263. 14 Oct. 1966, p. 6 (Sweden).

340 As the recent history of belated rescue missions in the Congo indicates, if it came to massive racial disorders, or mass slaughter, the British (and others as well) can be expected to be under pressure to intervene directly as rescuers. It is no less normal for the British electorate to be concerned over their "brothers" than it is for the Africans to demonstrate their interest in their kinsmen in South Africa; as Prime Minister Wilson's remarks suggest, this need not mean that they do not also recognize their more general obligations to the human race as well.

341 For other comments that they would prefer to "lack than go black," see *The Economist,* Aug. 7, 1965, p. xv.

342 For example, The Graaf plan has been described by Colin and Margaret Legum, who strongly support a unitary South Africa, as "much more equitable than that achieved in Ireland, Palestine and India." The plan is described in their book. Legum & Legum, *South Africa, Crisis for the West* 223. See also the suggestion of Jan Rabie, author of *Ons Die Afgod* (We the Idol), cited by Lelyveld, *New York Times Mag.*, Feb. 6, 1966, p. 9 at p. 47.

343 This is in fact a much easier question than those which a partition obviates, because it produces a once and for all division. These latter would include the question of what is a "fair" government to impose (a "fair" distribution system and the "good" institutional means of sustaining it for the interpersonal, interracial distribution of roles in a context of inherent scarcity of good roles over a socially divided human group) and again who will sanction failure. In the case of partition the difficult evaluation decisions have to be made only once. And there are some available, reasonable, if arbitrary, rules.

For example, there can be a division of the total value of territory and assets on a *per capita* basis, instead of "one-man, one-vote," "one-man, one-share." Though valuing these assets, including their potentials, is itself no easy matter, indeed to do it perfectly is in principle impossible, since it requires clairvoyance concerning future values, there are again many satisfactory accounting and statistical conventions for doing a reasonable, if arbitrary, asset evaluation. All countries, firms and individuals rely on these without which, for example taxes could not be calculated. For an insightful relevant comment on the "ritual" element in accounting see Boulding, *Conflict and Defense* 95 (1962).

344 Some of the economic problems sometimes raised are troublesome, but again, not necessarily insolvable. These include first the present achieved economic interdependence of the races, which seems to reduce ultimately to the claim that the white economy needs a cheap non-white labor supply and the labor supply needs their white bosses. A partition which cut the white economy back to size, which made it "poor and white," could largely end the first aspect of the economic problem. Temporary transitional massive technical assistance—which a newly independent rich Bantu South Africa could presumably well afford to support, and which the UN could provide as it has in the past, promises to make the non-white population in the new state independent in the supply of the various skilled technicians and administrators of a modern society much faster than the Republic, which bars non-white legal access to such roles. Furthermore it is reported that the Bantu experience of self-government in the Bantustans has laid a foundation in administrative skills upon which to build. The second major economic problem would be, of course, the effect of partition on foreign assets. This is clearly a political as well as an economic question. At the time of negotiation, even if the flag does not follow property officially, the capacity of threatened foreign investors to breed massive "private" intervention has been all too well demonstrated in the Congo, in Central America, etc. And, of course, where major overseas assets are involved of substantial importance to the investors' economy as is the case for Great Britain in southern Africa and even sometimes when important lobby or pressure groups' interests are involved, the flag has followed the investors (e.g., Iran, Cuba). Without examining the merits of these issues which are complex, the fact that this type of defense of investment now yields uneven success, especially in contexts where change is inevitable in the capital receiving state, suggests that these conflicts are bargainable. Only the confidence that the present government could be defended (perhaps with British help) can offer freedom from such a need to bargain by the British. This seems all the more true because British cooperation is in fact needed or preferable to British opposition by those who would gain most from a "fair" solution to the problems of South Africa. Western technical assistance, as well, is likely to be desired subsequent to victory.

345 Indeed *moderate* Arabs have recently been proposing to return to the original plan, while the others remain unyieldingly calling for the elimination of Israel. For a brief review of the inability of the UN to effectuate partition plans for Palestine and Trieste, see Jessup and Taubenfeld, *Controls for Outer Space* 74–83 (1959).

346 A rich *unitary* South Africa could afford to subsidize the export of its unwanted minorities in better style than the state of Mississippi. A partitioned South Africa could arrange for financing asset and population transfers, an arbitral court, and similar necessary transitional services.

PART TWO

THE FORUM

I. SUMMARY OF THE FORUM PROCEEDINGS

INTRODUCTION

The racial problems of southern Africa, in their international law aspects, were brought in focus at the tenth Hammarskjold Forum, held at the House of The Association of the Bar of the City of New York on December 5th, 1966. The focus was especially sharp because of the diversity of viewpoints presented. An American husband-wife team of scholars, a leading Black African diplomat, and South Africa's chief advocate in the International Court of Justice all were heard from. The timeliness of the topic was pointed out by the Moderator:

> Our subject of 'Race, Peace, Law, and Southern Africa' is particularly timely because of the events of the past weekend and today concerning the future of Rhodesia. The papers this evening report that the Cabinet of Mr. Ian Smith has rejected the terms worked out over the weekend between him and Mr. Wilson of the United Kingdom.

The American scholars, Professor HOWARD J. TAUBEN-FELD of Southern Methodist University Law School and RITA FALK TAUBENFELD, a Research Associate in political and economic studies at Southern Methodist University, concluded with respect to the areas in question that ". . . Portuguese Africa . . . seems likely, in the foreseeable future, to become independent;" that in Rhodesia ". . . the majority will some day prevail;" that ". . . there is still some room for hope for that happy phenomenon, a 'cheap' victory for the UN in South West Africa . . .;" but that ". . . international diplomatic sanctions and partial or even complete economic measures, even if backed by a credible threat of a military intervention, offer little hope for a 'cheap' South African success for the UN." Rather they urged that South Africa be partitioned into separate black and white states. To the TAUBENFELDS as outsiders, ". . . the rational move for a white South Africa that will not accept racial

155

integration would be a *fait accompli* . . . , by carving out a partition for itself. . . . It is obvious that white South Africa would not willingly elect to undergo a brutally 'fair' partition though it is repeatedly reported they might very well accept such an outcome rather than a unitary state in the face of imminent disaster.''

Partition of South Africa

That partition of a sort is already South African policy was indicated in the paper prepared for the Forum by Mr. D. P. de VILLIERS, a Senior Counsel of that country, its chief legal representative at the 1966 South West Africa case in the International Court of Justice, and a member of its delegation to the UN General Assembly in 1966. "While we are as much concerned with human rights as any other, our case is that the particular circumstances in our country virtually dictate the method to be applied in the realization of self-determination for the different population groups, viz. that each is to be treated as a separate political entity within a distinct territorial unit. It is with this object that the policy of separate development is applied in South Africa. A policy which is basically similar, in its broad approach, is also applied in South West Africa.''

South African belief in partition was made more explicit by Mr. D. C. REZELMAN, Editor of Publications of the Information Service of South Africa in New York City, who represented Mr. de VILLIERS at the Forum. "Independence was held out as the end policy of political separation, and independence for the Bantu homelands is still the policy of my Government. Is it wrong that Venda and Zulu and Xhosa should govern themselves? Is it wrong that white authority over their lands and their people should gradually be withdrawn? Surely this is a classic example of emancipating nations? . . . It happened in Ireland, White people, non-Anglo-Saxon Catholics, and Anglo-Saxon Englishmen, their destinies so different from each other . . . in effect they moved, they partitioned, they created apartheid between the two of them. . . . South Africa is a geopolitical complex with a number of disparate nations each with its own particular area of settlement. All that the South African Government has been doing in the past twenty years since the enunciation and articulation of its policies of apartheid is to give constitutional recognition to these existing national differences within areas delineated by historical processes.''

Mr. REZELMAN likened his country's Bantustans to newly independent Lesotho and Botswana: ''The South African Government is involved in exactly the same constructive process of recognizing its Bantu nations. The Kingdom of Lesotho is the traditional homeland of the Basuto people. The same with Botswana and in exactly the same way South Africa will be politically divided, not through fiat of government but because history has already divided it and now we must constitutionally recognize this. All that the South African Government at this stage of the development does is to recognize these claims of the Bantu and to go along with them as fast as is humanly possible in an extremely complex situation. To condemn separate development is to deny the Bantu self-determination.''

While the TAUBENFELDS and the South Africans thus both approved partition in principle, they differed on its application. The TAUBENFELDS asserted that, with only ''. . . 13 per cent of the land for 80 per cent of the people and . . . little of South Africa's special resource riches *** the Bantustans could not support more than a fraction of the people now allotted to them. . . .'' They appeared to prefer ''a partition which cut the white economy back to size, which made it 'poor and white' . . .'' To this Mr. REZELMAN replied that ''. . . when Ireland was partitioned, Britain didn't ask: what is a 'fair' partition of Ireland? Britain didn't say: what should we do to ensure a 'fair division of land? The land was partitioned upon the basis of historical settlement, and that is exactly the same thing that the South African Government is doing. We are not creating large ghettos and driving people in there.''

Partition of any kind was objected to by Ambassador COLLIER as a solution for South African racial problems. He commented that relegation to historic homelands would require the white South Africans to depart for Holland or England. He ''. . . was amused to hear the reference to Ireland. In the British Isles you have the Welsh, the Scot, you have the Irish, you have the English. They all live very happily together. They have one constitution. They are dif-

157

ferent people, very proud of their origins, going back to antiquity, not to talk about the United States, with people of very different backgrounds trying to live together. The crime of South Africa is that this attempt is not being made, to try to live together.''

Any factional bloodshed inside a multi-group country, such as Mr. REZELMAN pointed to in Nigeria, is, said Mr. COLLIER, ''. . . a problem we find all over the world. In Europe, . . . centuries have not solved the problems of wars amongst groups.'' However, he felt that white persons had no need to fear black majority rule in Africa. ''There has been this underlying suspicion all the time that if black rule exists in South Africa, the white population would be in danger. From the experience of independence in Africa, this thought is certainly mistaken. Nowhere in Africa today where there has been independence do we find the white elements in danger, nowhere. As a matter of fact, in every independent black African country more white people have come to live and to do business after independence than lived in these territories before independence.''

A statement to the same effect by President KENNETH KAUNDA of Zambia was quoted by the Moderator: ''Equally striking is the fact that everywhere in independent and free Africa white minorities are enjoying their life without discrimination by the majority. I have yet to find an African country where white people are subject to indignities and other inhuman practices purely on the basis of colour.''[*]

Partition in the South African form of apartheid being anathema to most of the world, the questions arise what corrective action lies within the international community's power, and upon what legal basis such action may be justified.

Availability of Force to Solve Southern Africa's Racial Problems

Ambassador COLLIER left no doubt of his continent's prevailing taste for the use of force in southern Africa. Said Mr. COLLIER, ''. . . it is only a question of time, if this

---

*UN Document A/PV. 1464 (prov.) (1966) at 31. Shortly after the Forum, President Kaunda appointed a white man as Zambia's Minister of Legal Affairs. New York Times, January 3, 1967, p. 36.

situation continues, before these African nations, when they get strong enough, will want to embark on military conflict with South Africa *** . . . the circumstances are now present . . . constituting a threat to the peace." And again, ". . . it is only a question of time before financing in all of these states gets to the point where everyone will have to agree, however reluctantly, that racial conflict is on in the African continent."

Some sources from which the tools for such racial war might come were graphically listed in Professor and Mrs. TAUBEN-FELD's Forum Working Paper. "For the African states the key question is which Major or Middle Powers would be their best ally.. . . we will confine ourselves to presenting a suggestive list of some apparently feasible alternative coalitions inside and outside the UN, which could presumably rely on the African states to furnish the bulk of the fighting men: *** I a) Africa plus China; b) Africa plus China and Communist bloc countries; II a) Africa plus U.S. and/or U.S.S.R. with possible parallel Chinese-aided insurgency," and so on.

White South Africa's answer to Black African force was given by Mr. de VILLIERS' representative, Mr. REZEL-MAN: "We have defended our nation and our country with arms before; if pressured we will do so again."

Legal Basis for Use of Force

Upon what legal grounds could South Africa be forced to change its racial policies? The TAUBENFELDS expressed the belief ". . . that a good case can be made that the deprivation of the human rights of a *racial majority* being subjugated politically, legally, economically and socially *by intent* by a racial minority is internationally unacceptable and illegal even when limited to their own homeland." Enforced compliance with such a prohibition is valid, they feel, despite the "domestic jurisdiction" limit of UN Charter Article 2(7), because ". . . in the scale of international values, as objectivized by the political organs of the international community, the human right of 'peoples' to 'self-determination' has for some decades outweighed the right of states to exclusive control of problems within their self-defined domestic jurisdiction," and such a prohibition ". . . can be viewed as a simple extension of the

159

concept of self-determination itself to apply against resident as well as foreign *racial* tyrannies." Further support for international force to compel compliance exists, said the TAUBENFELDS, because "these discriminatory acts against a racial majority are, like the intentional elimination of a racial, ethnic or religious minority for which Nazi leaders were tried, now considered 'of such a heinous character that they clearly violate basic principles of justice.' "

Ambassador COLLIER ". . . was very delighted to observe, to note that the distinguished Professor in his remarks referred to the Nuremberg trials. *** the UN of course came into existence after those trials, and much of the thinking which went into the drafting of the Charter derived inspiration from the circumstances of the times. *** the definition of crimes against humanity which was developed for the Nuremberg trials in every particular . . . could be applied to the situation in South Africa. This argument of . . . the sacredness of the sovereignty of the state . . . I find no difficulty in rejecting . . . in the context of what is happening in southern Africa."

Mr. REZELMAN was ". . . especially angered at the comparison . . . between the international effects of South African Government policy and the precedents of the Nuremberg tribunal. *** If the policies pursued by my Government are indeed similar, comparable to the policies pursued by Hitler, then today in South Africa we would have hundreds of thousands of black Africans fleeing South Africa and not entering South Africa in droves illegally as they do."

Law-Making by UN General Assembly

Aside from applying to present conduct rules established two decades ago at Nuremberg, what if any binding rules forbidding apartheid have been more recently created, and by what authority? As noted, the TAUBENFELDS believe in a process whereby rules can be "objectivized by the political organs of the international community." Ambassador COLLIER urged ". . . much attention to the constitution of the U.N., which I think includes not only the Charter but the case histories, so to speak, the resolutions which have been passed from time to time." He cited as one of such constitution-building case histories ". . . a recent resolution [in

160

which] the U.N. endorsed wars of liberation, that if persons are engaged in violence in overthrowing a colonial situation, such action should not only be recognized as proper but should in fact be encouraged and aided." The Ambassador went on to characterize the UN General Assembly's November 1966 resolution renouncing South African rule over South West Africa as a product of "the United Nations' legislative process" which had ". . . display[ed] a greater eagerness towards progressive international law making than the International Court of Justice" had shown in the July 1966 decision on South West Africa. Mr. COLLIER concluded by expressing ". . . the hope that the United Nations, through its existing legislative machinery, either through the Security Council or the General Assembly, would be able to produce that kind of consensus which would make it possible for the international community to use legal methods available to solve this problem, because if this problem is unsolved through legal means, it will unfortunately have to be resolved by other means."

The TAUBENFELD-COLLIER assertion that anti-apartheid law has been made by the General Assembly was staunchly resisted by Mr. de VILLIERS, who said: "I think it is axiomatic that there is no general rule of International Law (as distinct from ethical considerations) which prohibits a sovereign state from oppressing its own nationals." He argued however, that Ethiopia and Liberia in the South West Africa case had been unable to prove that apartheid was oppressive, and so were forced to contend for a *per se* rule, ". . . that United Nations condemnations of South African policies had created a norm to the effect, specifically, that apartheid was unlawful. The Court, it was submitted, was obliged to apply this norm without any enquiry into the factual situation in South West Africa or into the accuracy of the information upon which the United Nations had acted. From a practical point of view, this is equivalent to contending that the United Nations General Assembly possesses legislative power—a contention which not only runs counter to the clear intendment of the Charter but also to the contemplation of the authors of the resolutions relied upon." In any event, said Mr. de VILLIERS, the attempt to prove the existence of ". . . a rule which would prohibit official discrimination (or, to employ a more neutral term, 'differentiation') between different population groups even where the differentiation was intended to operate, and did in fact operate, for the benefit of the population as a whole, including the groups in question . . . was obviously doomed to failure—a formulation of this sort would render illegal systems such as the Minorities regime or provisions designed to protect the land and institutions of less advanced peoples, e.g., tribal communities in many African states, Indian groups throughout the Americas, etc.''

Mr. de VILLIERS described the international law-making process in the following terms: "At the moment the whole system functions on the basis that there is no international legislature. Apart from exceptional decisions which could be taken by the Security Council in *ad hoc* instances, the pressure which the United Nations system is intended to exert is that of persuasion, not compulsion. At the same time, depending on constructive handling, the force of persuasion may be considerable." He added that "concern about the absence of compulsive rules or measures" could be largely removed by correct understanding of "exactly what the South African Government claims to be doing," which is not to ''. . . set up or perpetuate systems which, openly and deliberately, contravene basic conceptions of morality as currently and generally holding sway in the international community." Rather, said Mr. de VILLIERS, South Africa is making ''. . . attempts at adaptation, even if gradual and even if manifesting differences as to matters of method and detail as may be considered appropriate in the particular circumstances, and designed to prevent disruption, through too rapid or too radical changes."

The South African position, according to Mr. de VILLIERS, ''. . . requires much more serious investigation than the superficial treatment usually accorded to it by adversaries at the United Nations. . . .'' The lawyer's role in the search for peaceful solution of southern Africa's racial problems could, he said, be a significant one. ''. . . if you as a body of lawyers are asked to interest yourselves in this matter, it seems to me to be fitting and proper that *you, par excellence,* should insist on a proper and impartial reconsideration and investigation of relevant facts before any further action of an international kind is decided upon. By doing so you may be making a much larger contribution to peace-keeping and the rule of law than you can probably imagine."

*　　*　　*

In presenting Professor HOWARD J. TAUBENFELD at the Forum, the Moderator made the following remarks: "Professor TAUBENFELD is the holder of three degrees from Columbia University, Bachelor of Arts, Bachelor of Laws and Doctor of Philosophy. He practiced law in New York for six years and in 1954 went to San Francisco where he both practiced law and taught at Golden Gate School of Law. He was also serving during this period as a Consultant to the School of Law of Stanford University. Since 1961 he has been a Professor of International Law and Organization at Southern Methodist University. In 1962 and 1963 he was here in New York as Visiting Research Scholar at the Carnegie Endowment for International Peace. In 1959 he published a book jointly with Judge PHILIP C. JESSUP of the International Court of Justice entitled "Controls for Outer Space." His other books and articles are too numerous to mention."

Mrs. TAUBENFELD, co-author of the Working Paper, was introduced as follows at the Forum: "Mrs. TAUBENFELD, has earned a Bachelor of Arts Degree at New York University and Master of Arts at the University of California. She and Professor TAUBENFELD, besides having jointly produced this paper, have also jointly produced not only other articles on various subjects but also three children, ranging at present from the age of two to six."

After Professor TAUBENFELD had presented the Working Paper, the Moderator introduced Ambassador COLLIER: "Our next speaker is a member of the English Bar, although his home is in Africa. He received his Bachelor of Arts degree from University College of Sierra Leone, and his Bachelor of Civil Law Degree from Durham University in England. He was called to the bar in the Middle Temple in London and is a Barrister at Law. He started his public career as City Solicitor in the community of Freetown. He practiced as a lawyer for five years prior to 1961, since which time he has been Ambassador and Permanent Representative of his country at the U.N. Since 1963 he has also served as Ambassador of his country to the United States.

"Our next speaker has represented his country in various international conferences, among them the Accra Conference in 1958; the 1960 conference on Sierra Leone's independence, where he was Constitutional and Legal Adviser; and the Parliamentary Ministers' Conference in London in 1964 and 1965, at Lagos in 1966, and in London also in 1966. In the 20th Session of the U.N. General Assembly a year ago he served as Vice President of the Assembly and at the present time he is the Chairman of the General Assembly's Committee on Decolonization, known as the 'Committee of 24' ''

II. STATEMENT OF GERSON B. O. COLLIER

Ambassador COLLIER made the following statement. "The subject before us this evening of 'Race, Peace, Law and Southern Africa' is particularly relevant at this time; what with the recent news we have from London, I think the timing of this forum was very, very apposite.

"The importance of law in the solution of international tensions and disputes cannot be overstated. The clear alternative to outright war and continued hostility amongst nations and groups of people in disagreement on particular issues can only be a serious effort to use peaceful methods to reach agreement, if people do not wish to resort to war. The alternative can only be this attempt to reach solutions of these problems by peaceful means.

"The process of such peaceful methods ought to have its basis in law. Unfortunately, public international law has not been developed to such an extent as to produce ready-made answers to all the problems which plague nations even if public international law had been established to provide these useful guidelines. The machinery for applying these principles does not now exist.

"When the U.N. came into existence after the second World War as the successor of the abortive League of Nations, the intent was largely to establish an organization through which international conflict could be prevented and the peace preserved. An important organ of the U.N. organization was conceived in the International Court of Justice. The hope certainly was the International Court of Justice would furnish legality to actions of the U.N. politically and otherwise through advisory opinions. Another function of the Court was to adjudicate amongst parties and nations who submitted to its jurisdiction.

"After twenty years of eventful existence, the U.N. is still with us as a force for the preservation of world peace, and indeed as the conscience of the world and a hope of mankind. In many areas it has failed to meet the expectations of troubled humanity. In many areas it has also failed to handle satisfactorily problems with which it has grappled. But in many areas, happily enough, it has managed to preserve the peace and at least prevent problems from escalating and thus endangering world peace.

"Indeed, through the years the possibilities of the U.N. as a powerful force in international affairs have been expanded. In the immediate aftermath of the last war at a time when men were more concerned with preserving the peace through a parent club of victors, when men were also desperately anxious to remove the causes of international war, the organs of the U.N. were clearly conceived to meet the demand of an adequate peace-keeping machinery. Further, because the fires of the last war had been kindled by a question of human rights when civilized humanity and indeed all of humanity had been shocked and ashamed by the evils of racism which the horrors of Nazi tyranny had revealed, the U.N. came to adopt as one of its more important areas of activity the eradication of colonialism in all its forms.

"Necessarily, to achieve the ultimate removal of all forms of colonialism, the attention of the U.N. has been directed in the first instance to those situations where traditional or classical colonialism exist at their worst. Thus we have seen in a short span of a dozen or so years many nations liberated from the shackles of colonialism to take their places as sovereign, independent states in the world community. Thus success has given impetus to the U.N.'s activities in this area and today it could properly be said that the most dramatic involvement of the U.N. in the problems of humanity has been in the field of colonialism. It has brought a new dimension to the possibilities of an international organization, thereby raising the prestige of the organization as a force for good in our time.

165

"Closely linked to the question of colonialism, unfortunately, has been the problem of race. Without going at this stage into the reasons for this, let us simply say that colonialism and racism have been working hand in hand through the centuries and we find in almost all of the areas of the world where traditional colonialism is most rampant, racism and racial discrimination in close attendance. In Africa we still find in spite of the great movement of decolonization of recent times the last bastions of colonialism in defiant posture.

"The area which has been described for the purpose of this forum as southern Africa comprises the so-called Portuguese territories of Mozambique and Angola, Southern Rhodesia and, of course, the racist Republic of South Africa. You could almost draw a line across that part of the African continent. It seems that the movement of decolonization which has been sweeping through the African continent from the north, west and east, has stopped short at this line and here we find the problem of race, of peace, and of law in southern Africa posing the greatest problems.

"At the U.N. today more time is given to problems which this situation has posed than to any other set of problems. It is right that it should be so, because it seems to me that the future of the organization as an instrument for the preservation of peace is involved. Unfortunately, or fortunately, depending on how we look at it, in the world of the middle 20th century no one could ignore the problems of race. Indeed, it may well be that when future historians come to write about this period they will describe it as a period of racial confrontation.

"We see these conflicts boiling to fever point all over our world today. In Europe, in Asia, in Africa, and indeed, in the United States men and women are suffering disabilities and nursing hatreds mainly because of skin pigmentation. Under these circumstances, the U.N.—in whose Charter are enshrined 'faith in fundamental human rights, in the dignity and worth of the human person, in the equal rights of men and women and of nations large and small'—the U.N. cannot fail to accept its responsibility to admonish, to cajole and, indeed, to condemn those nations still persisting in preserving colonialism and thus violating fundamental human rights.

166

"To what further extent the U.N. as an organization conceived for the preservation of world peace and the maintenance of international law could go in securing these fundamental human rights is one of the problems before us. One of the sacred provisions of the U.N. Charter is the respect for the sovereignty of states. Indeed, Professor TAUBENFELD in his very well prepared Working Paper has dwelt at great length on this problem. But I think it is also important to remember that side by side with this concept, this principle of the sovereignty, the sacredness of the sovereignty of states, has also developed, particularly in recent times, the idea and indeed the importance of respect for fundamental human rights.

"I was very delighted to observe, to note that the distinguished Professor in his remarks referred to the Nuremberg traisl. It seems to me very important that attention be given to the Nuremberg trials because the U.N. of course came into existence after those trials, and much of the thinking which went into the drafting of the Charter derived inspiration from the circumstances of the times.

"We were told that the Nazi atrocities were terrible. We were told that the actions of the Nazis constituted a crime against humanity. Therefore, they were heinous, they were offensive to decency and these persons who have been guilty of such action should be condemned and indeed they were condemned. That to me was the hallmark of this development of international thought as to the level to which one could uplift human rights. And that thinking continued after the U.N. came into existence. Indeed, the famous Declaration of Human Rights subscribed to by all nations—and I must say championed to a very commendable extent by the United States delegation—has to some extent constituted the Magna Charta of thinking on human rights in international circles.

"If it was possible to justify the Nuremberg trials and the judgment from those trials on the principle of crimes against humanity committed within the jurisdiction of the sovereign state, using judges who were drawn from countries outside that particular sovereign state, it seems to me that the principle had come to receive a certain respectability and a certain authority in legal international circles. And if the principle was received with such approval at that time, I do not see

167

why, today, some people find it difficult to understand why the principle of the dignity of human rights could not be applied in the situation of South Africa, because the definition of crimes against humanity which was developed for the Nuremberg trials could in every particular, and indeed to a vast extent, be applied to the situation in South Africa.

"This argument of the sovereignty and the sacredness of the sovereignty of the state is forceful and to some extent convincing, but I find no difficulty in rejecting it in the context of what is happening in southern Africa. I believe that this principle of sovereignty and the need for non-intervention is valid only insofar as the practices within particular states are not likely to injure the relations of such states within the international community. Indeed, states must be made responsible, and here I am quoting from Professor TAUBENFELD, to the international community when their actions cause substantial international effects. The U.N. as an organization for the preservation of international peace can only rise to its noblest expectations if it demonstrates a desire to block those steps which in fact militate against the preservation of international peace.

"This brings me to the second point on this question of law, peace and southern Africa. The U.N.'s charter describes circumstances under which the Security Council, which is the policing organ of the U.N., can act if there is a threat to the peace. When African nations have brought this matter of South Africa before the U.N. Security Council calling for action under the Charter under Articles 41 and 42 of Chapter VII of the Charter, it has been argued by some of our friends that the circumstances do not now exist, circumstances which could well be regarded as a threat to the peace, implying, of course, by that argument that unless there is such a threat to the peace, these relevant articles of the Charter could not be invoked.

"It seems to me that presented with the situation we find in southern Africa today when all the African states, the black African states, have declared their attitude to this problem through their own individual pronouncements and through pronouncements of the Organization of African Unity, as has been recognized in the Working Paper, it is only a question of time, if this situation continues, before these African na-

168

tions, when they get strong enough, will want to embark on military conflict with South Africa. It is only a question of time. Indeed, these nations, today, have declared their willingness to aid all sorts of liberation struggles within these territories.

"In the face of this reality one would think that the circumstances are now present which could well be regarded as constituting a threat to the peace. It seems to me most unfortunate that the international community should wait until blood is shed, because that can be the only next step for those who think that the threat does not now exist whereby the U.N. can consider itself, within its own Charter, able to interfere. There could well be persuasive argument for intervening at this stage when this threat has not developed into wide scale bloodshed.

"There is evidence of fighting in Portuguese territories, in Mozambique and Angola, and in South Africa, because we cannot ignore the incidents of Sharpeville and other places. Indeed, even in Southern Rhodesia one might reflect why Mr. Smith has been so anxious to preserve a blanket of censorship and secrecy as to what is happening there, if there were not in fact fighting and a threat of overthrow of the regime.

"In Chapter VII of the Charter of the U.N., where acts with respect to threats to the peace, breaches of the peace and acts of aggression are considered, direct responsibility is given to the Security Council to determine the existence of any threat to the peace, breach of the peace, and acts of aggression. Authority is also given to that chapter to the Security Council to decide what measures should be taken to maintain or restore international peace and security. The question in this situation seems to me to be whether international peace is in fact threatened by the continued truculence and intransigence of the colonial powers and the Government of the Republic of South Africa in that part of the continent.

"My submission is that there is a clear threat to international peace in the situation in southern Africa. The world is fully aware of the attitude of all the African states on this question. The U.N. has in fact endorsed the relentless determination of the African states to eradicate colonialism from the face of their continent. Indeed, the U.N. has in a significant resolution recognized the legality of just wars and of wars of liberation generally.

"After all, if the U.N. is the organ, the international organ of our times, it is useful to pay much attention to the constitution of the U.N., which I think includes not only the Charter but the case histories, so to speak, the resolutions which have been passed from time to time. In a recent resolution the U.N. endorsed wars of liberation, that if persons are engaged in violence in overthrowing a colonial situation, such action should not only be recognized as proper, but should in fact be encouraged and aided.

"And as a matter of fact, the U.N. in recent times has gone much further by giving aid to refugees, by in fact providing educational opportunities for persons engaged in these liberation struggles that have had cause to leave their homeland. This important decision of the United Nations has done much to encourage and hearten liberation fighters all over Africa, and it is only a question of time before financing in all of these states gets to the point where everyone will have to agree, however reluctantly, that racial conflict is on in the African continent. In such a development there will be no knowing how far the conflagration will extend. Should the international community wait until that much blood has been spilled before it becomes aware of this threat to international peace?

"Another problem in this matter is, of course, how should the international community proceed to tackle this problem, in the face of the defiant and determined attitude of the colonial powers and of the government of the Republic of South Africa, without violating the principle of sovereignty of independent states? It seems to me that a prior consideration would be the acceptance of the consensus by all nations, particularly the permanent members of the Security Council, that such action is desirable and just.

"We have precedents in United Nations practice for investing such actions with legality. I shall not say more than to refer to the United Nations action in Korea, where the U.N. was involved in a struggle authorized by its own resolution, and this intervention was made in defense of certain principles. I will not go into an examination of the validity of that intervention. I am just stating the fact that there are precedents of such United Nations intervention. Granted this

170

intervention in Korea was buttressed and made possible by the arms and troops of the United States, a powerful member of the United Nations, and it was possible for action to take place in Korea without much conflict within the United Nations for the crucial vote took place at a time when other great powers were temporarily absent from their seat at the United Nations. But the qualification really needed was the legality, if I may use that word, that the United Nations resolution gave to that action.

"There is another example in the Congo. The United Nations has intervened in the Congo. That was of course a different situation because it was not a situation of one big power providing most of the forces and most of the necessities for war. It was a situation where many small states in part at least supplied forces and materials for war. But that action also had the legality which United Nations resolutions gave it. In the same Congo, not too long ago, certain Western powers, the United States, Belgium, the United Kingdom, in the name of human rights used paratroopers in Stanleyville to rescue persons whose human rights were endangered. It seems to me that the international community has conveniently not found the same moral consciousness to want to intervene in similar situations like Southern Rhodesia where human rights have been trampled upon by Mr. Smith's minority racist regime.

"If the international community can accept a consensus and be of the mood to justify intervention within a particular state, as I have cited instances where this has been done before, then we will be left with only one question: how can it actually be done?

"It can be done by a resolution or resolutions of the Security Council. Indeed, we have seen in very recent times a great precedent established by the British Government when they took the question of Rhodesia to the Security Council in April of this year and got the Security Council to pass a resolution which clearly falls under Article 41 of the United Nations Charter authorizing the British to use force, if necessary, to prevent ships off the coast at Beira from unloading their cargo of oil in Portuguese Mozambique—oil destined for Rhodesia. So it seems to me that it is possible for the United Nations to pass resolutions which would give this

171

authority to nations in a position to do so to use sanctions in the first instance, and if sanctions fail, to use force, if necessary, to bring about the intention of the international community.

"Of course, the prior consideration is whether the international community is as of now ready to produce that intention. We have in this context to be aware of certain realities, that there are major partners of South Africa who have told us, for instance, the British Prime Minister has stated publicly that he will not—his Government will not do anything at this stage that will injure South Africa. It seems to me that if we do not even consider the other permanent members, United Kingdom is a permanent member of the Security Council, and what with the existence of the veto, you can see the difficulties at this stage in getting the Security Council to pass any meaningful resolution for this desirable intervention.

"I only want to end on this note: if you agree that such an international consensus could be produced, we will only be left with the question of what active measures should be adopted to challenge the situation in South Africa within the legally acceptable context. Those, of course, who had reposed much confidence in the International Court of Justice as presently constituted, as a custodian of international law and as a source of progressive reflection of the development in international thinking were rudely shocked by the clearly partisan and purely political decision recently handed down by the International Court of Justice on the South West African case. I would prefer to dismiss this particular exercise in futility by approving with great emphasis the remarkable and historic comment in his very learned minority judgment by Mr. Justice Jessup of the United States when he said, amongst other things, that the majority judgment had no foundation in law.

"I think it is useful to emphasize that the so-called machinery of development of international law such as it is today seems to have broken down. No wonder the United Nations was so swift in taking direct action on this question of South West Africa. We were very gratified to find that important members of the United Nations, permanent members of the Security Council like the United States, the Soviet Union, voted for this resolution, thereby allowing the United

Nations' legislative process to display a greater eagerness towards progressive international law-making than the International Court of Justice had done.

"Finally, the problems in southern Africa will be resolved one day. It should be the hope of all civilized humanity that they will be resolved peacefully. And if we hope that they will be resolved peacefully, we ought to have great confidence, great reliance on law, legal process, either through the International Court or through that law-implementing machinery which the Security Council provides. It is a pity as has been noted on many occasions that the International Court of Justice in 1966 was not willing to reflect the evolution of thought on this matter.

"Let us hope that the United Nations, through its existing legislative machinery, either through the Security Council or the General Assembly, would be able to produce that kind of consensus which would make it possible for the international community to use the legal methods available to solve this problem, because if this problem is unsolved through legal means, it will unfortunately have to be resolved by other means.

*　　*　　*

After Ambassador COLLIER's statement, the Moderator introduced Mr. de VILLIERS, and his representative, Mr. REZELMAN. "The third principal speaker, the one who is present with us by proxy, Mr. DAVID P. de VILLIERS, who holds the title of Senior Counsel, comparable to the English Queen's Counsel, was born 47 years ago in Paarl in the Western Cape Province of South Africa. He attended schools there and went to Stellenbosch University where he obtained B.A. and LL.B. degrees. He started practicing law in Capetown and has been involved in a variety of constitutional cases in South Africa. He has published books and articles on aspects of South African law and also on the implications of the South West Africa judgment. During the last six years, he has been the South African Government's advocate in the World Court Case concerning South West Africa.

173

"Mr. de VILLIERS was a delegate to the 21st session of the General Assembly, the current session, where he presented South Africa's main policy statement on South West Africa. On October 27, 1966, the General Assembly adopted a resolution supported by the United States deciding that the mandate of South Africa over South West Africa was '. . . terminated, that South Africa has no other right to administer the Territory and that henceforth South West Africa comes under the direct responsibility of the United Nations.' Shortly thereafter Mr. de VILLIERS was recalled by his Government for consultations preparatory to the Special Session of the General Assembly which is to be held not later than April 1967 to hear the report of an *Ad Hoc* Committee on 'practical means by which South West Africa should be administered, so as to enable the people of the Territory to exercise the right of self-determination and to achieve independence . . .'

"Before leaving New York, Mr. de VILLIERS was kind enough to tell me that he would send us a paper to be presented by one of his colleagues. We are fortunate in having here tonight for the purpose of presenting Mr. de VILLIERS' paper, as well as to present additional remarks of his own, Mr. DIRK C. REZELMAN of the South African Information Service.

"Mr. REZELMAN was born in Port Elizabeth in the Eastern Cape Province of South Africa. His family have been in South Africa since 1680. He attended schools in the Cape and Transvaal Provinces and obtained a law degree from Rhodes University in Grahamstown. As a student he worked for 'Die Oosterlig', an Afrikaans language newspaper in Port Elizabeth, and then moved to Natal, a predominantly English speaking part of South Africa, where he helped to establish 'Die Nataller', a weekly Afrikaans language newspaper. While in Natal he obtained the degree of B.A. with honors at Natal University, specializing in literary stylistics and comparative literature. After lecturing at Natal College, he joined the South African Department of Information as Associate Editor of its magazine 'South African Panorama'. He was transferred in 1962 to New York as Editor of Publications for the Information Service. He has published many articles in both English and Afrikaans in South African magazines and newspapers."

174

III. STATEMENTS OF DIRK C. REZELMAN AND DAVID P. DE VILLIERS

"Mr. Carey, Mr. Ambassador, ladies and gentlemen, South Africans always find themselves appealing. Tonight I am going to make a few appeals. First of all, I am going to appeal for, in essence, equal time. I have, in effect, President Kaunda of Zambia against me; I have Professor TAUBENFELD'S learned expose of conditions in South Africa and southern Africa; and I have the most articulate analysis by His Excellency, the Ambassador of Sierra Leone.

"I have a few comments on my own behalf to make to place this question into proper perspective. I believe that we should deal with facts as they are, not as we would imagine them to be. We must deal with realities. When we deal with questions of law, particularly, we must deal with things as they really exist, not as we project them.

"I am especially angered at the comparison, even if it was implicit, that was made between the international effects of South African Government policy and the precedents of the Nuremberg tribunal. I believe if one takes this analogy a bit further and analyzes why the Nuremberg tribunal took place, it doesn't require much imagination to see that at the time of the rise of the Third Reich hundreds of thousands of people of Jewish descent were fleeing Germany.

"If the policies pursued by my Government are indeed similar, comparable to the policies pursued by Hitler, than today in South Africa we would have hundreds of thousands of black Africans fleeing South Africa and not entering South Africa in droves illegally as they do. My Government resents this analogy very deeply, and I believe that a kind of consensus is being sought upon the basis of this false comparison. It's something that should not be pursued in a body as distinguished as yours. On the other hand, I find myself thinking of the Old Testament story of King Ahab, who I think was not really interested in how Naboth administered his vineyard. When people with motives that are suspect criticize South Africa, we tend to write off this criticism. In the same way most African states today care very little for what we say the position really is in the Republic of South Africa. In the same way also I could add here how one might regard cer-

175

tain stories about the state of Israel if they emanate from Arab sources, or vice-versa.

"The Working Paper to my mind does not try to resolve the issues facing South Africans. Prof. TAUBENFELD's thesis appears to me to raise issues as to how the white nation in my country can be most effectively brought to its knees. A fruitful dialogue can only be initiated with the authors of the Working Paper if they accept our thesis that, aware of the whole range of problems facing South Africa, we are not under any circumstances prepared to commit national suicide. We have defended our nation and our country with arms before; if pressured we will do so again.

"We find it regrettable that one particular incident out of South Africa's varied history, that of Sharpeville where rioters died while attacking the police, should be used and belabored consistently for six years. In the rest of the African continent our critics themselves are unable to control the conflicts, often bloody, between groups, the tribal disparities, and the ideological dichotomies that exist within their own states. The rivalries in the Sudan between Arab and Negro are very real factors. Again, they might be unpalatable, but they do exist. In Ruanda and Burundi within the last few years tens of thousands of people have died in tribal uprisings. The recent bloody rioting in Nigeria is no advertisement for bundling different tribes together under one government.

"Many black African spokesmen are today employing the exclusive language of a previous dark age and destroying all dialogue. They refer to "their" Africa and perpetuate the myth that only black men may have rights in that continent. Africa, for heaven's sake, is big enough to accommodate all those divergent groups. It always has. Moses was an African. One of the men who drew up the Charter of the United Nations, Jan Smuts, was an African. Ian Smith and John Vorster are Africans. The continent is big enough certainly to accommodate many races and cultures if due respect is paid to the separate identity of each people. Many of these spokesmen start with black racism which we find directed against South Africans and South African spokesmen in particular. This is something which should be very critically surveyed in the United States of America.

176

"I would again like to apologize on Mr. de VILLIERS' behalf for his absence here tonight, and I would now like to read his comments into the records of the Forum."

COMMENT BY D. P. DE VILLIERS, S.C.:—

"I am grateful for the opportunity to make a contribution, from the South African point of view, to the discussions at this Forum. It is naturally impossible to comment fully on the many interesting matters raised in the lengthy Working Paper, which testifies to great industry, ability, and keen thought on the part of its authors. This is so both because of the time limit of thirty minutes, and because the last instalment of the Working Paper only reached me on the last day before the scheduled despatch of my contribution from South Africa. Had it not been for my colleagues Muller and Grosskopf, who made this a joint effort even to the extent of writing about two-thirds of the text, and to whom I am exceedingly grateful, this written comment could never have been furnished in time.

"I must confine myself to brief consideration of certain main aspects of the subject. It will be noticed that I concentrate on South Africa and South West Africa: I cannot speak with any authority on Rhodesia or the Portuguese territories. And despite my professional association with the South African Government in regard to the South West Africa case and in regard to the current session of the General Assembly, I speak on this occasion in my personal capacity, as a lawyer to respected colleagues. My only regret is that I am unable to be present in person.

"The Working Paper invites consideration of a topic having both political and legal implications, namely, what can be done within the present international system to compel certain countries in Southern Africa to abandon domestic policies considered to be in conflict with so-called currently accepted international standards or norms.

"In raising this question the authors of the Working Paper proceed from a fundamental premise, and that is that the policy of apartheid, or separate development, as practised in South Africa and South West Africa, contravenes some of the most fundamental standards of currently agreed international

177

morality, and denies to the peoples concerned, or at least sections of them, certain basic human rights. In particular it is said that they are denied the right of self-determination and of non-discrimination on racial and ethnic lines.

"Indeed, the Working Paper describes South Africa's policy as a 'tyranny . . . employed by a racial minority intent on retaining exclusive political control of the nation itself, to enchain a racial majority with a minority of political power and thus delimit their political and economic roles and their lives'.

"In stating this conclusion the authors rely not on personal knowledge of circumstances and conditions in these territories, but on critical comment and condemnation emanating from other sources, including organs and agencies of the United Nations. Although brief mention is made of statements by South African representatives on the objectives underlying the policy of Separate Development, it can hardly be said that justice is done in the Paper to that cause. The adverse conclusions are stated as if they are beyond controversy. Indeed, the authors say 'this case does not have to be made now'. This is my first point of comment, and one of basic importance.

"It is true that the policy of apartheid, or separate development, has been widely criticized and even condemned not only by large majorities in the United Nations but also outside the organization; but that is only one side of the picture. There is also another side represented by numbers of responsible persons who consider that a policy of separate development is the only realistic approach to the particular circumstances prevailing in South Africa and South West Africa with a view to a just solution in the interests of all concerned —in other words, precisely with a view to the most equitable satisfaction of their human rights.

"As a body of lawyers you will agree that if there is to be an objective and impartial enquiry into the matter under discussion, all relevant facts must be considered to see whether there is a wrong, and if so, to establish its precise nature and scope before exploring the possibilities of remedial action.

"Time does not permit me to enter into any detailed factual discussion, or to deal with each of the so-called 'reported intolerable conditions' in South Africa and South West Africa

178

as are mentioned in the Working Paper. To those of you who are really interested in the problem, who seek the truth and wish to see both sides of the picture, I recommend a reading of the pleadings and record of oral proceedings in the South West Africa case. Although that case was concerned with policies and conditions in South West Africa it dealt also with the development and implementation of the policy of separate development in South Africa itself.

"In making that recommendation I must at the same time warn you that the Court record is a lengthy one and that a proper study thereof would be time-consuming. But you will agree that a true view of the relevant facts is of absolute and fundamental importance. A brief summary is to be found in the recently published book 'Ethiopia and Liberia versus South Africa'; I am sure the South African Permanent Mission to the U.N. or the South African Information Office would gladly assist you to obtain copies. Though the summary is brief, it should at least indicate to you that the facts cannot unquestionably be assumed to be as stated in the Working Paper.

"I cannot in this discussion attempt even a brief review of the case presented by South Africa to the Court. At most I can point out certain issues of basic importance.

"In the first place I must emphasize that in order to appreciate the real objectives of the policy there must be a clear understanding of the particular circumstances prevailing in South Africa and South West Africa, and particularly of the composition of their populations. In South Africa there are a number of different ethnic groups, each with its own traditions, cultures and language. Historically the groups developed separately from each other, occupying to a large extent separate areas, each group regarding itself as distinct from the others, and desiring on the whole to be treated as such. Having regard to these differences between the various groups and to the history of their relation to one another, South Africans are generally convinced that they are unassimilable and cannot be treated as a single political unit. But we do not plead these circumstances as justification for denial of self-determination to any of the groups. While we are as much concerned with human rights as any other, our case is that the particular circumstances in our country virtually dictate

179

the method to be applied in the realization of self-determination for the different population groups, viz. that each is to be treated as a separate political entity within a distinct territorial unit. It is with this object that the policy of separate. development is applied in South Africa. A policy which is basically similar, in its broad approach, is also applied in South West Africa. But this is so not for the reason suggested in the Working Paper, namely, that of extending to the Territory an ideological concept. The reason is simply that the particular circumstances of the Territory present broadly similar problems. The existence there, as in South Africa, of a number of distinct and unassimilable population groups does not realistically permit of an integrated political system within a single territorial unit.

"In both cases the ultimate aim is self-determination for the different groups, separate development being the method adopted to attain that end.

"The charge that the policy of apartheid or separate development constitutes a denial of the basic human right of self-determination is therefore unfounded, and so also is the more extreme charge that the policy is intended to keep a racial minority in perpetual domination of a majority, politically or otherwise. One can hardly believe that a system of territorial separation would have been devised if that were the object.

"Turning now to a consideration of the charge that the policy is one of discrimination on racial and ethnic lines, I must at the outset plead for clarity as to what is intended to be conveyed by the expression 'discrimination'.

"If what is intended to be conveyed is that the policy is one of differentiation between persons by reason of membership in an ethnic group, then there is no denial that that is the case, and that in implementation of the policy rights, duties and burdens are allotted on the basis of membership of an ethnic group. But then the question immediately arises whether there is any international legal norm or standard which outlaws such differentiation *per se*. This matter was dealt with very fully in the South West Africa case and I invite you to study the arguments and evidence presented in that regard. I shall return to this topic later in my comment.

"If, however, the essence of the charge is *oppression* of certain population groups—as indeed is the case sought to be made in the Working Paper which refers to South Africa as a 'pigmentocracy', to allegations of arbitrary treatment of certain sections of the community, to subordination of the interest and rights of the great majority of the people of South Africa to the preference of a minority, and to alleged discriminatory treatment of the Native population of South West Africa—then again I must in all fairness ask that you consider all the facts before accepting that a case of oppression has been established.

"Implementation of a policy of separate development must of necessity in certain stages of development cause hardships for members of some groups who temporarily find themselves in areas reserved for other groups. But it is a complete distortion of the situation to represent the policy of separate development in South Africa and South West Africa as operating in such a way that in the allotment of rights and burdens, the white people always got the right and the non-whites are saddled with the burdens.

"Such a charge was in fact made in the South West Africa case with respect to the Natives of the Territory and was based mainly on false and distorted versions of fact furnished to the United Nations and accepted by majorities in that organization. After the matter had been fully canvassed in the pleadings before the Court, this charge was abandoned by the Applicants.

"Space does not permit me to re-plead the case here. But if you as a body of lawyers are asked to interest yourselves in this matter, it seems to me to be fitting and proper that *you, par excellence,* should insist on a proper and impartial reconsideration and investigation of relevant facts before any further action of an international kind is decided upon. By doing so you may be making a much larger contribution to peace-keeping and the rule of law than you can probably imagine.

"This brings us to the next aspect on which I wish to comment, viz. the international law-creating process, insofar as relevant to the subject under discussion. Again there is a background of fact which requires to be duly noted for purposes of perspective.

181

"The authors of the Working Paper state that the 'concept of self-determination as a politically achieved "right" ends, in the eyes of many (or perhaps all) of the Afro-Asian countries, and certainly of the Soviet bloc, with the decolonization, "old style".' This statement provides the key to the situation in southern Africa and the attitude of the world thereto. In international politics the opposition to the policies of Portugal, Rhodesia and South Africa arises, not primarily from the nature of the policies themselves, but because they are regarded as forming part and parcel of a colonial system. Thus the major (although sometimes unexpressed) complaint against the Governments concerned is not that they govern badly, but that they govern at all. To rationalize this situation, various methods are employed, of which one has been mentioned already, viz. a distortion of the factual situation in an attempt to bring it within the ambit of generally accepted principles of law or ethics. As noted, this was attempted in the South West Africa case. When the Applicants were put to the proof of their factual allegations, they switched their position and sought to find a legal norm which would render illegal certain admitted aspects of South African policy in South West Africa. This is a further method commonly employed in seeking a valid legal basis for condemning South African policies, and the problems encountered by the Applicants in the South West Africa case effectively demonstrate the limitations of this expedient.

"The major problems in establishing the existence of a norm of this sort are two-fold: firstly, to define the content of the norm, and, secondly, to identify the source of law which gave rise to it. The problem of definition arises essentially from the circumstance that the whole process is one of rationalization— an expedient is sought to remedy an *ad hoc* situation in southern Africa which is regarded for political reasons as undesirable. The result is that any general formulation of a norm suffers from one or other defect: either it fails to cover the facts in southern Africa, or else it covers too many other situations as well.

"Thus, for example, unconditional insistence on a rule of one man one vote would indubitably strike at the political systems in southern Africa, but would at the same time affect a host of dictatorships, monarchies, peoples' democracies, military juntas, etc., throughout the world.

"This problem becomes no easier of solution when the attention is directed to questions of discrimination. It is, of course, fairly easy to define a rule which would prohibit any form of oppressive discrimination against certain sections of the population. Application of such a rule would, however, require proof of oppression, a task which the Applicants in the South West Africa case did not see fit to essay. Instead they sought to formulate a rule which would prohibit official discrimination (or, to employ a more neutral term, 'differentiation') between different population groups even where the differentiation was intended to operate, and did in fact operate, for the benefit of the population as a whole, including the groups in question. This attempt was obviously doomed to failure—a formulation of this sort would render illegal systems such as the Minorities regime or provisions designed to protect the land and institutions of less advanced peoples, e.g. tribal communities in many African states, Indian groups throughout the Americas, etc.

"It is consequently not surprising that there has arisen a tendency in recent times to single out South Africa for *ad hoc* condemnation without attempting to define any generally applicable norm which has allegedly been contravened. Typical examples are to be found in Article 5 of the U.N. Declaration on the Elimination of all forms of Racial Discrimination, G.A. Res. 1904 (XVIII) of November 20, 1963, and in Article III of the International Convention on the Elimination of all Forms of Racial Discrimination, G. A. Resolution 2106 (XX) of December 20, 1965.

"In short, the only workable norm would be either one relating specifically to South Africa, or one prohibiting discrimination only when it is injurious or oppressive. In the South West African case, the Applicants were ultimately forced to opt for the former. They contended that United Nations condemnations of South African policies had created a norm to the effect, specifically, that apartheid was unlawful. The Court, it was submitted, was obliged to apply this norm without any enquiry into the factual situation in South West Africa or into the accuracy of the information upon which the United Nations had acted. From a practical point of view,

183

this is equivalent to contending that the United Nations General Assembly possesses legislative power—a contention which not only runs counter to the clear intendment of the Charter but also to the contemplation of the authors of the resolutions relied upon.

"The possibility of a norm which prohibits injurious or oppressive discrimination must be taken more seriously—at least in theory—since, as noted, the premise that the South African policies as a fact discriminate in an injurious or oppressive manner cannot be assumed to be correct. But even on a purely abstract plane, there is at least extreme difficulty in affirming the existence of a *legal* norm of this content. I think it is axiomatic that there is no general rule of International Law (as distinct from ethical considerations) which prohibits a sovereign state from oppressing its own nationals. I leave out of account, for the moment, the suggestion in the Working Paper regarding 'pathological cases'. Of course, a prohibition on the oppression by a state of its own nationals may be assumed in defined respects by treaty or convention. A number of examples exist, such as the European Convention for the Protection of Human Rights and Fundmental Freedom. Obligations of a similar type may be created in respect of particular international regimes, such as the Mandate System or the Trusteeship System. Further than this point International Law has not proceeded. As demonstrated in the Working Paper, generally applicable rules protecting human rights, including freedom from injurious discrimination, are still limited to non-legal statements of principle.

"It is interesting to observe that the authors of the Working Paper, in searching for a norm which would be appropriate for conditions in Southern Africa, as they see them suggest a content which is directed against tyranny and *oppressive* discrimination. They do so towards the end of the Working Paper, evidently as part of what they earlier call 'some possible approaches to a solution . . . and their implications for the international system'. This is the final aspect on which I wish to comment briefly.

"Throughout the Working Paper the accent in regard to possible international action falls heavily on *compulsion*—i.e. on the generation of rules that would *bind* the South African Government, preferably without its consent, and on machinery for *enforcement* and the like. Such an approach flows naturally from the factual premise which I have repeatedly mentioned and which ascribes to the South African Government a rigid policy and course of deliberate tyranny and oppression.

"It is not surprising that the search for a legal basis for compulsion has turned out to be an unrewarding effort. In substance the authors bring the matter no further than two somewhat tentative suggestions, which on their own acknowledgement would require important changes in the legal and enforcement systems of the world in order to be of real practical value.

"The first suggestion is that the South African situation may be brought under a possible special rule for so-called 'clearly pathological cases' of 'shocking crimes' against mankind, rendering the perpetrator liable on a non-censensual basis. It is in this context that the authors suggest the possible norm which I have mentioned. I do not intend to enter into all the legal intricacies of the suggestion, but will confine myself to certain basic considerations. Firstly it will be observed that the suggested norm is also tailor-made for Southern Africa. The authors correctly insist upon specific content in implementable form for norms sought to be applied in practice. They thereupon proceed to provide such a content as being directed against a tyranny of a minority, explicitly intended to keep a majority in permanent subjection purely on the discriminatory basis of the pigment of their skins. In other words, their definition rests essentially on the very premise of tyranny and oppression which the Applicants in the South West Africa case were unable to establish and forced to abandon. Failing the factual premise, the formulation therefore fails to achieve anything. A second notable feature, emerging on a more abstract approach, is this: even if one were for the sake of argument to assume the correctness of the factual premise, the Working Paper leaves the basic logical and ethical question unanswered—why would White oppression of Black in southern Africa be more reprehensible than the numerous other examples of oppression in Africa and the world, often amounting to expulsion or even extermination, some of which have been noted in the Working Paper? The answer has, of course, already been given. The issue in regard to southern Africa is a political one, which is in its real essence not concerned with questions of human rights. This is in itself a strong red light for lawyers against becoming involved, as lawyers, in the suggestion of the authors.

"The second tentative suggestion is that the International Court could adopt a more 'aggressive, law-making' role, similar to that attributed by the authors to the United States Supreme Court; and the majority Judges in the 1966 Judgment in the South West Africa case are criticized for 'timorous conduct' and the like. As to the general suggestion, the authors virtually answer it themselves. I may merely add that American lawyers are on the whole possibly not fully conscious of the depth and intensity of the objections of lawyers of other systems against assigning anything in the nature of an 'aggressive, law-making' role to a Court of law at all. The subject is too large for proper debate on this occasion.

"As for the criticism of the 1966 majority in the International Court, I respectfully regard it as extremely unfortunate and wholly unfounded. I say so despite my strong view—contrary to the suggestions in the Working Paper—that on the substantive issues the indications favored South Africa more than the Applicants: this will be evident from what I have already said about the course of the proceedings regarding the issue of South Africa's policies.

"As to the Judgment itself, Judge Jessup's comment that it was 'completely unfounded in law' was merely an emphatic way of expressing his difference of opinion on the conclusion of law arrived at. The mere fact that an expression of dissent, however strong, was made, obviously cannot establish by itself that the conclusion was indeed wrong. On the contrary, the reasoning in favor of the conclusion is a model of lucidity, and on analysis not one of the dissenting opinions, nor the contrary reasoning in the 1962 Judgment, weighs up to it.

"Finally, the suggestion that the Judges were timorous, or acted absurdly, is an extremely strange one. It seems to mean that the Judges should not have given a Judgment in accordance with their honest opinion as to the law. Having concluded that the Applicants had no legal right or interest in the subject matter of the claims, should the Judges have disregarded that conclusion and adjudicated on the substantive aspects of the claims? The Working Paper seems to suggest

186

not only that they should have done so, but even that they should have given 'the generally expected decision', i.e. one in favor of the Applicants. I can hardly think of anything more improper, unjudicial and even dishonest. The Judges themselves gave the answer to all invitations to overstep the bounds of their judicial function. They stated, in terms well worth remembering:

> Law exists, it is said, to serve a social need: but precisely for that reason it can do so only through and within the limits of its own discipline. Otherwise it is not a legal service that would be rendered. (1966 Judgment, p. 34)

In my view the cause of international co-operation, and of advancement of international institutions, is best promoted by strict adherence to the agreed limits which exist at any particular stage of development, and by the instilling of confidence that international bodies do and will adhere to those limits. This applies not only to the International Court but to all other international bodies. At the moment the whole system functions on the basis that there is no international legislature. Apart from exceptional decisions which could be taken by the Security Council in *ad hoc* instances, the pressure which the United Nations system is intended to exert is that of persuasion, not compulsion. At the same time, depending on constructive handling, the force of the persuasion may be considerable. This is so particularly in a modern world in which constantly improving media of communication are not only shrinking distances but are also establishing ever new links of interdependence.

"Under these circumstances it becomes less and less likely that any Government would, particularly in the sphere of human relations, set up or perpetuate systems which, openly and deliberately, contravene basic conceptions of morality as currently and generally holding sway in the international community. One would rather expect attempts at adaptation, even if gradual and even if manifesting differences as to matters of method and detail as may be considered appropriate in the particular circumstances, and designed to prevent disruption, through too rapid or too radical changes. This is exactly what the South African Government claims to be doing: and it must be obvious that the claim requires much more serious investigation than the superficial treatment usually accorded to it by adversaries at the United Nations and, indeed, in the Working Paper itself. Correction in respect of this basic premise should go far towards removing the concern about the absence of compulsive rules or measures, as well as the suggested need for changes in the international systems which seem incapable of achievement in the foreseeable future. Moreover, an approach of keeping faithfully within the existing limits would facilitate and encourage processes of peaceful adaptation in countries such as South Africa and South West Africa—whereas attempts at exercising non-existent powers of enforcement could well have exactly the opposite effect, and overall disastrous consequences.''

*   *   *

Following the formal statements of the principal Forum speakers, questions and statements from the audience were received. The following question was put to Mr. REZEL-MAN: "What parliamentary representation was given to Africans in the decisions that separate representation of the races should be the South African Government official policy?'' Mr. REZELMAN replied:

"I think the basic premise underlying the question is loaded. Separate representation of the Bantu in South Africa must not be seen as an attempt to destroy the vestigial elements of representation which existed in the South African parliament for the Bantu at that time.

"True, representation in the white parliament was abolished. But direct representation in the Bantu homeland was instituted and, in the case of the Transkei, home of the Xhosa people, universal adult suffrage— 'one man, one vote' was instituted. The diaspora of the Xhosa nation were also recognized by the extension of political rights to them. For the first time they could vote for their own people in their own parliament. Does the world condemn this too when it assails apartheid? A more effective system of liaison was created through the institution of envoys from the white nation to the homelands of the Bantu. Independence was held out as the end policy of political separation, and independence for the Bantu homelands is still the policy of my government. Is it wrong that Venda and Zulu and Xhosa should govern themselves? Is it wrong that white authority over their lands and

188

their people should gradually be withdrawn? Surely this is a classic example of emancipating nations.

"Separate representation for the Bantu, removed out of the central white parliament, out of the parliament of white South Africa, proceeds on the very logical premise that representation of the Bantu within the central parliament of South Africa would, if it were logically extended, ultimately lead to a position in South Africa of greater and greater representation for this group in the central parliament. Now, the basis of the South African Government's policy is not that there shall be no representation for all of the disparate nations in South Africa now, but that there shall be separate territorial political representation for these groups.

"If I might use an analogy, when Britain withdrew from the Indian subcontinent and left Muslims and Hindus in that subcontinent, she could quite easily, as she did in the case of South Africa, have left all political power in the hands of one group. She could have, if we take a hypothetical example, left all political power in India in the hands of the Muslims. And today it's conceivable that the world could be agitating for Muslims in India to become more democratic in their institutions by allowing majority Hindu representation. Instead we saw what happened in India.

"It happened too in Israel with respect to Israel's arguments with the Arab countries. Partition took place. It happened in Ireland, White people, non-Anglo-Saxon Catholics, and Anglo-Saxon Englishmen, their destinies so different from each other . . . in effect they moved, they partitioned, they created apartheid between the two of them.

"Now in the Republic of South Africa we have seen these things. We live in Africa. We see every day the clashes that are occurring between tribe and tribe, between group and group. Certainly, like everybody else I think in an international community, we do not worship the chasms that tragically exist between man and between nations, but to deny the existence of those chasms is to be politically unwise.

"So when the South African Government removed what representation the Bantu had in our parliament it was not done as an act of depriving the Bantu of all political representation which they had had in the white parliament. A separate machinery of Bantu representation was then created.

189

And we could not have these two separate machines operating with some representation in the white parliament and with other representation in the Bantu homeland area.

"Now, I would like to comment on one particular issue which is often raised when this point is mentioned. People say that the division of land in South Africa is unfair. Professor TAUBENFELD mentioned that only 13 per cent of the land is earmarked for Bantu settlement. It often seems to me that in South Africa we are damned if we do and we are damned if we don't. Whatever we happen to propose, whatever we happen to say, is always wrong, and is always rejected.

"Now again, when Ireland was partitioned, Britain didn't ask: what is a 'fair' partition of Ireland? Britain didn't say: what should we do to ensure a 'fair division' of land? The land was partitioned upon the basis of historical settlement, and that is exactly the same thing that the South African Government is doing. We are not creating large ghettos and driving people in there. South Africa is a geopolitical complex with a number of disparate nations each with its own particular area of settlement. All that the South African Government has been doing in the past twenty years since the enunciation and articulation of its policies of apartheid is to give constitutional recognition to these existing national differences within areas delineated by historical processes.

"One last point in this connection. Within the geopolitical area of southern Africa, there are three other areas as you know: Basutoland, Bechuanaland and Swaziland. They are, or were, British-controlled. Two of these countries have become independent nations on our borders now. The Kingdom of Lesotho and the Republic of Botswana. Now, in effect, these are the ethnic homelands of the Bantu Basuto and Tswana nations.

"The South African Government is involved in exactly the same constructive process of recognizing its Bantu nations. The Kingdom of Lesotho is the traditional homeland of the Basuto people. The same with Botswana and in exactly the same way South Africa will be politically divided, not through fiat of government but because history has already divided it and now we must constitutionally recognize this. All that the South African Government at this stage of the development

190

does is to recognize these claims of the Bantu and to go along with them as fast as is humanly possible in an extremely complex situation. To condemn separate development is to deny the Bantu self-determination.''

*　　*　　*

IV. *STATEMENT OF FRANCIS T. P. PLIMPTON*

A statement from the audience was made by Mr. FRANCIS T. P. PLIMPTON, a member of The Association of the Bar of the City of New York, who formerly served as Deputy United States Representative to the United Nations:

"Mr. Chairman, I would like to make a statement that I suppose is out of order because it relates to what happens from now on. However, I think that what happens from now on is a problem that all of us must give very serious thought to.

"I would think it was fairly obvious that South Africa would not agree to the taking over by the United Nations of South West Africa, for South Africa, I think quite wrongly, regards the I.C.J. opinion as some sort of a blessing of its mandate over South West Africa—which of course it is not. In fact the opinion was merely a procedural one which, to the astonishment of a great many of us and despite the fact that the Court had already decided that it did have jurisdiction, held that the parties bringing the proceeding had no interest or standing, and therefore that the proceeding must be dismissed. I would have thought myself that the prior decision that the Court had jurisdiction included the concept that the case was properly brought before it, but that is an aside.

"Granting that South Africa will not accept the termination of its mandate by the General Assembly (and I suppose a constitutional argument could be made that the General Assembly did not have any legal power to do so), what then? I think it's generally assumed that somehow or other, presumably by the Security Council, economic sanctions will be imposed on South Africa until it yields. This is where I think we have to leave the legal stratum and think about another stratum—that is, the economic effect of sanctions.

191

"The Security Council made a special study about two years ago as to sanctions against South Africa, and it came to the conclusion that it was possible that sanctions might work after quite a long time, but that sanctions would have to involve, almost certainly, a naval blockade because virtually the only economic weakness of South Africa is in petroleum and, particularly, heavy lubricants. Now, if economic sanctions were imposed on South Africa they would first have to be enforced by a navy, and second they would most certainly involve counter-sanctions against the United Kingdom, and that is where I think the difficulty arises. One has to assume for the purpose of argument that the United Kingdom would be willing to impose sanctions and of course if they were to be imposed mandatorily, United Kingdom consent would be necessary in the Security Council. Calculations vary, but it's quite clear, I think, that if sanctions were imposed by Great Britain against South Africa—the loss in foreign exchange to the United Kingdom would be almost astronomical, and that in turn would almost certainly result in the devaluation of the English pound and worldwide currency chaos.

"I simply pose this eventual economic problem as one for your serious consideration, quite apart from the legal problems—what actually can be done by way of economic sanctions against South Africa without concomitant damage to all of us? I am not speaking about damage to American investments. But there is a real problem here of world concern as to what would happen if sanctions were adopted, and I think our South African friends must also consider, very seriously, the practical economic aspects of a problem which is terribly, terribly, difficult from every single viewpoint.

"I apologize for introducing economic considerations into what is a legal discussion, but in the last analysis we do have to think about other things than law and we do have to think about the welfare of all of us in an extremely difficult situation."

Selected Bibliography
on Race, Peace, Law and Southern Africa*

GENERAL

Bishop, William W.   International law: cases and materials. 2d ed. Boston, Little, Brown. 1962. 964p.

Brierly, James L.   The law of nations; an introduction to the international law of peace. Ed. by H. Waldock. 6th ed. New York, Oxford Univ. Press. 1963. 442p.

Brierly, James L.   The sovereign state today. 1949. 61 Jurid. Rev. 3–15.

Claude, Inis Lothair.   Power and international relations. New York, Random House. 1962. 310p.

Cleveland, H.   Peace and human rights. 1963. 49 Dep't State Bull. 38–43.

Coyle, David C.   The United Nations and how it works. New ed. New York, Columbia Univ. Press. 1966. 256p.

Detter, Ingrid.   Law making by international organizations. Stockholm, P. A. Norstedt & Soners Forlag. 1965. 353p.

Fenwick, Charles G.   International law. 4th ed. New York, Appleton-Century-Crofts. 1965. 849p.

Goodrich, Leland M. and Hambro, Edward.   Charter of the United Nations; commentary and documents. Boston, World Peace Foundation. 1946. 413p.

Goodrich, Leland M. and Simons, Anne P.   The United Nations and the maintenance of international peace and security. Washington, Brookings Institution. 1955. 709p.

Goodspeed, Stephen S.   The nature and function of international organization. New York, Oxford Univ. Press. 1959. 676p.

Great Britain.   Foreign Office. United Kingdom draft of an international bill of human rights, June 1947. London, H.M.S.O. 1947. 13p.

Gross, Ernest A.   The United Nations: structure for peace. New York, Published for the Council on Foreign Relations by Harper. 1962. 132p.

Guggenheim, Paul.   Traité de droit international public . . . Genève, Georg. 1953–54. 2v.

Higgins, Rosalyn.   The development of international law through the political organs of the United Nations. London, New York, Oxford Univ. Press. 1963. 402p.

Hudson, Manley O.   International tribunals; past and future. Washington, Carnegie Endowment for International Peace and Brookings Institution. 1944. 287p.

Jenks, Clarence Wilfred.
The common law of mankind.   London, Stevens. 1958. 456p.
Law, freedom and welfare.   Dobbs Ferry, N.Y., Oceana Pub. 1963. 162p.
The prospects of international adjudication.   London, Stevens; Dobbs Ferry, Oceana Pub. 1964. 805p.

* Compiled by Anthony P. Grech, Reference Librarian of The Association of the Bar of the City of New York.

Jessup, Philip C.   A modern law of nations . . . New York, Macmillan. 1948. 236p.

Kaplan, Morton A. and Katzenbach, Nicholas de B.   The political foundations of international law. New York, John Wiley & Sons. 1961. 372p.

Kelsen, Hans.   Principles of international law. New York, Rinehart. 1952. 461p.

Lauterpacht, Hersh.   The development of international law by the international court. London, Stevens. 1958. 408p.

Lipsky, George Arthur.   Law and politics in the world community. Berkeley, Univ. of California Press. 1953. 373p.

Liska, George.   International equilibrium; a theoretical essay on politics and organization of security. Cambridge, Harvard Univ. Press. 1957. 233p.

McNair, Arnold Duncan.   The expansion of international law. Jerusalem, Magnes Press, Hebrew University. 1962. 68p.

Mezerik, A. G.   Colonialism and the United Nations: decolonization declaration. Committee of 24. Neo colonialism, border questions, Africa's colonial heartland. New York, International Review Service. 1964. 105p.

Morganthau, Hans J.   Politics among nations: the struggle for power and peace. 3d ed. rev. New York, Knopf. 1965. 630p.

O'Connell, Daniel P.   International law. London, Stevens; Dobbs Ferry, N.Y., Oceana Pub. 1965. 2v.

Preuss, Lawrence.   Article 2, paragraph 7 of the charter of the United Nations and matters of domestic jurisdiction. Hague, Academy of International Law. Recueil des Cours 1949, I, v.74, pp.553–653.

Robinson, Jacob and others.   Were the minorities treaties a failure? New York, Institute of Jewish Affairs. 1943. 349p.

Rosenne, Shabtai.   The law and practice of the International court. Leyden, A. W. Sijthoff. 1965. 2v.

Sandifer, D. V. and Scheman, L. Ronald.   The foundations of freedom. New York, Praeger. 1966. 139p.

Schachter, Oscar.   The relation of law, politics and action in the United Nations. Hague. Academy of International Law. Recueil des Cours 1963, II, v.109, pp.169–256.

Schapiro, L. B.   Domestic jurisdiction in the covenant and the charter. 1947. 33 Grotius Soc'y Transactions 195–211.

Schwarzenberger, Georg.
    The frontiers of international law.   London, Stevens. 1962. 320p.
    International law as applied by international courts and tribunals.   London, Stevens. 1949. 681p.

Taubenfeld, Rita Falk and Taubenfeld, Howard J.   The "economic weapon": the League and the United Nations. 1964. 58 Am. Soc'y Int'l L. Proc. 183–205.

Tucker, Edwin W.   Has the individual become the subject of international law? 1965. 34 U. Cin. L. Rev. 341–66.

United Nations.   Repertory of practice of United Nations organs. New York. 1955. 3v.

Virally, Michael.   La valeur juridique des recommandations des organisations internationales. 1956. 2 Ann. Français de Droit International 66–96.

Visscher, Charles de.   Theory and reality in public international law. Princeton, Princeton Univ. Press. 1957. 381p.

Volio-Jimenez, F. International protection of human rights: balance sheet of a promising action. 1964. 1 (7) U.N. Monthly Chronicle 75–81.

Waldock, C. H. M. The plea of domestic jurisdiction before international legal tribunals. 1954. 31 Brit. Yb. Int'l L. 96–142.

Wainhouse, David W. Remnants of empire: the United Nations and the end of colonialism. New York, Harper. 1964. 153p.

Whiteman, Marjorie M. Digest of international law. Washington, U.S. Department of State; for sale by the Superintendent of Documents, U.S. Gov't Print. Off. 1963–65. 5v.

Wright, Quincy.
International law and the United Nations. New York, Asia Pub. Co. 1960. 134p.
Is discussion intervention? 1956. 50 Am. J. Int'l L. 102–10.

SOUTHERN AFRICA

PORTUGUESE AREAS

Assembly condemns "colonial war" in Angola: asks Portugal to halt repressive acts in African territory. Feb. 1963. 10 U.N. Rev. 42–49.

Assembly urges independence for Portuguese territories. Jan. 1963. 10 U.N. Rev. 16–28.

Bains, J. S. Angola, the U.N. and international law. 1963. 3 Indian J. Int'l L. 63–71.

Cabral, Joao. Portugese colonial policy. 1965. 5 Africa Q. 153–73.

Duffy, James E.
Portugal in Africa. 1961. 39 For. Aff. 481–93.
Portugal in Africa. Cambridge, Harvard Univ. Press. 1962. 239p.

Ehnmark, Anders and Wästberg, Per. Angola and Mozambique: the case against Portugal. New York, Roy Publishers. 1963. 176p.

Goldberg, Arthur J. U.S. urges Portuguese-African talks on self determination. 1965. 53 Dep't State Bull. 1034–38.

International Labor Organization. Report of the commission appointed under article 26 of the constitution of the International labour organization to examine the complaint led by the government of Ghana concerning the observance by the government of Portugal of the abolition of forced labour convention 1957 (no.105). April 1962. 45 Int'l Lab. Off. Official Bull. Supp. 2. 1–253.

Martelli, George.
Portugal and the United Nations. 1964. 40 Int'l Aff. (Lond.) 453–65.
The Portuguese in Guinea. 1965. 21 World Today 345–51.

Neumann, Heinzgeorg. Portugal's policy in Africa: the four years since the beginning of the uprising in Angola. 1965. 41 Int'l Aff. (Lond.) 663–75.

Security council asks Portugal to end "repressive measures" in Angola. July 1961. 8 U.N. Rev. 8–11.

Stevenson, Adlai E.
U.N. general assembly urges Portugal to promote self-determination for Angola. 1962. 46 Dep't State Bull. 385–92.
United States explains position on Portuguese territories. 1963. 49 Dep't State Bull. 303–09.

195

United Nations. General Assembly. Special committee on territories under Portuguese administration established under General assembly resolution 1699 (XVI).

Draft report. July 24, 1962. 22p. (mimeo) (1962, A/AC.108/L.4)

Report of the special committee . . . Aug. 15, 1962. 144p. (mimeo) (1962. A/5160)

Some measures relating to the territories under Portuguese administration promulgated since Jan. 1961: prepared by the secretariat Oct. 15, 1962. 40p. (mimeo) (1962. A/AC.108/L.5)

Some measures relating to the territories under Portugese administration promulgated since 1 Jan. 1961; pt. 4. Texts of legislation prepared by the secretariat Oct. 19, 1962. 77+ 15p. (mimeo) (1962. A/AC.108/L.5/Add.1)

General policies in territories under Portuguese administration: background paper prepared by the secretariat Feb. 1, 1963. 46+ 7p. (mimeo) (1963. A/AC.108/67)

Constitutional status of territories under Portuguese administration: background paper prepared by the secretariat Feb. 4, 1963. 45p. (mimeo) (1963. A/AC.108/L.6)

Draft report of the special committee on the situation with regard to the implementation of the declaration on the granting of independence to colonial countries and peoples, covering its work during 1963: territories under Portuguese administration. July 10, 1963. 83p. (mimeo) (1963. A/AC.109/L.67)

Special committee on the situation with regard to the implementation of the declaration on the granting of independence to colonial countries and peoples. Territories under Portuguese administration: working paper prepared by the secretariat June 9, 1964. 73p. (mimeo) (1964. A/AC.109/L.126)

Special committee on the situation with regard to the implementation of the declaration on the granting of independence to colonial countries and peoples, draft report: territories under Portuguese administration Aug. 26, 1964. 114p. (mimeo) (1964. A/AC.109/L.140)

Special committee on the situation with regard to the implementation of the declaration on the granting of independence to colonial countries and peoples. Report chap. 5: territories under Portuguese administration Jan. 5, 1965. 117p. (mimeo) (1965. A/5800/Add.3)

Special committee on the situation with regard to the implementation of the declaration on the granting of independence to colonial countries and peoples. Territories under Portuguese administration: draft report Aug. 23, 1965. 125p. (mimeo) (1965. A/AC.109/L.244)

Wohlgemuth, Patricia. The Portuguese territories under the United Nations. Nov. 1963. 545 Int'l Conciliation.

Yates, Sidney R. U.S. restates views on colonialism and Portuguese African territories. 1963. 48 Dep't State Bull. 581–83.

REPUBLIC OF SOUTH AFRICA

Apartheid: a "dangerous drift of events;" special committee reports to general assembly and security council. May 1963. 10 U.N. Rev. 33–37.

Apartheid in South Africa: committee adopts report to security council and general assembly. July 1965. 2 U.N. Monthly Chronicle 42–47.

Apartheid in South Africa: report of expert committee. April 1965. 2 U.N. Monthly Chronicle 23–27.

Baker, John T. Human rights in South Africa. 1965. 11 How. L.J. 549–82.

Dale, . South Africa and the international community. 1966. 18 World Politics 297.

De Kiewiet, C. W. South Africa's gamble with history. 40 Va. Q. Rev. 1–17.

Dugard, C. J. R. The legal effect of United Nations resolutions on apartheid. 1966. 83 S.A.L.J. 44–59.

Duncan, P. Toward a world policy for South Africa. 1963. 42 For. Aff. 38–48.

Fraser, G. L'O.N.U. et l'apartheid. 1964. 37 Ann. Politique et Economique 207–12.

Gonze, C. et al. South African crisis and United States policy. New York, American Committee on Africa. 1962. 63p.

Graefrath, B. On the subject of the prohibition of racial discrimination under international law. 1964. 3 German For. Policy 285–90.

Haekkerup, P. The South African racial crisis and the world (in Segal, R. M. Sanctions against South Africa. Baltimore, 1964, pp.42–47)

Hahlo, H. R. and Maisels, I. A. The rule of law in South Africa. 1966. 52 Va. L. Rev. 1–31.

Houghton, Desmond H. The South African economy. London, Oxford. 1964. 261p.

International Commission of Jurists. South Africa and the rule of law. Geneva. 1960. 239p.

International conference on economic sanctions against South Africa. Papers submitted to the . . . held in London from 14–17 April 1964. Aug. 17, 1964. 142p. (mimeo) (U.N. 1964. S/AC.14/L.2)

International conference on economic sanctions against South Africa, London, 1964. Sanctions against South Africa, ed. by Ronald Segal. Harmondsworth, Eng., Penguin. 1964. 272p.

International Labor Organization. Declaration concerning the policy of "apartheid" of the Republic of South Africa. 1964. 3 Int'l Leg. Materials 973–76.

International Labor Office. Proposed declaration concerning the policy of "apartheid" of the Republic of South Africa. Genève. 1964. 53p.

Landis, Elizabeth S. South African apartheid legislation. 1961. 71 Yale L. Rev. 1–52, 437–500.

Legum, Colin and Legum, M. R. South Africa: crisis for the west. London, Pall Mall. 1964. 333p.

Leiss, Amelia C.
    American policy and the future of southern Africa (review article of African battleline, American policy choices in southern Africa by Waldemar A. Nielsen). 1966. 19 World Politics 151–65.
    Apartheid and United Nations collective measures. New York, Carnegie Endowment for International Peace. 1965. 170p.

Lewin, Julius. Politics and law in South Africa: essays on race relations. New York, Monthly Review Press. 1963. 115p.

Malhatra, R. C. Apartheid and the United Nations. 1964. 354 Annals 135–44.

197

Marquard, Leopold. The peoples and policies of South Africa. 3d ed. London, Oxford. 1962. 284p.

Measures against South Africa urged because of racial policies. 1962. 9 (12) U.N. Rev. 19–25.

Measures to counter apartheid: special political committee's recommendation. Dec. 1963. 10 U.N. Rev. 25–28.

Mezerik, A. G., ed. Apartheid in the Republic of South Africa: Bantustans, boycotts, U.N. action. New York, International Review Service. 1964. 109p.

Pierson-Mathy, P. La politique raciale de la république d'Afrique du Sud. 1964. Chronique de Politique Etrangère (Bruxelles) 253–660.

Report on apartheid. 1963. 10 (9) U.N. Rev. 35–41.

Roberts, H. V. Race relations in South Africa as an international problem. 1958. 34 Int'l Aff. (Lond.) 164–73.

Security council calls on South Africa to promote racial harmony and to abandon apartheid and racial discrimination. May 1960. 6 U.N. Rev. 16–19.

Security council resolutions on apartheid in South Africa. 1964. 3 Int'l Leg. Materials 793–97.

Soubeyrol, J. L'action internationale contre l'apartheid. 1965. 69 Rev. Gén. de Driot des Etats 326–69.

The South African issue in the United Nations. 38 Current History 360–66.

Stevenson, Adlai E. U.N. Security council condemns apartheid in South Africa: sets up committee to study sanctions. 1964. 51 Dep't State Bull. 29–33.

Sun-Nusret-Ali. La discrimination raciale et l'organisation des Nations Unies. Thèse. Paris. 1954.

Tambo, O. Apartheid, the indictment (in Segal, R. M. Sanctions against South Africa. Baltimore, 1964, pp.15–20)

United Nations. Commission on the racial situation in the Union of South Africa. Third report. 1955. 105p. (Gen. Ass. official recs.: tenth sess. supp. no. 14(A/2953)

United Nations. Department of Public Information. Apartheid in South Africa. New York. 1965. 52p.

United Nations. General Assembly. Special Committee.

Question of race conflict in South Africa resulting from the policies of apartheid of the government of the Union of South Africa, report Jan. 22, 1957. 7p. (mimeo) (1957. A/3508)

Question of race conflict in South Africa resulting from the policies of apartheid of the government of the Union of South Africa. Nov. 12, 1959. 5p. (mimeo) (1959. A/4271)

Policies of apartheid of the government of the Republic of South Africa. Second interim report July 19, 1963. 11p. + v.p. (mimeo) (1963. A/5453)

The policies of apartheid of the government of the Republic of South Africa, July 23, 1963. 42p. (mimeo) (1963. A/5454)

On the policies of apartheid of the government of the Republic of South Africa. Report, Sept. 16, 1963. 154p. (mimeo) (1963. A/5497); also issued as (S/5426)

On the policies of apartheid of the government of the Republic of South Africa, report: addendum Sept. 26, 1963. 169p. (mimeo) (1963. A/5497/Add.1); also issued as (S/5426/Add.1)

On the policies of apartheid of the government of the Republic of South Africa. Report: addendum Oct. 31, 1963. 18p. (mimeo) (1963. A/5497/Add.2.); also issued as (S/5426/Add.2)

On the policies of apartheid of the government of the Republic of South Africa. Report, May 25, 1964. 70p. (1964. A/5707)

United Nations. Office of Public Information.

Apartheid in South Africa: summary of the report of the special committee on the policies of apartheid of the government of the Republic of South Africa. 1963. 48p. (Sales no. 63.1.42)

A new course in South Africa: report of the group of experts established in pursuance of the Security council resolution of 4 Dec. 1963. 1964. 35p. (Sales no. 64.1.13)

United Nations resolution on apartheid in South Africa. 1966. 5 Int'l Leg. Materials 369–73.

The United Nations resolution on South Africa. Dec. 1963. 45 Current Hist. 366.

United Nations. Security Council.

Expert committee established in pursuance of Security council res. S/5773. Report. March 2, 1965. v.p. (mimeo) (1965. S/6210)

U.N. Security council resolutions on apartheid in South Africa. 1964. 3 Int'l Leg. Materials 793–97.

United Nations. Security Council.

Special comm. on the policies of apartheid of the government of the Republic of South Africa. Report Dec. 7, 1964. 227p. (1964. S/6073); also issued as (A/5825)

Special comm. on the policies of apartheid of the government of the Republic of South Africa. Report: addendum. Repressive measures against opponents of the policies of apartheid, Dec. 10, 1964. 129p. (mimeo) (1964. S/6073/Add.1.); also issued as (A/5825/Add.1.)

Whitehead, M. J. The elimination of racial discrimination; the United Nations proposed solution. 1965. 11 How. L.J. 583–93.

SOUTH WEST AFRICA

Action on South-west Africa. Jan. 1, 1951. 10 U.N. Bull. 48–52.

Arden-Clarke, Charles. South-west Africa, the Union and the United Nations. 1960. 59 African Aff. 26–35.

Assembly makes solemn appeal on status of South-west Africa: South Africa asked to reconsider its stand on former German colony and place it under trusteeship. 1953. 15 U.N. Bull. 593–99.

Ballinger, R. B.

The International court of justice and the South West Africa cases: judgment of 21st December 1962. 1964. 81 S.A.L.J. 35–62.

South-West Africa: the case against the Union. Johannesburg, South Africa Institute of Race Relations. 1961. 56p.

The territory of South-west Africa. 1963. 45 Current Hist. 361–65.

Bisson, J. Le statut international du sud-ouest Africain. These. Paris. 1954. 175p.

Bradford, The origin and concession of the League of Nations' class "C" mandate for South-west Africa and fulfillment of the sacred trust, 1919–1939. Unpublished diss., Yale. 1965.

Bravo. L. F. Note in margine alla recente sentenza della corte internazionale di giustizia nel caso dell'Africa sud-occidentale. 1963. 46 Riv. di Diritto Internazionale 337.

Castaneda, J. La question du Sud-ouest Africain. 1962. 5 Cahiers de Droit 7–18.

Chowdhuri, Ramendra Nath. International mandates and trusteeship systems; a comparative study. The Hague, Nijhoff. 1955. 328p.

Committee is invited to study conditions in South West Africa. 1961. 8 U.N. Rev. 16–20.

Conditions in South West Africa: committee's report to the General assembly. Sept. 1959. 6 U.N. Rev. 28–31.

Dugard, C. J. R. Objections to the revision of the 1962 judgment of the International court of justice in the South African case. 1965. 82 S.A.L.J. 178–91.

Effective United Nations presence proposed for South West Africa. 1963. 10 (1) U.N. Rev. 29–38.

Favoreu, Louis.

L'arrêt du décembre 1962 sur le Sud-Ouest africain et l'évolution du droit des organisations internationales. 1964. 9 Ann. Français de Droit International 303–57.

Récusation et administration de la preuve devant la cour internationale de justice. A propos des affaires du Sud-Ouest Africain. 1965. 11 Ann. Français de Droit International 233–77.

Feinberg, Nathan. La juridiction et la jurisprudence de la cour permanente de justice internationale en matière de mandats et minorities. Hague, Academy of International Law. Recueil des Cours 1937, I, v. 59, pp. 591–733.

Fishel, Murray I. The international aspects of South West Africa: the historical perspective. 1965. 13 J. Human Relations 196–207.

Fitzmaurice, Gerald (Sir). Judicial innovation—its uses and its perils—as exemplified in some of the work of the International court of justice during Lord McNair's period of office (in Cambridge essays on international law. Dobbs Ferry, N.Y., Oceana Pub., 1965, pp. 24–47)

Goldblatt, I. The mandated territory of South West Africa in relation to the United Nations. Cape Town, Struik. 1961. 67p.

Gross, Ernest A.

The South West Africa cases: on the threshold of decision. 1964. 3 Colum. J. Transnat'l L. 19–25.

The South West Africa case: what happened? 1966. 45 For. Aff. 36–48.

Hague. International Court of Justice.

International status of South-west Africa, request for advisory opinion, list of documents accompanying the request, written statements, articles 65 & 66 of the statute. The Hague. 1950. 89p.

International status of South-west Africa: pleadings, oral arguments, documents; advisory opinion of July 11, 1950. 373p. (Sales no.46)

Voting procedure on questions relating to reports and petitions concerning the territory of South-west Africa. Advisory opinions of June 7, 1955. 1955. 1v.

Reports of judgments, advisory opinions and orders: admissibility of hearings of petitioners by the Committee on South West Africa: advisory opinion of June 1, 1956, July 24, 1956. 71p. (Sales no.151) (A/ 3147)

Reports of judgments, advisory opinions and orders: South West Africa cases (Ethiopa v. South Africa; Liberia v. South Africa), preliminary objections; judgment of 21 Dec. 1962. 347p. (Sales no.207)

Communique regarding the South West Africa case. 1963. 2 Int'l Leg. Materials 199–204.

Reports of judgments, advisory opinions and orders. South West Africa cases (Ethiopa v. South Africa; Liberia v. South Africa). Second phase judgment of 18 July 1966. 505p. (Sales no.299)

Hall, Hessel Duncan.

Mandates, dependencies and trusteeship. Washington, Carnegie Endowment for International Peace. 1948. 429p.

The trusteeship system and the case of South-West Africa. 1947. 24 Brit. Yb. Int'l L. 385–89.

Hambro, Edward. The authority of the advisory opinions of the International court of justice. 1954. 3 Int'l & Comp. L.Q. 2–22.

Imishue, R. W. South West Africa: an international problem. London, Pall Mall Press. 1965. 80p.

Johnson, O. Contribution of the International court to the international law through the South-West Africa case. 1963. 4 Nigerian B. J. 46.

Kahn, Ellison. The international court's advisory opinion on the international status of Southwest Africa. 1951. 4 Int'l L.Q. 78–99.

Landis, Elizabeth S.

South West Africa in the International court of justice. April 1964. 11 Africa Today 10–12.

South West Africa in the International court: act II, scene I. 1964. 49 Cornell L.Q. 179–227.

Leroy, P. La nature juridique des accords de tutelle. 1965. 69 Rev. Gén. de Droit International Public 977–1018.

Logan, Rayford W. The African mandates in world politics. Washington, Public Affairs Press. 1948. 220p.

Mason, Philip. Separate development and South West Africa: some aspects of the Odendaal report. April 1964. 5 Race 83–97.

Nordau, R. N. The South West Africa case. 1966. 22 World Today 122–30.

Robinson, K. The dilemmas of trusteeship. London, Oxford Univ. Press. 1965. 95p.

Roskan, K. L. Mandaat Zuid-West-Afrika—"a sacred trust" (in Volkenrechtelijke opstellen aangeboden aan Prof. Dr. Gesina H. J. van der Molen. . . . Kamken, J. H. Kok, N. V., 1962, p.111)

Scott, Michael. The international status of South-West Africa. 1958. 34 Int'l Aff. (Lond.) 318–39.

Security council again condemns apartheid in South Africa. 1964. 50 Dep't State Bull. 92–96.

South Africa. South West Africa and the Union of South Africa. The history of a mandate. New York, Manhattan Print. Co. 1947? 108p.

South Africa. Commission of Enquiry into South West Africa Affairs. Report 1962–1963. Pretoria, Government Printer. 1964. 557p.

South West Africa. 1962. 9 U.N. Rev. 27–31.

The South West Africa cases: a symposium. The developing concept of treaty by Gerald M. Feder; Parties in interest by David A. Rice and Justiciable disputes: a jurisdictional and jurisprudential issue by Aaron Etra. 1965. 4 Colum. J. Transnat'l L. 47–118.

South-West Africa: the crisis and its background. March 1962. Round Table 155–61.

South West Africa: decisions by the South African government. 1964. 2 Int'l Bull. (Africa Inst.) 173–80.

South West Africa: a new approach, assembly renews appeals on mandated territory. Jan. 1955. U.N. Rev. 44–51.

Steward, Alexander. The sacred trust: South West Africa. Johannesburg, Da Gama Publications. 1963. 46p.

Sud, Usha.

Committee on information from non-self-governing territories: its role in the promotion of self-determination of colonial peoples. 1965. 7 Int'l Studies 311–36.

United Nations and the non-self-governing territories. Jullundur, University Publishers. 1965. 219p.

Suy, E. Nieuw arrest van het internationaal gerechtshof over Zuid-West-Afrika. 1963. 26 Rechtskundig Weekblad 1981.

Thullen, George. Problems of the trusteeship system: a study of political behavior in the United Nations. Genève, Librairie Droz. 1964. 217p.

Toussaint, Charmian Edwards. The trusteeship system of the United Nations. New York, Praeger. 1957. 288p.

United Nations. Statement by the Union of South Africa on the outcome of their consultations with the peoples of South West Africa as to the future status of the mandated territory and implementation to be given to the wishes thus expressed. 1946. 56p. (A/123. 19 Oct. 1946)

United Nations. General Assembly. Fourth Committee. Question of South West Africa: statement made by the representative of the United Kingdom at the 666th mtg. Oct. 10, 1957. 5p. (1957. A/C.4/358)

United Nations. Secretariat. Progress of the non-self-governing territories under the charter. New York. 1961. 5v.

United Nations. Special committee on the situation with regard to the implementation of the declaration on the granting of independence to colonial countries and peoples. Report: South West Africa, Dec. 18, 1964. 78p. (mimeo) (1964. A/5800/Add.2)

United Nations. General Assembly. Comm. on South West Africa.

Report 1954. (Gen. ass. official recs.: 9th sess. supp. no.14 (A/2666)

Information and documentation in respect of the territory of South West Africa, May 11–24, 1954. 3pts. (mimeo) (1954. A/AC.73/L.3/Add.2)

Report. 1955. 50p. (Gen. ass. official recs. 10th sess. supp. no.12 (A/29/13)

Information and documentation in respect of the territory of South West Africa: chapter M, social, moral and material condition of the natives. May 12, 1955. 99p. (mimeo) (1955. A/AC.73/L.7/Add.1)

Information and documentation in respect of the territory of South West Africa. May 13, 1955. 434p. (1955. A/AC.73/L.7)

Information and documentation in respect of the territory of South West Africa, addendum June 26, 1956. 129p. (mimeo) (1956. A/AC.73/L.8/Add.1)

202

Information and documentation in respect of the territory of South West
Africa. June 1956. 173+ 6p. (mimeo) (1956. A/AC.73/L.8)
Question of South West Africa: report of the committee . . .; report of the
fourth committee, F. H. Soward. Feb. 15, 1957. 21p. (1957. A/3541)
Report. 1957. 43p. (Official recs.: 12th sess. supp. no.12 (A/3626)
Special report: a study of legal action to ensure the fulfillment of the ob-
ligations assumed by the mandatory power under the mandate for South
West Africa. 1957. 8p. (Official recs.: 12th sess., supp. no.12A (A/3625)
Information and documentation in respect of the territory of South West
Africa: submitted by the secretary-general, Aug. 19, 1957. 263p. (1957.
A/AC.73/L.10)
Subcommittee on legal questions. Report 31 Aug. 1959. 82p. (processed)
(1959. A/AC.73/2)
Report. 1959. 68p. (Official recs.: 14th sess., supp. no.12 (A/4191)
Information and documentation in respect of the territory of South West
Africa: submitted by the secretary-general, Sept. 2, 1959. 119p. (1959.
A/AC.73/L.13)
Petitions and communications relating to South West Africa dealt with in
the report of the committee. . . . to the General assembly at its fifteenth
session, Sept. 9, 1960. 248p. (mimeo) (1960. A/AC.73/3)
Question of South West Africa: report of the committee . . . concerning the
implementation of general assembly resolutions 1568(XV) and 1596(XV).
Oct. 26, 1961. 65p. (1961. A/4926)
Report. 1963. 23p. (Official recs.: 17th sess., supp. no.12 (A/5212)
Special committee on the situation with regard to the implementation of
the declaration on the granting of independence to colonial countries
and peoples. South West Africa: report. July 26, 1963. 72p. (mimeo)
(1963. A/5446/Add.2)
Vedovato, Guiseppe. Les accords de tutelle. Hague. Academy of Interna-
tional Law. Recueil des Cours 1950, I, v.76, pp.609–700.
Verzijl, J. H. W. International court of justice—South West Africa and
Northern Cameroons cases (preliminary objections). 1964. 11 Nederlands
Tijdschrift voor International Recht 1–33.
Wynne, G. Grounds for revision of the judgment of the International court
of justice of 21 Dec. 1962, on jurisdiction in the South West Africa case.
1964. 81 S.A.L.J. 449–57.

SOUTHERN RHODESIA

Fischer, Georges. Le problème Rhodésien. 1965. 11 Ann. Français de Droit
International 41–69.
Ghana. A memorandum in regard to Southern Rhodesia submitted to the
security council on the 2d Aug. 1963: together with documents and notes
supplementary thereto. Accra, Ghana Information Service. 1963. 84p.
Mezerik, A. G., ed. Rhodesia and the United Nations: U.N. imposition of
mandatory sanctions, 1966; sanctions, actions and reactions. New York,
International Review Service. 1966. 109p.
Nyerere, Julius K. Rhodesia in the context of southern Africa. 1966. 44 For.
Aff. 373–86.
Perham, Margery. The Rhodesian crisis: the background. Jan. 1966. 42 Int'l
Aff. (Lond.) 1–13.

Southern Rhodesia constitutional conference. Report . . . Salisbury. Feb. 1961. 10p.

Southern Rhodesia—human rights and the constitution. March 1964. Int'l Comm'n Jurists Bull. 43–48.

Southern Rhodesia: special committee resumes consideration of question. April 1964. 11 U.N. Rev. 16.

United Nations general assembly resolutions on Rhodesia. 1966. 5 Int'l Leg. Materials 161–68.

United Nations. General Assembly. Special Committee.

Question of Southern Rhodesia: report of the special committee on the situation with regard to the implementation of the declaration on the granting of independence to colonial countries and peoples. May 21, 1962. 18p. (mimeo) (1962. A/5/24)

Draft report of the committee on the situation with regard to the implementation of the declaration on the granting of independence to colonial countries and peoples: Southern Rhodesia. July 19, 1963. 91p. (mimeo) (1963. A/AC.109/L.72)

On the situation with regard to the implementation of the declaration on the granting of independence to colonial countries and peoples: Southern Rhodesia. Report. July 30, 1963. 91p. (1963. A/5446/Add.3)

On the situation with regard to the implementation of the declaration on the granting of independence to colonial countries and peoples. Question of Southern Rhodesia: working paper prepared by the secretariat: action taken by the special committee in 1963, by the security council and by the general assembly during its 18th session, March 4, 1964. 22+ 14p. (mimo) (1964. A/AC/109/L.99)

On the situation with regard to the implementation of the declaration on the granting of independence to colonial countries and peoples. Draft reports: Southern Rhodesia. Rapporteur, K. Natwar Singh. June 25, 1964. 147p. (mimeo) (1964. A/AC/109/L.133)

On the situation with regard to the implementation of the declaration on the granting of independence to colonial countries and peoples. Report: Southern Rhodesia. Aug. 10, 1964. v.p. (mimeo) (1964. A/5800/Add.1)

On the situation with regard to the implementation of the declaration on the granting of independence to colonial countries and peoples. Question of Southern Rhodesia: working paper prepared by the secretariat. March 18, 1966. 82p. (mimeo) (1966. A/AC.109/L.264)

On the situation with regard to the implementation of the declaration on the granting of independence to colonial countries and peoples. Question of Southern Rhodesia: working paper prepared by the secretariat. May 10, 1966. 36p. (mimeo) (1966. A/AC.109/L.4264/Add.2)

INTERNATIONAL LAW AND HUMAN RIGHTS

Abranches, C. A. D. de. Proteção internacional dos direitos humanos. Rio de Janeiro, Freitas. 1964. 159p.

Acosta Díaz de Martín, E. J. Protección internacional de los derechos humanos (in Rosario, Argentine Republic (Santa Fé) Universidad nacional del litoral. Instituto de derecho internacional. Curso de preparación para la enseñanza sobre Naciones Unidas, pp. 243–56, Rosario, 1961)

Allen, Florence E. Human rights and the International court. 1949. 35 A.B.A.J. 713–16, 788–89.

Anoneau, Eugène. L'intervention d'humanité et la declaration universelle des droits de l'homme. 1955. Rev. de Droit International 126–33.

Bibliography of works on human rights (in United Nations. Department of economic and social affairs. Yearbook on human rights for 1958. N.Y., 1960, pp.315–26.)

Bilder, R. R. The international promotion of human rights: a current assessment. 1964. 58 Am. J. Int'l L. 728–33.

Biörklund, E. A world movement in favour of human beings. 1963. 33 Nordisk Tidsskrift for International Ret 112–20.

Cadieux, M. Les droits de l'homme en regard du droit international. 1962. 22 Rev. du Barreau 18–38.

Ciasullo, Aldo L. El hombre y la comunidad internacional. Montevideo. 1954. 153p.

Concepción, R. International law and human rights. 1963. 2 Phil. Int'l L.J. 572–76.

Coursier, M. Henri. L'évolution du droit international humanitaire. Hague. Academy of International Law. Recueil des Cours 1960, I, v.99, pp.361–465.

Drost, Pieter Nicolaas. Human rights as legal rights, the realization of individual human rights in positive international law; general discussions and tentative suggestions on an international system of human rights. Leiden, Sijthoff. 1951. 272p.

Dumas, Jacques. La sauvegarde international des droits de l'homme. Hague. Academy of International Law. Recueil des Cours 1937, I, v. 59, pp.1–97.

Ezijiofor, Gaius. Protection of human rights under law. London, Butterworth's. 1964. 292p.

Fernando, Enrique M. An international bill of rights. Manila, P.C.F. Publications. 1948. 72p.

Ganji, Manouchehr. International protection of human rights. Genève, Droz, 1962. 317p.

Garcia Bauer, C. Los derechos humanos preocupación universal. Guatemala, Editorial Universitaria. 1960. 532p.

Hamburger, Ernest. Droits de l'homme et relations internationales. Hague. Academy of International Law. Recueil des Cours 1959, II, v.97, pp.293–429.

Hendrick, James Pomeroy. Progress report on human rights. Washington, Gov't Print. Off. 1948. 16p. (U.S. Dep't of State pub. 3262, Int'l org. & conf. series, III 13)

Herrera Gutierrez, J. C. La protección internacional de los derechos de hombre filosofia y realizaciones. México. 1965. 147p.

International protection of human rights (in Inter-parliamentary Union. 53rd econference. Copenhagen, 1964, Compte rendu, pp.469–77 (Genève 1965)

Jakovijević, B. The problem of the protection of human rights and international law. 1962/63. 32/33 Hague. Acad. Int'l L. Annuaire 162–71.

Jenks, Clarence W. Human rights and international labour standards. New York, Praeger. 1960. 159p.

205

Juvigny, P.   The legal protection of human rights at the international level.
1966. 18 Int'l Social Sci. J. 55–68.
King, D. B. and Gormley, W. P.   Toward international human rights. 1963.
9 Wayne L. Rev. 294–307.
Kunz, Josef L.
Present-day efforts at international protection of human rights: a general
analytical and critical introduction.   1951. 45 Am. Soc'y Int'l L. Proc.
109–20.
The present status of the international law for the protection of minorities.
1954. 48 Am. J. Int'l L. 282–87.
Lauterpacht, Elihu.   Some concepts of human rights. 1965. 11 How. L.J.
264–74.
Lauterpacht, Hersh.
International law and human rights.   New York, Praeger. 1950. 475p.
The international protection of human rights.   Hague. Academy of Inter-
national Law. Recueil des Cours 1947, I, v.70, pp.1–108.
Mosler, Hermann.   The protection of human rights by international legal
procedure. 1964. 52 Geo. L.J. 800–23.
Nova, R. de.   Human rights and the protection of minorities. 1965. 11 How.
L.J. 275–290.
Pollack, Rosalind S.   The individual's rights and international organization.
Northampton, Mass. 1966. 122p.
Rimanque, K.   Human rights. Legal implications in an historical and phil-
osophic context. 1965. 7 World Justice 170–93.
Sharma, S. P.   The promotion of international protection of human rights:
problems and prospects. 1965. 7 Int'l Studies 262–78.
Sperduti, G.   La personne humaine et le droit international. 1961. 7 Ann.
Français de Droit International 141–62.

UNITED NATIONS AND HUMAN RIGHTS

Asamoah, Obed.   The legal effect of resolutions of the general assembly.
1965. 3 Colum. J. Transnat'l L. 210–30.
Alladi, Krishnaswami Aiyar (Sir).   Human rights. 1952. 1 Indian Yb. Int'l
Aff. 179–84.
Asbeck, Frederick Mari, baron van.   The universal declaration of human
rights and its predecessors (1679–1948). Leiden, E. J. Brill. 1949. 99p.
Assembly action on human rights and freedom of information.   1961. 8 U.N.
Rev. 36–48.
Azcárate y Flórez, Pablo de.   League of nations and national minorities.
Washington, Carnegie Endowment for International Peace. 1945. 209p.
Blaustein, J.   Human rights: a challenge to the United Nations (in Cordier,
A. W. & Foote, W. The quest for peace: the Dag Hammarskjöld memorial
lectures. N.Y., 1965, pp.315–30)
Briggs, H. W.   Implementation of the proposed covenants on human rights.
1948. 42 Am. J. Int'l L. 389–97.
Buergenthal, T.   The United Nations and the development of rules rela-
ting to human rights. 1965. Am. Soc'y Int'l L. Proc. 132–35.
Carey, John.
Implementing human rights conventions—the Soviet view.   1964. 53 Ky.
L.J. 114–34.

The UN and human rights; who should do what? July 1966. 10 (3) Int'l & Comp. L. Bull. 9–29.

Cassin, Rene. La declaration universelle et la mise en oeuvre des droits de l'homme. Hague. Academy of International Law. Recueil des Cours 1951, II, v.79, pp.237–367.

Chakravarti, R. Human rights and the United Nations. Calcutta, Progressive Pub. 1958. 218p.

Cohen, Benjamin V. Human rights under the United Nations charter. 1949. 14 Law & Contemp. Prob. 432–37.

Collier, H. E. Gershon B. O. Committee of twenty-four. 1966. 1964/65 Ann. Rev. U.N. Aff. 35–51.

Consultative Council of Jewish Organizations. A United Nations attorney-general or high commissioner for human rights; a memorandum submitted to the Commission on human rights. New York. 1950. 17p.

Convention on the elimination of all forms of racial discrimination. New York. December 21, 1965. 1966. 60 Am. J. Int'l L. 650–61.

Declaration on elimination of racial discrimination. 1965. 11 (1) U.N. Rev. 35–39.

Declaration on the elimination of all forms of racial discrimination. 1964. 3 Int'l Leg. Materials 164–68.

Fawcett, Sandford. A British view of the convenant. 1949. 14 Law & Contemp. Prob. 438–50.

Ferguson, Clarence Clyde, jr. The United Nations convention on racial discrimination: civil rights by treaty. 1964. 1 Law in Transition Q. 61–75.

Gardner, Richard N.
Fifteenth anniversary of universal declaration of human rights. 1964. 50 Dep't State Bull. 19–24.
Human rights: some next steps. 1963. 49 Dep't State Bull. 320–28.
The United Nations and human rights: illusion and reality. 1964. 1962/63 Ann. Rev. U.N. Aff. 131–38.

Green, James Frederick. The United Nations and human rights. Washington, Brookings Institution. 1956. 194p.

Henkin, L.
The United Nations and human rights. 1965. 19 Int'l Org. 504–17.
The United Nations and human rights (in Padelford, N.J. & Goodrich, L.M. The United Nations in the balance. N.Y., 1965, pp.140–53)

Holcombe, Arthur N.
The covenant on human rights. 1949. 14 Law & Contemp. Prob. 413–29.
Human rights in the modern world. New York, New York Univ. Press. 1948. 162p.

Holman, Frank E. International proposals affecting so-called human rights. 1949. 14 Law & Contemp. Prob. 479–89.

Humphrey, John P.
Human rights. 1962/63. Ann. Rev. U.N. Aff. 113–30.
The United Nations and human rights. 1965. 11 How. L.J. 373–78.

Hyman, Jacob D. Constitutional aspects of the convenant. 1949. 14 Law & Contemp. Prob. 451–78.

International convention of the elimination of all forms of racial discrimination. 1966. 3 (1) U.N. Monthly Chronicle 103–15.

International protection of human rights: the proposal for a U.N. high commissioner. 1966. 5 Colum. J. Transnat'l L. 150–58.

International protection of human rights (in Inter-parliamentary Union. 53rd conf. Copenhagen, 1964. Compte rendu, Geneva, 1965, pp.469–77)

Kelsen, Hans. The law of the United Nations; a critical analysis of its fundamental problems. London, Stevens. 1950. 903p.

—Recent trends in the law of the United Nations; a supplement. New York, Praeger. 1951. pp.909–94.

Kunz, Josef L. The United Nations declaration of human rights. 1949. 43 Am. J. Int'l L. 316–23.

Lauterpacht, Hersh. Human rights, the charter of the United Nations and the international bill of the rights of man; preliminary report. Lake Success. 1948. 63p.

McDougal, Myres S. and Bebr, G. Human rights in the United Nations. 1964. 58 Am. J. Int'l L. 603–41.

McDougal, Myres S. and Leighton, Gertrude C. K. The rights of man in the world community: constitutional illusions versus rational action. 1949. 14 Law & Contemp. Prob. 490–536.

Malik, Charles. Human rights in the United Nations, with text of draft covenants. New York, United Nations, Department of Public Information. 1952. 21p.

Mirkine-Guetzevitch, Boris. Quelques problèmes de la mise en oeuvre de la déclaration universelle des droits de l'homme. Hague. Academy of International Law. Recueil des Cours 1953, II, pp.255–376.

Moskowitz, Moses. Human rights and world order; the struggle for human rights in the United Nations. Dobbs Ferry, N.Y., Oceana. 1959. 239p.

Mousheng, L. The human rights program. 1961/62. Ann. Rev. U.N. Aff. 102–36.

Munro, H. Human rights and the United Nations. 1964. 114 L.J. 399.

Neal, Marian. The United Nations and human rights. New York, Carnegie Endowment for International Peace. 1953. (Int'l conciliation no.489)

Padilla, A. Universal declaration of human rights: expression of past achievements and future aspirations. 1962. 37 Phil. L.J. 739–47.

Schwelb, Egon.
    Human rights and the international community; the roots and growth of the universal declaration of human rights 1948–1963. Published by the B'nai B'rith International Council, Anti Defamation League and the U.S. Committee for the United Nations. Chicago, Quadrangle Books. 1963. 96p.
    International conventions on human rights. 1960. 9 Int'l & Comp. L.Q. 654–75.
    The United Nations and human rights. 1965. 11 How. L.J. 356–72.

Simsarian, James.
    Economic, social and cultural provisions in the human rights covenant; revisions of the 1951 sessions of the commission on human rights. Washington, Department of State, Office of Public Affairs. 1951.
    Progress toward completion of human covenants. Washington, Gov't Print. Off. 1952.

Slim, Taieb. The work of the committee of 24. 1963/64. Ann. Rev. U.N. Aff. 1–22.

Tchirkovitch, Stevan. La déclaration universelle des droits de l'homme et sa portée internationale. 1949. 53 Rev. Gén. de Droit International Public 359–86.

Tiwari, S. C. Forms of international organization action for the protection of human rights. 1964. 13 Indian Yb. Int'l Aff. 28–58.

The United Nations commission on human rights. 1960. 11 Bull. Int'l Comm'n Jurists 51–55.

United Nations. Commission on Human Rights. Draft international covenants on human rights. New York, United Nations, Dep't of Public Information. 1955. 16p.

United Nations. Convention on elimination of racial discrimination. 1966. 5 Int'l Leg. Materials 350–68.

United Nations declaration on the elimination of all forms of racial discrimination. 1963. 34 Current Notes Int'l Aff. 5–13.

United Nations declaration on the elimination of all forms of racial discrimination. 1964. 44 Inter-Parliamentary Bull. 41–46.

United Nations. Department of Social Affairs. Yearbook on human rights. 1946–.

United Nations. Economic and Social Council. Commission on human rights. Working group on the covenant of human rights. Report. Lake Success. 1947/ 15p.

United Nations Education, Scientific and Cultural Organization. Human rights, comments and interpretation; a symposium by UNESCO with an introd. by Jacques Maritain. New York, A. Wingate. 1949. 287p.

United Nations. General Assembly. Universal declaration of human rights. Lake Success, United Nations, Department of Public Information. 1949. 12p.

United Nations. Secretariat. Collation of the comments on the draft international declaration on human rights, draft international covenant on human rights and the question of implementations. Lake Success. 1948. 103p.

United Nations. Secretariat. Dep't of Public Information.
For fundamental human rights; an account of the work of the United Nations "in promoting and encouraging respect for human rights and for fundamental freedoms for all without distinction as to race, sex, language or religion." Lake Success. 1948. 126p.
These rights and freedoms. Lake Success. 1950. 214p.

United Nations. Secretary General.
Activities of the United Nations and of the specialized agencies in the field of economic, social and cultural rights; report. New York, United Nations Commission on Human Rights. 1952. 74p.
Comments from governments on the draft international declaration on human rights, draft international covenant on human rights and the question of implementation; memorandum. Lake Success. 1948. 25p.
Draft first international covenant on human rights and measures of implementation; subject analysis of discussions and solutions in the general assembly. Geneva. 1951. 65p.

Verdodt, Albert. Naissance et significance de la déclaration universelle des droits de l'homme. Louvain, E. Warny. 1964. 366p.

209

EUROPEAN COMMISSION ON HUMAN RIGHTS

Bement, R. H. The European convention for the protection of human rights and fundamental freedoms. 1963. 24 U. Pitt. L. Rev. 263–86.

British Institute of International and Comparative Law. The European convention on human rights. London. 1965. 106p.

Comte, P. The application of the European convention on human rights in municipal law. 1962. 4 J. Int'l Comm'n Jurists 94–133.

Council of Europe.
European convention on human rights: collected texts. Convention européenne des droits de l'homme: recueil de textes. Text up to date on 1st Sept. 1965. 4th ed. Strasbourg. 1965. v.p.
European convention on human rights. Strasbourg. 1963. 147p.

Dupuy, René-Jean. La commission européenne des droits de l'homme. 1957. 3 Ann. Français de Droit International 449–77.

Eissen, M. A.
La cour européenne des droits de l'homme. 1959. 5 Ann. Français de Droit International 618–58.
The European convention on human rights and the duties of the individual. 1962. 32 Nordisk Tidsskrift for International Ret 230–53.

European Commission of Human Rights.
Documents and/et decisions 1955–57. The Hague, Nijhoff.
Yearbook 1958–59. The Hague, Nijhoff. 1960. 684p.

Greenberg, J. and Shalit, A. R. New horizons for human rights: the European convention, court and commission of human rights. 1963. 63 Colum. L. Rev. 1384–1412.

Lee, L. K. European integration and the protection of human rights. 1963. 31 Geo. Wash. L. Rev. 959–76.

McNulty, A. The practice of the European commission of human rights. 1965. 11 How. L.J. 430–41.

Modinos, P. Effects and repercussions of the European convention on human rights. 1962. 11 Int'l & Comp. L.Q. 1097–1108.

Pilling, A. M. The European convention on human rights. 1963. 21 Toronto U. Faculty L. Rev. 93–116.

Rolin, H. Has the European court of human rights a future? 1965. 11 How. L.J. 442–51.

Schindler, D. The European convention on human rights in practice. 1962. 162 Wash. U. L.Q. 152–65.

Schwelb, Egon.
On the operation of the European convention on human rights. 1964. 18 Int'l Org. 558–85.
The protection of the rights of nations under the first protocol to the European convention on human rights. 1964. 13 Am. J. Comp. L. 518–51.

Smith, G. A. The European convention on human rights and the rights of derogation: a solution to the problem of domestic jurisdiction. 1965. 11 How. L.J. 594–606.

Smyth, J. F.   The European commission of human rights (in Rowat, D.C. The ombudsman. London, Allen & Unwin, 1965, pp.162–72)

Vasak, K.   The European convention of human rights beyond the frontiers of Europe. 1963. 12 Int'l & Comp. L.Q. 1206–31.

Verdross, A.   The status of the European convention for the protection of human rights and fundamental freedoms in the hierarchy of rules of law. 1965. 5 Indian J. Int'l L. 455–63.

Weil, Gordon L.
Decisions on inadmissible applications by the European commission of human rights.   1960. 54 Am. J. Int'l L. 874–81.

The European convention on human rights: background, development and prospects.   Leyden, Sithoff. 1963. 260p.

The evolution of the European convention on human rights.   1963. 57 Am. J. Int'l L. 804–27.

Yearbook of the European convention on human rights—the European commission and European court of human rights. V.1–, 1955–57–. The Hague, Nijhoff.

CENTRAL AMERICAN CONVENTION ON HUMAN RIGHTS

The Central American draft convention on human rights and the Central American court.   1965. 6 J. Int'l Comm'n Jurists 129–35.

Salgado, A. y Tapiador, R.   Observaciones al proyecto de convención centroamericana sobre derechos humanos. 1965. 19 (677) Boletin de Informacion 3–7.

INTER-AMERICAN COMMISSION ON HUMAN RIGHTS

Inter-American Commission on Human Rights.   Basic documents. Rev. ed. Washington, Pan American Union. 1963. 36p.

Proyecto de convencion interamericana sobre derechos humanos.   1963. 14 Revista de Derecho 117–44.

Sandifer, D. V.   Human rights in the inter-American system. 1965. 11 How. L.J. 508–28.

Scheman, L. Ronald.   The inter-American commission on human rights. 1965. 59 Am. J. Int'l L. 335–44.

Thomas, Ann Van Wynen and Thomas, A. J., jr.   The inter-American commission on human rights. 1965. 20 Sw. L.J. 282–309.